THE ILLUSTRATED HISTORY OF HYPNOTISM

FROM FRANZ ANTON MESMER TO MILTON H. ERICKSON

JOHN C. HUGHES, D.C.

Published by the National Guild of Hypnotists, Inc.
P.O. Box 308, Merrimack, New Hampshire 03054.

*This book is dedicated to the real pioneers
in the field of hypnotism,*
THE LAYMEN
*who labored long and hard, braving age-old
prejudices, to gain acceptance of hypnosis
by the public and the medical and dental
professions . . . and who now face
an uncertain future.*

Acknowledgments

The author is indebted to his professional friends and colleagues for their support and encouragement. Of the many people who contributed to this book, one deserves special thanks. Andrew Rothovius read at least two versions of every chapter and — to separate facts from fiction — searched libraries for material that my inquiry demanded. I am deeply grateful to the founder of the National Guild of Hypnotists, the late Rexford L. North. Those of us who are still alive and active in hypnosis remember Dr. North with keen affection. I also wish to extend my appreciation to the late Ormond McGill, the "Dean of American Hypnotists," and a very special thanks to my esteemed friends Edith Fiore, the noted author, and Dwight Damon, the President of the National Guild of Hypnotists.

I am thankful to Professor Brian Aubrey for reading the manuscript, and amending its literary shortcomings. Kimberly Martin is a paragon of efficiency and I am particularly grateful for her skillful layout and formatting expertise, and to Suzzanne Connolly who prepared all the images in this book.

Foreword

This engaging book makes an original contribution to the literature on hypnotism. With hypnosis coming into rapidly widening use as a therapeutic modality, it is important to have an expanded awareness of the long and difficult struggle that hypnotism has had in attaining scientific recognition and acceptance. This awareness can most easily be gained through acquaintance with the great pioneers who fought for the inclusion of hypnosis in the therapeutic arsenal against both physical and mental illness. This book will provide readers with this acquaintance.

It traces the roots of hypnotism from ancient times to the present. "Sleep temples" dedicated to Aesculapius, the god of medicine, arose in Greece and flourished about 500 B.C. There were hundreds of these "sleep temples" throughout ancient Greece and the Roman Empire. Sleep and dream healing continued to be used during the Middle Ages and the Renaissance, but without any understanding of its true nature.

The author has restored a giant from the shadows of misunderstanding. Franz Anton Mesmer's life and career are covered comprehensively. Reading about his contributions, we begin to realize the depth, scope, and vision of his thinking. Far from being the charlatan or fraud that he is all too often depicted as, Mesmer was a highly intellectual product of the 18th Century Enlightenment. He was well educated, a practicing physician in the highest circles of Viennese society, and a man of cultured tastes. He discovered a therapeutic method for treating numerous ailments through the projection of what he thought was a universal, invisible fluid, in which all bodies were immersed. He called it "animal magnetism," because he believed it was transmissible through the animate matter of the human body. He further believed that all persons possessed, in some degree, the ability to direct this magnetic fluid through the power of their minds, to heal disorders in others' but that only a very few (such as himself) had this gift in sufficient measure to do widespread good.

Despite the remarkable cures he performed, he was spurned in Vienna and sought recognition in Paris, regarded in the 1780s as the intellectual capital of the world. After initial favorable response in France, his teaching and therapeutic method was officially condemned by a royal commission of inquiry. Mesmer had unwittingly brought about his own downfall by failing to realize that his cures and other effects were psychological phenomena, and not caused by his postulated magnetic fluid.

Yet Mesmer had sown the seed from which a whole new scientific discipline would grow and flourish. And in its turn hypnotism, and the study of mental states that it encouraged, in time led to the emergence of modern psychiatry and its many offshoots. All these, and the incalculable ways in which they have shaped and continue to influence our world today are traceable in direct line from the original findings and work of Mesmer.

Mesmer was a man of powerful intellect and personality, and won a wide following. Many of his adherents achieved new discoveries of how the mind works. Eventually the notion of magnetic fluid would be discarded and replaced with the concept of suggestion and visualization, the real elements of hypnosis.

Individual chapters are devoted to each of the following remarkable pioneers:

The Marquis de Puységur, who had observed Mesmer at first hand and advanced a new dimension with his discovery of "artificial somnambulism."

The Abbé Faria, who investigated lucid dreaming, and anticipated some of the modern concepts of hypnosis.

John Elliotson, an English medical trailblazer who introduced the stethoscope in England, and founded a mesmeric hospital and the first journal of mesmerism.

James Braid, a British physician who began a scientific study of mesmerism and discovered validity in some of its phenomena, though disagreeing with the mesmerists as to the causes. Experiments convinced Braid that a peculiar condition of mind and body could be induced by a fixed gaze at an inanimate object. He named this condition *hypnotism* from the Greek root *hypnos* meaning sleep. Although the trance state resembles sleep, he established the fact that hypnosis is very different from natural sleep.

James Esdaile, a Scottish surgeon who a century and a half ago, in government hospitals for natives in India, performed several thousand minor operations and over three hundred major surgeries (including amputations of limbs and breasts and the removal of huge scrotal tumors) without pain on mesmerized patients. To undergo surgery in those days was often tantamount to signing one's death warrant. In the pre-anesthesia era many surgery patients died of neurogenic shock. Esdaile's use of mesmeric anesthesia reduced the mortality rate from 50% to only 5%.

Charles Poyen, a Frenchman, and others who in the pre-Civil War era introduced mesmerism to an America eager for novelty; leading to important advances in psychology, including the work of William James on mystical experiences.

Jean-Martin Charcot, a distinguished neurologist, who hypnotized hysterical and other mentally disturbed patients at the Salpêtrière hospital in Paris. Charcot laid many of the foundations on which Freud and his followers would erect psychoanalysis and psychiatry.

Auguste Ambroise Liébeault and Hippolyte Bernheim, contemporaries and rivals of Charcot, who founded the Nancy School which achieved important advances in the correct conception and therapeutic uses of hypnotism, setting right several errors that had led Charcot into some blind alleys.

Concluding chapters focus on the leading 20th century contributors to the further evolution of hypnotism to its present high and still growing eminence among the healing arts. Particular prominence is given to the life and work of Milton H. Erickson, who overcame a crippling boyhood illness to become the acknowledged father of modern hypnotherapy. Erickson was a tremendously creative practitioner, as well as a remarkably effective teacher. Therapists came to him from all over the world to participate in his seminars. The book closes on a positive note of looking forward to an even wider application of hypnotherapy by the medical, dental, and mental health professions.

John C. Hughes has produced a highly readable work that is both illuminating and historically informative. *The Illustrated History of Hypnotism* is destined to become a classic.

Ormond McGill, Ph.D.[1]

Palo Alto, California

---

[1] *Author's note:* The Foreword was amended for this expanded edition. Ormond McGill wrote the Foreword for the first edition of this book in 1996. Ormond was known world-wide as the Dean of American Hypnotists and was actively engaged in hypnosis until his death in 2005 at the age of 92.

Table of Contents

Introduction

T he *Illustrated History of Hypnotism* was written for a
general audience, to provide a non-technical yet
authoritative account of how modern hypnosis
evolved. The further aim is to portray the human side of the
history of hypnotism.

It was more than five years since I conceived the idea of
this book and began the research for it. Numerous books
relating to the theoretical and experimental foundations of
hypnosis, along with texts on the clinical uses of hypnosis as
an adjunct to medical and psychological treatment were
found. I did not find, however, any adequate history of how
hypnotism has grown since it was introduced — under the
name of "animal magnetism" — by the Viennese physician
Franz Anton Mesmer over two centuries ago.

This book, then, fills that gap. It will introduce you to the
many fascinating and colorful personalities who pioneered
and developed hypnotherapy. Though their achievements
were of a magnitude comparable in the field of psychology to
those of Pasteur, Lister, and other giants of physical medicine,
these great hypnotists remain virtually unknown to general
readers, beyond perhaps the recognition of Mesmer as the
founder of "mesmerism" (an early form of hypnotism).
Although we still use the word "mesmerized" as a synonym

for "spellbound," few know anything of the man himself, or of his successors into our own time.

Hypnotism has had to wage a long and difficult struggle to gain scientific credibility and acceptance by the medical profession. In the past few decades—although little noticed by the general public or the news media—there has been a growing recognition and use of hypnosis in all of the advanced nations around the globe.

The variety of problems for which hypnosis is useful makes it a healing tool of tremendous importance. Hypnosis is the preferred method in the healing of severe burns. A second degree burn can often be kept from going third degree, if hypnosis is promptly employed. It is an effective treatment for skin conditions, such as itching, eczema, herpes, psoriasis, warts, and many others. It has been used beneficially in the treatment of anorexia, bulimia, and other eating disorders, as well as for gastrointestinal disorders such as irritable bowel syndrome, and colitis. Hypnosis is used in the alleviation of pain in dentistry, in childbirth, and in the relief of chronic pain problems such as arthritis and cancer. It is used successfully in the treatment of anxiety and stress, and in the management of fears and phobias. The employment of hypnosis in treating psychosomatic disorders, and in psychotherapy in general, is now virtually routine.

Hypnotism has thus come of age and is being used more effectively with more people than ever before. The evolution of the many uses of hypnosis is continuing, with the promise of even greater achievements in the century ahead.

I have enjoyed writing this history of the pioneers and standard-bearers of hypnotism. I hope your reading of it will be an equally interesting and rewarding experience.

John C. Hughes, D.C.
Las Vegas, NV

I.

BEGINNINGS: THE ROOTS OF HYPNOTISM

Asklepios, the Greek god of healing

Sleep Temple of Aesculapius

CHAPTER 1
Temples of Sleep

A century and a half have passed since the Scottish surgeon, James Braid, introduced the term "hypnotism" (from the Greek *hypnos* meaning sleep) into common usage. Its derivatives, "hypnosis" and "hypnotherapy," the first meaning the state of the hypnotized person and the second the therapeutic uses of hypnosis, have also long been a part of everyday speech. And the term "mesmerism" — which originally was used for what we now call "hypnotism" — has had an even longer life, now a little over two centuries. The word "mesmerism" is derived from the name of the discoverer of "animal magnetism," Franz Anton Mesmer, who was the first true practitioner of the art. Although mesmerism was founded on unscientific premises, it was the first step toward the development of scientific hypnotism.

For Mesmer "animal magnetism" referred to a mysterious ethereal fluid, which he believed he was able to direct and control. He visualized animal magnetism as an invisible, impalpable, all-pervading fluid, a force analogous to physical magnetism. This misconception continued to prevail, though diminishing in influence, long after the terms "animal magnetism" and "mesmerism" went out of use, which was within a decade or two of Braid's introduction of the word "hypno-tism." We now understand that mesmerism was a psychologi-cal phenomenon. There was no invisible "fluid," magnetic or otherwise, but only the subconscious mind, enormously powerful and enormously susceptible to direction through suggestion. Gradually, step by significant step, hypnosis has become one of the most potent weapons in the armories of medical and psychological science for dealing with illness both of mind and body. Even now, however, the public recognition of this lags severely behind the reality. The term "mesmerism" continues to be used loosely for domination of a person's mind. We say for instance that Nazi audiences were "Mesmer-ized" by Hitler's incendiary speeches. We even apply the term to animals, referring to stalking predators "mesmerizing" their victims. All the while, most are only vaguely aware of how this faculty, first employed as a healing modality by Mesmer, is now helping increasing numbers of people to gain purpose-ful control of their emotions, their bodily processes, and the functioning of their immune systems to combat infections.

To a substantial degree, this lack of general recognition of the present high and still rising status of hypnotism can be traced to a widespread ignorance of how it has developed over the two centuries since Mesmer. Like the proverbial wheel, the therapeutic applications of hypnosis have had to be rediscovered — if not re-invented — in each generation over that two-century span. Every new generation of medical practi-tioners has had to rediscover for itself what hypnotherapy can do and how best to utilize it. Every generation has had one or more figures, comparable in stature to Mesmer himself, arise to re-emphasize the basic facts of hypnotism, dispel lingering misconceptions, and initiate fresh advances toward a fuller understanding of its nature and uses. To the lay public, however, and even to a surprising proportion of the medical and mental health professions, these pioneers of hypnotism's growth and development are either unknown or no more than names. To make their acquaintance is to meet remarkable personalities who strove to expand the borders of knowledge of how the mind works, and how all the functions of the physical body are linked to and affected by it. They were often mistaken, in some of their concepts, as Mesmer had been, but each one left hypnotism and its proper clinical application on a sounder base than before. Humanity is deeply in their debt and will be even more so as hypnosis becomes a still more effective method of treatment in medical specialties, psychotherapy, and dentistry.

In this book I will first present in detail the life and achievements of Mesmer, and then those of his foremost successors, the greatest hypnotists of the world to the present time. But first it is essential to sketch in the background of what had preceded Mesmer and why no one before him had attempted to reduce the phenomenon of hypnosis to a standard discipline and practice.

Certainly the trance state had been known from the earliest beginnings of the human race. It is the bedrock of shamanism in all its variations among primitive peoples, from Siberia to South America, from Australia to West Africa. The shaman induces himself into an autohypnotic trance state through techniques that are extremely similar everywhere. This has led several scholars to propose that such techniques are the strongest argument in support of the theory that all peoples have sprung from a common ancestry. In this self-hypnotic trance, the shaman enters into the realm of the subconscious, in which his imaging faculties have full play. He returns to waking consciousness to predict the future, to perform healings, to cast spells and counter-spells.

All of this, however, is far removed from any normalized corpus of doctrine and application. While a variety of clearly hypnotic methods of inducing trance were known to all the civilizations of antiquity, there is no evidence that a form of clinical hypnosis was anywhere established as a separate discipline with accepted modes of procedure. The closest approach to this was in the *Asklepeia* sleep temples that appeared in the final, Hellenistic phase of the ancient Greek civilization. These seem to have derived from models in late Pharaonic Egypt, which in turn were probably elaborated from more individualized forms of treatment that had persisted through close to two thousand years.

The difficulty in antiquity, which carried through into the Middle Ages and the early modern period, was that there was neither an adequate understanding of the subconscious or of the power of suggestion, nor any general body of doctrine into which the induction of the trance state and its effects could be fitted. Countless healers and practitioners of healing magic employed the trance state, benignly or otherwise, but each did so in their own way. No one tried to write an exposition or instructions (at least none have survived or come to modern knowledge) that others could follow and replicate their results. Mesmer virtually had to create both the discipline of animal magnetism — the precursor of modern hypnotism — and its doctrinal context. The culture of the eighteenth century enlightenment, of which he was a product, provided him with the necessary intellectual framework, which had never previously existed on such a scale.

Eye fixation by the subject, either on the eyes of the operator or on the movements of his hands, or more frequently on some luminous object, has from the remotest times been a favored mode of induction. The late Egyptian treatise known as the Demotic Magical or Leiden Papyrus (from the Dutch city in whose museum it has been stored since its discovery in 1829) describes the induction of a boy into a trance by eye fixation on a lighted lamp. The boy then acted as a voice medium for demons. Actually, his utterances were evocations from his subconscious, and provided information, such as diagnoses of illness, which was sought by the operator. There is no precise dating of this papyrus but it appears to be from the second or third century A.D.. It is representative of a long antecedence of similar practices, of which some indications — especially of hypnotic passes by the hands — can already be found in the Ebers Papyrus (the oldest known compendium of ancient Egyptian medical writings) believed to date from about 1550 B.C.

Yet no widespread, formalized employment of hypnotism can be shown to have existed in ancient Egypt. There was no context of understanding in which it could have developed. However, after the Persian conquest of the Pharaonic kingdom in the sixth century B.C., temples dedicated to promoting healing through sleep, during which gods either effected a cure or directed a mode of treatment, started to be built in Egypt. These temples were usually dedicated to the goddess Isis, or later to the new syncretic god Serapis, who was introduced by the Ptolemaic dynasty following the Greek conquest under Alexander the Great in 330 B.C. The customary regimen was a stay of nine days for the patient, who was daily induced into a trance-like sleep by the priest-physicians. What method of induction they used is not known; perhaps they employed a variety of techniques.

Along with numerous other exotic practices the returning veterans of Alexander's campaigns brought back to Greece with them, temples of sleep soon became popular. At least 186 sleep temples are known to have been built in Greece between about 325 B.C and the second century A.D.; the bulk of them within the first fifty years of that span. Since many others were probably destroyed without a trace in the later barbarian invasions, the actual total may have been around three hundred. They were uniformly dedicated to Asklepios, the Greek god of healing—supposed to be a deification of an actual physician of the ninth or eighth century B.C.—and hence were called Asklepeia. Their principal feature was the *abaton* (sleep room), which the patient could enter only after ritual purification and a large donation to the temple. After induction into sleep—again, we do not know the methods employed—the patient was visited in a dream by Asklepios, who prescribed the proper treatment, or sometimes healed the ailment immediately. Though the surviving descriptions ascribe a large number of cures to temple sleep, other records indicate the cult—for such it seems to have become—had detractors who ridiculed it as an imposture by which the temples and priests became rich. At this remove from the actuality, no objective judgment can be made; but it would seem reasonable to assume some rudimentary form of hypnosis was used, with at least a limited amount of success.

The Romans were late in being attracted to the temple sleep cult; it is not until about 150 A.D. that we find a Temple of Aesculapius (the name was Latinized) being frequented on an island in the Tiber at Rome. Once established, the cult persisted and was adapted into early Christian worship. Saints instead of pagan gods responded to the need of the sick person. The practice continued until about the year 1000 A.D. in the Western Church but then became frowned on, as liable to various abuses, during the period of the Cluniac and other reforming movements. In the Eastern (Orthodox) Church healing continued to be sought through being touched during worship ritual, or by sleeping within the church precincts. This continued until the Turkish Conquest in 1453. It is said to have persisted in some remote rural areas of Greece into the beginning of the twentieth century.

There was thus a predisposition in the mindset of Western Christian culture, stretching back into Hellenistic times, to accept the possibility of healing being effected through the unconscious activity of the mind in an induced sleep. There is little doubt this contributed to the receptivity which Mesmer and his immediate successor, the Marquis de Puységur, met with in the early stages of their advocacy of animal magnetism.

Jewish culture also contained a substratum of hypnotic practices for inducing trance and effecting healing. The thirteenth century kabbalist mystic Abraham Abulafia described a hypnotic fixation of the letters of the Hebrew alphabet, which induced a state of mystical exaltation. Eye fixation for healing seems to have been an accepted practice in the Jewish communities of the New Testament period; the first Christian apostles, who came out of those communities, are described as employing it in their miracles of healing, as for instance St. Peter (Acts 3:4) and St. Paul (Acts 14:8). Paul also used the technique to induce psychosomatic blindness in the sorcerer Elymas (Acts 13: 9-11), as well as to give him a posthypnotic suggestion that he would regain his sight "after a season."

Additional instances of the use of hypnotic methods to induce trance for various purposes could be cited from all levels and periods of culture in every part of the world. They would not alter the basic premise here stated, that nowhere before Mesmer was a form of hypnotism recognized, studied, and practiced as a therapeutic discipline separate from others.

The one person who appears to have possessed the capacity to anticipate Mesmer, though he failed to do so, was Theophrastus Bombastus von Hohenheim Paracelsus (1493-1541), a largely self-taught genius from northern Switzerland whose life spanned the first half of the sixteenth century. This was the period during which Luther commenced the Protestant Reformation, and the New World of the Americas became revealed to Europe, with the Spanish conquest of the hitherto hidden civilizations of Mexico and Peru. It was a time that was open to daring innovations, and Paracelsus was attuned to its spirit in his often violent attacks on the hidebound, unimaginative ways into which the practice of medicine had degenerated in the later Middle Ages. He denounced physicians in general as ignorant swindlers preying equally on the rich and the poor, and having no understanding of the human body and its organs. A keenly observant traveler, he had journeyed as far as India and spent eight years studying the Tartar cultures of Central Asia. He kept company with gypsies and peasants, learning about medicinal plants and folk remedies. Magnets fascinated him and he formulated a theory, that was very close to Mesmer's, that there were two magnetic forces, one that linked everything in the universe, and another that was the "vital spirit" in all living matter. This latter force was, he insisted, capable of being directed in whatever way the human mind willed it to act, whether in its own physical body or that of others.

Paracelsus was thus on the threshold of an operative doctrine of hypnotherapy, but he did not attain to it. He left no instructions for the induction of trance and there are no indications that he ever sought to use it in any regulated way. More of a theorist than a pioneer of actual practice, he was a needed gadfly who stirred the somnolent medical establishment into long overdue experimentation and investigation. Paracelsus was too far ahead of his time to be the introducer of hypnosis into medical usage.

Another theorist who anticipated many of Mesmer's ideas of a century later was William Maxwell of Scotland, who constructed an elaborate hypothesis of a universal magnetic fluid that could be utilized for overcoming all forms of disease in humans. He published this hypothesis in his book *De Medicina Magnetica* (Of Magnetic Medicine), written in Latin, which came out in 1679 in Frankfurt, Germany. As far as is known, Maxwell never attempted any practical demonstrations of this healing force, and toward the end of his book he seems to have become frightened of what he had written about it, suggesting that this all-pervading force could easily be abused in obtaining absolute control over other persons, especially women. "It is not wise to talk about these things," he concluded, "because of the problems it can create. Fathers could not trust their daughters, husbands their wives, or women themselves." Maxwell really need not have worried, for the book attracted little notice, and in any event he had not provided any instructions on how to induce the trance state in which the magnetic force could be exerted. Nevertheless, his speculations on its nature and effects were so similar to Mesmer's the latter was accused by his enemies of lifting his ideas without apology from Maxwell's book. Mesmer vehemently denied ever having seen it, and modern analysis supports him, showing that the resemblances are only superficial.

All the same, there is enough in Maxwell's tedious volume to suggest that he did have some roughly correct notion of the subconscious level of mind and its susceptibility to suggestion. However, it is also clear that he largely derived this notion from the confused conceptions of magnetism and its supposed medical properties which appeared in the writings of Robert Fludd (1574-1637), an Englishman who followed Paracelsus in attacking conventional medicine. Fludd failed to develop any coherent doctrine, but left enough in the way of possibilities for Maxwell to adapt to his own theorizing.

While neither Fludd nor Maxwell did much in the way of practical demonstration of what they asserted about magnetism, there appeared in the same century a practitioner who rivaled Mesmer in what he achieved in cures, but who lacked the intellect to propose a solid theory to explain what he was able to do. This was Valentine Greatrakes (1628-1680), of an English family settled in County Waterford in southern Ireland. There was nothing in the first thirty-odd years of his life to show Greatrakes possessed any extraordinary powers of mind or had interests other than the usual ones of his time and social class. He was educated in England as a lawyer, and served a stint as a lieutenant in Cromwell's army. Returning to Ireland, he became a justice of the peace and clerk of the court in a town near his birthplace. Then suddenly, sometime in 1660, there came upon him a strange conviction he had been chosen by God to heal the sick. The method he employed was to stroke them with his hands — an induction technique later used by mesmerists — though he never stated clearly whether the stroking was his own idea or was imparted to him from the divine instruction to go forth and heal.

At first he believes that his healing ability extended only to the various skin afflictions that were common in that age of poor sanitation. For these ailments his power was very effective and there is attested evidence of his healing hundreds of people that were suffering from them. After three years he had a further conviction that he could now heal the malarial fevers or "agues" that were prevalent in that marshy part of Ireland. Using his stroking technique he successfully instilled the conviction (via indirect hypnosis) that the ailing body would quickly expel the infection. Those who came to him believed this and were healed.

Early on the morning of Easter Monday, April 2, 1665, Greatrakes received a third divine revelation, that God was now imparting to him the power to heal all diseases. For a time he did seem endowed with such all-embracing power.

The barns and stables at his residence were continually filled with thousands seeking relief. To keep from being overwhelmed by them, he set up office hours from 6:00 a.m. to 6:00 p.m., three days a week. Medical records exist of his having healed cases of epilepsy, migraine and edema. However, he was eventually called to account by the authorities for practicing medicine without a license. The (Protestant) Church of Ireland ordered him to desist because he was infringing on the Biblical miracles. In addition to these troubles, he started to experience failures. Some illnesses were resistant to his power. On being called to England in 1666 to treat Lady Anne Conway, who suffered from severe and frequent migraine, he accepted money for the first time and failed to bring her any relief. Though he was presented to King Charles II and had some further spectacular successes in London, Greatrakes was unable to fully regain the healing power he had possessed in the first years of his mission. Gradually his failures increased and his fame dwindled. It seems that once his confidence in his healing gift was shaken; his ability to exert it also eroded. He was almost a forgotten man when he died in 1680 at the age of fifty-two.

Had he lived a century later, Greatrakes might well have been greater than Mesmer. By then a scientific context had developed in Western European thought, which, though rudimentary by present standards, would have provided a theoretic rationale for Greatrakes' healings and promoted the framing of a new therapeutic discipline to accommodate and practice it. In his time, however, such a context did not exist. There was no base on which to build. The prevailing mindset was that there had always been miracle-workers, some genuine and some not. They came and went, and there was no way to account for them or explain what they did or how they did it, beyond ascribing it to God — or the Devil. So another hundred years had to pass before hypnotism came to be recognized as a mode of medical practice. That first recognition — though flawed and mistaken in part — would come through a pioneering breakthrough that was the work of a trained medical man, Mesmer.

In the interval, however, there was an episode of the kind that is generally dismissed as "religious hysteria." Occurring as it did in Paris, where Mesmer would make his greatest impact and attract his most influential immediate successors the episode can be regarded as having prepared a climate of acceptance for phenomena attributable to the mind. It is identified in history as the Convulsionaries of St. Medard, from the name of the cemetery where the manifestations took place. Its background was the doctrinal battle that had lasted since the 1630s, between the Roman Catholic state church of France and those of its adherents who followed the teachings of Cornelius Jansen. Jansen was a Dutchman who asserted that while the rituals and practices of the official Church were good and acceptable as far as they went, any assurance of salvation had to rest on strict austerities and spiritual fervor that individuals had to develop for themselves. The Jansenists were in great vogue for a while, probably because of the contrast they provided to the dissoluteness of the French royal court, and they controlled the section of Paris called Port-Royal. After 1700, however, they came increasingly under official disfavor; in 1713, Pope Clement XI condemned them as schismatics, and a peace settlement in 1720 was largely on Rome's terms.

Jansenism as a movement within the Church was then dead and discredited, but many of its followers continued to feel they had not been mistaken. They kept praying heaven would, by some miraculous sign, manifest its approval of what they still believed. In 1727 their prayers appeared to have been answered by phenomena which began to occur at the St. Medard cemetery grave of François de Pâris, a Jansenist who had practiced austerities and deprivation of bodily needs to the point of starvation, from which he died that same year at the age of thirty-seven. Die-hard Jansenists claimed that instantaneous cures of cripples were taking place at the grave. These afflicted people had gone there to pray, and gone into ecstatic convulsions from which they came out with all their physical faculties restored. Over the four following years these and similar manifestations increased as thousands flocked to the St. Medard cemetery in hope of miraculous cures. Among them were many devotees who believed François was a Jansenist saint, and who went into trances in which they were insensible to the pain from repeated blows from heavy iron bars and hammers. They begged for these blows, to prove their faith, in a remarkable demonstration of ecstatic self-hypnosis on a mass scale.

Finally, the authorities put a stop to these activities, which were fast becoming a public nuisance and a danger to morals. Most of the convulsionaries were women and in many cases it was apparent they were experiencing a self-induced hysterical state of sexual excitation in which they derived masochistic pleasure from being hit, kicked, and stepped on. By order of

Louis XV the cemetery was closed to visitors on January 27, 1732. A placard was posted on its gate stating, "By the King's decree it is forbidden for God to do miracles in this place."

"Perhaps surprisingly, God obeyed," was Voltaire's sardonic comment. The activity, however, had only gone underground; for at least thirty years longer, well into the 1760s, the authorities were breaking up groups who continued the masochistic practices of being beaten and maltreated while in a self-induced trance. In a few cases, women were found to have submitted to actual crucifixion, while claiming to feel no pain from the nails driven through their hands and feet. It is estimated up to four thousand persons were involved in these secret groups, and at least five hundred had undergone the "assistances," the strange name given to the batterings. Rational people scorned and derided this sort of behavior, but it had made many aware that the human mind was capable of controlling the body to the extent of making it insensible to the cruelest pain. A public that had seen, or heard at first hand of what was done at St. Medard and in the secret groups, was a public prepared to believe the message of Mesmer, that these mental powers could be brought under leash and used beneficently.

After nearly three millennia in which Western humanity had acquired only a vague awareness of the hidden power of hypnotism, the eighteenth century's cultural ambiance of enlightened reason was at last providing the context in which that awareness could expand to an active knowledge. A dynamic personality was needed to ignite that expansion. He appeared, in the person of Franz Anton Mesmer, the Viennese physician. From his day to ours hypnotism has progressed steadily through the efforts of many dedicated successors of Mesmer, who each in turn assumed his mantle as the world's greatest hypnotist.

II.
THE EMERGENCE OF MESMERISM

Franz Anton Mesmer
1734 - 1815

CHAPTER 2
Mesmer Revives an Ancient Art

A s we have seen, hypnotism has had a long ancestry of both doctrine and practice, going back to the remotest antiquity of primitive peoples, and continuing through the classical high civilizations and the medieval and Renaissance cultures of Europe. Yet not until a little over two centuries ago was it forcefully brought to the notice of the medical, legal, and religious establishments of Western society, then at the peak of that phase of widening outlooks generally known as the Enlightenment.

This came about through the widely publicized claims, and demonstrated results, of a new mode of healing introduced by a Viennese physician, Franz Anton Mesmer, a man of high education, culture and refinement who could confront the Enlightenment on its own terms. Even so, he met with opposition that finally discredited him and drove him into the obscurity in which his life ended. He was, arguably, the architect of his own downfall; his conception of how his method functioned was tragically in error and all too open to critical attack. He did not understand the true nature of hypnotism, nor the effect of suggestion on the subconscious mind.

Mesmer believed the effects he was able to produce in the thousands of patients who came to him for treatment were due to the operation of a mysterious magnetic fluid that permeated the entire universe, and which he was somehow able to tap and direct to healing purposes.

Erroneous though this concept was, the results he obtained were, with few exceptions, so beneficial, and brought such genuine relief to sufferers from both physical and psychological ailments, he could justly claim his animal magnetism, as he called it, was safe and effective, as well as a wholly new therapy.

Mesmer's name became permanently attached to his method, which continued to be periodically revived by several followers and rediscoverers for decades after his own withdrawal from the public scene. Even today "mesmerism" is sometimes used as a synonym for the term hypnotism. We also still refer to people being "mesmerized" by someone's personality or powers of influence. By whatever measure he is judged, Mesmer was one of those extraordinary individuals who left a permanent imprint upon history. All subsequent development of hypnotism, and of psychoanalysis and allied disciplines, can be traced directly to his pioneering accomplishment.

Had he not come forward when he did to promote his animal magnetism concept effectively and widely, the practice and understanding of hypnotism as a therapy could not have made the substantial advances that it did over the span of the nineteenth century. The great progenitors of hypnotherapy in the Victorian Era — Braid, Elliotson, Esdale, Liébeault, Bernheim, and several others — all followed in the path Mesmer had originally laid out, even though frequently diverging from his interpretations and techniques. It is thus necessary for an understanding of the progress of hypnotism from its revival for modern times by Mesmer, to be acquainted with his fascinating personality, his keen and searching mind, and the vast extent of his influence on Western thinking and views on mental processes.

Above all it is important to examine critically the various accounts of Mesmer's life and activities. They abound in misstatements of fact and opinion, and often fail to correct long-standing errors. The following account, based on the best available sources, presents Mesmer's career as accurately and impartially as possible.

Mesmer was a product of the Enlightenment society and culture. He sought to enlarge and widen their reach through his innovative therapy. This was possible because there had come into existence, through the widely read writings of Diderot, Rousseau, Voltaire, and others, an elitist mental climate that was ready to accept a rational basis and explanation for unusual mental phenomena. These had hitherto been solely the preserve of religion, which had tended to attribute them to demoniacal possession. In this new mind-set Mesmer found both an audience and a clientele.

Yet his claims went beyond what the Enlightenment milieu was ready for, and this was largely because he presented them in language that was as far from the real nature of hypnotism as his whole doctrine of animal magnetism. His results were genuine, however, and from them his successors would develop a new science and discipline. Because he failed to understand the mechanism behind the results, he could not convince the best scientific minds of his time, and they dismissed him as a fraud and charlatan. His early success and general acceptance by the lay public were mainly due to his openness, sincerity, and personal warmth toward others. Later, as he became embittered by opposition and disappointment, he grew more suspicious and taciturn.

Mesmer was born on May 23, 1734, in the small village of Iznang on Lake Constance, in the extensive lands held by the Prince-Archbishop of Constance in the western Alpine tip of the Habsburg Empire of Austria. He was the third of nine children of Anton Mesmer, a forester in the service of the Prince-Archbishop. At eighteen, already noted as a bright and studious youth, he decided to become a Roman Catholic priest. Through his family's connections with the Prince-Archbishop, he easily obtained a scholarship to the Jesuit seminary at Dillingen in Bavaria. He went on to the University of Ingolstadt, also a Jesuit institution, to study philosophy, then seems to have decided he was not suited to the priesthood after all, and turned to the study of science and astronomy. Both these disciplines still came under the general heading of philosophy, in which he gained a doctorate degree from Ingolstadt in 1759.

He was now twenty-five and faced with the problem of making a living, and there were not many openings for philosophers in general, or scientists or astronomers in particular. Law now attracted him, and he went to Vienna to study, but the work soon palled on him. Turning to medicine, he underwent a six-year course of training by the Medical Faculty of Vienna. Among his instructors were Gerard van Swieten, the director of the Faculty, and Anton de Haen, court physician to the Empress Maria Theresa, both of whom took a personal interest in him. Mesmer appears indeed to have cultivated contacts with prominent and wealthy persons, some of whom must have contributed to the cost of his prolonged higher education. Once he had given up the idea of the priesthood, it is unlikely the Church would have subsidized him any further, and his own family was certainly not able to do it. (One of his brothers, named Johann, did become a priest, doubtless with the aid of a Church scholarship.)

Mesmer graduated from the Medical Faculty in 1766 at the age of thirty-two. His doctoral thesis was on the influence of the planets on the human body. It was largely plagiarized from a Latin work on that subject by the Englishman Richard Mead, first published in 1704. That does not seem to have handicapped Mesmer, who launched into an immediately large and profitable practice, his cultivation of contacts in the higher levels of Vienna society again paying off for him.

A year after his graduation he entered into a professionally advantageous marriage with the widow of Ferdinand von Bosch, who had been an influential adviser of the Imperial Court. Ten years older than her new husband, and not much taken with him romantically, Maria Anna von Bosch was nevertheless very valuable to him in widening his circle of acquaintances among those who could pay well for his services. She was herself from a medical background, being the daughter of Georg Friedrich von Eulenschenk, an apothecary to the medical service of the Austrian Army, and had many other contacts that proved helpful to Mesmer.

In short, he prospered. He was able to live on a splendid Viennese estate, with a garden adorned with classical statues, and a private theater. Mesmer was a lover of music, and one of the first in Europe to play expertly on the glass harmonica that had been perfected in America by Benjamin Franklin. He attracted visitors like Leopold Mozart, who declared the garden incomparable, and the leading composers Christoph Willibald Gluck, and Franz Joseph Haydn. Young Wolfgang Amadeus Mozart, whose first opera *Bastien und Bastienne* had its premiere in Mesmer's private theater, later composed the Adagios in C minor and C Major (Opuses K 617 and K 617a) for Mesmer to play on the glass harmonica.

As for the nature of the medical treatments he provided his wealthy and titled clientele, they were the standard ones of the time, such as bleeding and purgative emetics—his favorite was cream of tartar, made from the acidic residue of fermented grapes, and less harsh than the more commonly used calomel and arsenical compounds—along with herbal medicines. He also experimented, as did many of the Viennese physicians of that period, with recent innovations such as magnets and electric shocks from the crude generators then existing, actually no more than toys. He was eager to discuss these and similar methods with those who did not shun novelties. Among them the one who influenced him most was Father Maximilian Hell, a Jesuit priest who also practiced medicine, then a not infrequent combination. He was also an astronomer.

The Jesuit employed magnets in the shape of the bodily parts whose ailments he treated, and claimed a high number of cures or alleviations of symptoms. Mesmer, observing these ministrations and their results, became convinced that the shape of the magnets had nothing to do with the effects.

Indeed, the metal magnets themselves were unnecessary. He tried magnetizing materials ranging from liquids to a variety of solids, and was able to achieve relief or healing in his patients as well as or even better than Father Hell.

The conclusive experiment which settled the matter for Mesmer, and led to the break between him and the Jesuit healer, involved Francisca Oesterlein, a young woman of twenty-seven, and a distant relation of his wife. Fraulein Oesterlein became a resident patient at Mesmer's home at the end of 1773, seeking relief for fifteen different symptoms that appear to have been primarily psychogenic.

Over a period of several months, Mesmer tried various forms of treatment involving magnets. The one that finally brought relief consisted of having the woman drink a decoction of iron salts and then attaching magnets to her abdomen and legs, with the aim of inducing a "tide" that would sweep the afflictions right out of her body. This indeed happened; she claimed to feel powerful streams of some mysterious fluid coursing downward inside her, and in a few hours she was perfectly well. She soon thereafter married Mesmer's stepson and bore children to him without difficulty.

This historic cure took place on July 28, 1774. Mesmer realized that it confirmed the conclusions he had already arrived at—none of the physical materials employed had any healing effect of themselves. At most, they acted as channels, directing the true healing force, which was an invisible magnetic fluid he was somehow able to accumulate within his own body and then transmit into another body in which it would have a curative result.

Since this magnetic force—which he was unable to define better, or even to explain what he meant by its being magnetic—came out of a living, i.e., animated, body and was transmissible to other living bodies, he called it animal magnetism. It was an unfortunate term that has continued to confuse all who do not realize its derivation from "animation," and thus tend to give it a sensual connotation.

Mesmer did at times use another term, natural magnetism, to indicate that the force he was dealing with had a natural origin and existed independently of any magnetizing by artificial means. However, again his definitions were not altogether clear and this term also was confusing to many.

By whatever name, Mesmer's healing force was anathema to Father Hell, who denounced it as a delusion, insisting that any cures Mesmer might have effected were solely due to his having employed magnets, even if clumsily. From this time on, the growing antagonism between Mesmer and Hell increasingly divided medical opinion in Vienna—and eventually across all Europe—into opposing camps.

It continued to be a localized squabble until early in 1775, when Mesmer submitted a summary of his animal magnetism concept to a scientific journal in Altona, Germany. He attributed the benefits of his treatments to an invisible and immaterial universal fluid, similar to electricity in that it could be generated and stored through a large number of intermediary substances.

We now know that both Mesmer and Father Hell—who took great offense at Mesmer's paper when it was published, saying it was written out of sheer spite and jealousy of his own work with magnets—were employing suggestion to achieve their results, and that no such magnetic healing forces actually existed. Neither of them understood this.

Mesmer's reputation as an effective healer was still on the rise. In the early summer of 1775, he was invited by Baron Horeczky de Horka, a Hungarian nobleman, to his castle at Rohow in Slovakia, to treat the Baron's nervous spasms which the other Viennese physicians had been unable to relieve. In a two-week stay at the castle Mesmer demonstrated some fascinating effects, even though he too was not able to fully allay the Baron's spasms. Simply by pointing at people, Mesmer could make them stop or resume singing, or have them fall into sleep—or, as we would now understand it, hypnotic trance—when he played music. Others would feel ill when he made certain gestures, then immediately be relieved by different ones. All these were recorded in detail by the resident tutor of the Baron's children, one Seyfert, who had been highly skeptical of Mesmer's abilities but was convinced by what he witnessed—not least by Mesmer's restoring, as he was leaving, the hearing of a peasant who had suddenly lost it six weeks before.

Mesmer noted that the intensity of the effects produced by the magnetic force he now believed he possessed within himself, was in direct ratio to his approach or retreat from the persons upon whom he was exerting it. He had already observed, when assisting at the bleeding of a patient, the flow of blood increase as he came closer, and decrease as he withdrew. While treating the Baron, and seeking to remove his nervous spasms by cathartic convulsions, the paroxysms always intensified as Mesmer moved closer to him. These observations convinced Mesmer he had the ability to accumulate and store within himself so powerful a quantity of the force-fluid, he could do away with the magnets and electrical shocks he had previously used as adjuncts. He gradually abandoned them all over the months following his visit to the Baron's castle.

While there he kept hearing additional reports — earlier ones having already been ciculating in Vienna since the preceding winter — of cures verging on the miraculous performed by Father Johann Gassner, a Catholic parish priest from northeast Switzerland. Mesmer was greatly interested in these reports and told those who asked about them he believed Father Gassner possessed an even greater store of magnetic force-fluid than he himself did, but the priest did not understand its nature or how to apply it properly. Mesmer added that he hoped to have an opportunity to study Gassner's effects at first hand and then make a further judgment. The opportunity was not long in coming. Soon after returning to Vienna, Mesmer received an invitation from the Electoral Prince of Bavaria, Max Joseph, to appear before a Commission of Inquiry the Prince was setting up at Munich to look into the cures attributed to Father Gassner. Since Mesmer was himself reputed to be performing extraordinary cures, the Prince felt he would be a helpful expert witness. Mesmer accepted the invitation, and, as the Commission was not to meet for some months yet, decided to visit some of the areas where Gassner had been doing his cures and find out more about them. They were said to involve a ritual exorcism of evil spirits.

This tour extended as far as Zurich and Bern on the Swiss side of the upper Rhine, in both of which cities Mesmer demonstrated magnetic cures in the public hospitals. Primarily, however, he went to the smaller localities, on both the Bavarian and Swiss sides of the Rhine, where Father Gassner had performed his cures, and heard descriptions of how he had done them. There is no firm documentation of his ever having met the priest in person; a reputed meeting at the court of the Prince-Bishop of Regensburg (Ratisbon) appears to have no foundation in fact. Mesmer was probably not eager to confront Father Gassner personally, looking rather to discredit him by showing that all the effects produced through his rites of exorcism could be obtained without them.

Gassner was born into a poor peasant family in the Vorarlberg Alps of western Austria, in 1727, and was ordained a priest in 1750. He was then sent to the small Swiss parish of Kosterle, not far from Lake Constance on whose shores Mesmer was born. Being troubled with violent headaches and dizziness that came only when he was celebrating Mass, Gassner decided they were symptoms of possession by evil spirits, and banished them through prayer and the Church's rite of exorcism. This gave him confidence to start using these methods to heal others who were sick in various ways. He met with considerable success, his fame spread, and ailing persons from parishes beyond his own started to come to him for treatment. In 1774 he healed a noblewoman, the Countess Maria Bernardine von Wolfegg, and was besieged by requests from hundreds of miles around to perform cures in many cities and towns.

To fend off some of this torrent, he wrote and published a small booklet explaining his procedure. He distinguished three grades of demoniacal possession and the proper invocations to determine if any of them were present in the sick person. If not, the illness was of an ordinary kind and the patient was referred to medical physicians. Cure from demoniacal possession was achieved through properly following the ritual prescribed by the Church, and absolute faith in Christ was essential in both the patient and the healer. Where these basic principles were met, he implied, others could be just as successful as he was. None had yet tested that, however, and so strong were the importunities from the diocese of Constance—though its Bishop, Cardinal Roth, was noticeably cool toward him—that Gassner finally went there and performed numerous cures by exorcism.

He was next invited by the Prince-Bishop of Regensburg, Count Fugger, to come to that diocese, and in November 1774 he settled there in Ellwangen, a town just inside the Duchy of Wurttemberg. Here he became the center of both adulation and criticism, which crossed the usual sectarian lines. Among his ardent supporters was the Protestant pastor in Zurich, Johann Kaspar Lavater, propounder of the doctrine of physiognomy (the determining of people's character from their facial expressions) while prominent among his detractors was a Catholic theologian, Sterzinger.

By the spring of 1775, the controversy over Gassner's healing exorcisms, which he continued to perform in increasing numbers, had reached such a fever pitch the Prince-Bishop held a formal inquiry in his court in June. This followed an independent inquiry on May 27 by the faculty of the Jesuit University of Ingolstadt that Mesmer had once attended, which concluded that on the whole Gassner was conducting his exorcisms properly and obtaining favorable results. However, the Prince-Bishop's inquiry came to a more negative determination; it cautioned Gassner he was attracting excessive publicity, and asked him to reduce his activities, accepting only those patients referred to him by their parish priests.

Shortly afterward, the Prince-Elector of Bavaria decided to hold his own official inquiry, to which he then invited Mesmer as a witness. There are indications this further inquiry was set in motion by the Imperial Court in Vienna, which had expressed strong reservations to the Prince-Elector concerning the propriety of Father Gassner's public use of a private ritual of the Church. The Imperial Court may also have suggested the invitation to Mesmer, seeking perhaps to convict him out of his own mouth on the nature of his innovative animal magnetism therapy that was arousing mounting suspicion and hostility among the Viennese physicians.

However that may be, Mesmer did, as we have seen, follow up his acceptance of the Prince-Bishop's invitation to testify regarding Gassner, with a thorough inquiry into the priest's methods, in the places where he had performed his cures. On November 23, 1775, Mesmer finally arrived in Munich for the sitting of the Commission of Inquiry, which was to begin the following day. He preceded it with a public demonstration of his animal magnetism, inducing various symptoms in volunteer subjects and then instantly removing them. Father Kennedy, secretary of the Electoral Academy in Munich, was an epileptic, and Mesmer induced an immediate seizure in him and then halted it just as quickly.

He performed various other demonstrations before the Commission of Inquiry, in effect duplicating all of Gassner's results without any recourse to the exorcism ritual. This showed clearly, Mesmer declared, that no demoniacal possession was involved; Gassner was simply possessed of a very strong amount of animal magnetism and was exerting it, without knowing what he was really doing, on the imaginations of his patients. What Mesmer saw as the priest's possession of an unusually powerful animal magnetism, we can now understand to have been a manifestation of the remarkable power of suggestion. In short, Father Gassner was a potent hypnotist without knowing it. He was employing therapeutic suggestion and imagery, much as in modern hypnotic usage, except he did not understand them for what they were.

Mesmer's verdict undermined Gassner's sincere claim that he effected his cures through the use of a religious rite. As a result, the priest was ordered by his superiors in the Church to retire to the small rural parish of Pondorf and to cease all public healing activities. A further inquiry into them by the Papal Curia, ordered by Pope Pius VI, resulted in Father Gassner being absolved of any violation of Church usages or doctrine, other than an immoderate employment of the rite of exorcism. He seems to have declined rapidly in health after his removal to Pondorf, where he died April 4, 1779. The Latin inscription on his tombstone eulogizes him as the most noted exorcist of his time.

Mesmer himself did not gain as much support for his animal magnetism concept as he had expected from his triumph at the Munich Commission of Inquiry. To many in the influential levels of Viennese society where Mesmer sought acceptance, it seemed his victory was a hollow one in that Father Gassner had not been allowed to be present to defend himself. In addition, Mesmer was assuming an arrogant attitude of mental superiority, asserting that only he understood these matters properly. Also, in the eyes of his critics, he had shown lack of respect for the Church's stand on exorcism.

On his return to Vienna, Mesmer found this unfavorable impression of him was spreading. It was causing him to lose favor in those circles of society where he had been a favorite, and from which he drew the patients able to pay the high fees that enabled him to live comfortably. Moreover, a crisis was at hand in his relations with the Habsburg Court that would cost him his welcome in the exalted company he had been keeping.

Mesmer's magnetic induction

CHAPTER 3
The Paradis Case Leads to Mesmer's Exile

Mesmer confessed he was unpleasantly surprised by the coolness he encountered on what he had thought would be his triumphant return from Bavaria to the charming pleasure-estate where he resided at No. 261 on the Landstrasse, overlooking the Danube. The high Viennese socialites who had found such enjoyment in being his guests amid the rococo splendors of his gardens and elegant chambers, now began to reject his invitations more often than they accepted them. They claimed "other engagements" or sudden indispositions, or sometimes did not respond at all. It came to his ears that there was a whispering campaign afoot, to the effect that he was not even a practicing physician in any real sense. He only dabbled in the medical art to gain the fees that enabled him to live in such high style. His palatial estate wasn't really his; it came to him through his marriage with the wealthy widow. Not satisfied even with that, he was reaching out for fame — rather, for notoriety — by hoodwinking the Bavarian Electoral Court with his absurd hocus-pocus of animal magnetism.

These were the sort of stories that were bandied around in the Imperial Court at Vienna and in the social circles around it, and carried back to Mesmer by the tale-bearers common in such situations. Clearly the impression he had made among officials and the scientific fraternity in Munich had aroused intense jealousy in the medical faculty of Vienna, and his old enemy Father Hell was making the most of the opportunity to spread further calumnies about him.

Particular resentment appears to have been aroused by Mesmer having treated Councilor Osterwald of the Electoral Court, reputed to have been a total paralytic and barely able to see. When Mesmer applied his magnets to his paralyzed limbs and weak eyes, Osterwald regained their full use and proclaimed himself restored to health. The Bavarian Academy of Sciences at Augsburg investigated this healing and declared, "Doctor Mesmer has indeed discovered one of nature's most mysterious energies." It would be the last time any professional body would give its official sanction to Mesmer's method and results.

Writing in March 1776 to acknowledge the Bavarian Academy's approval, Mesmer stated the gratification he felt was shadowed by the "coldness with which my ideas are received here in Vienna . . . it has surprised me greatly . . . I am accused of being a common cheat, and my friends taunted as dupes and fools."

This opposition, which had at its head the President of the Vienna Faculty of Medicine, Baron Anton von Stoerck, personal physician to the Empress Maria Theresa, was nevertheless aware that it lacked any single overriding charge to bring against Mesmer. He had, after all, acquired a reputation that extended across half of Europe. He had done nothing criminal, blasphemous, or outright scandalous.

He did take young women in as resident patients, and there had been some complaints about this, but the women were always placed strictly under the care of his wife, and no improprieties had yet been alleged.

His enemies were looking for some solid ground of accusation on which to lastingly discredit him. It was the most celebrated cure he had yet performed that finally provided the occasion his foes sought. The patient was Maria Theresa Paradis, a girl of eighteen, the daughter of middle-class parents, blind from the age of four, and severely manic depressive. Talented musically—she had learned to play the piano as a small child—and having come to the notice of the Empress, her education was paid for and a pension of two hundred gold ducats annually was granted to her parents. Arrangements were made for her to play at concerts. Mozart heard her once and rated her performance as competent. She even created compositions of her own on the piano, which others, of course, had to score for her.

Nevertheless she was unhappy, had fits of severe depression, and went from doctor to doctor seeking a cure for her blindness. The leading oculist of Vienna, Professor Barth, who had successfully operated for cataracts many times, told her he could not help; the optic nerve had atrophied beyond hope of repair. Baron Stoerck expressed the same opinion. Desperate, she finally went to Mesmer. His examination convinced him her blindness was not caused by damage to the optic nerve. To treat it by his method would be a challenge, to which he rose. He accepted Fraulein Paradis as a resident patient. Because he wished to be completely objective in treating her and evaluating the results, he assured her that he would charge no fees.

Her sight returned gradually, by stages, as the treatment progressed. Mesmer's magnetic treatment ritual induced a trance state. In this state Fraulein Paradis' subconscious mind assimilated Mesmer's suggestions that she would be able to see. Her father, who followed the process closely, compiled a written report of her reactions as she regained her sight and was increasingly able to distinguish objects, people, colors and landscapes. This account is consistent with many other cases in medical literature relating to the gradual attainment of sight by blind persons.

However, the medical fraternity of Vienna was outraged. Professor Barth was adamant in his assertion that the girl was faking her new-found capability of sight. He said Mesmer was influencing her to pretend that she was really seeing. Yet the long and exhaustive documentation her father compiled, day-by-day, of her recovery is clear proof to the contrary. She was not finding sight an unmixed blessing. Bright sunlight made her giddy. She stumbled over doorsteps she had traversed easily while sightless. The quality of her piano playing fell off, as she found herself laboriously watching her fingers on the keys instead of moving quickly and easily over them as she had learned to do when sightless.

It was this last difficulty that gave Mesmer's opponents the opportunity they had sought to discredit him. They went to Fraulein Paradis' parents and indicated that the Empress would soon discontinue the annual pension, because with their daughter's sight restored, the original consideration for the grant of the pension no longer existed. It was unfortunate, they added, that the girl could no longer play the piano so well; that would seriously reduce her desirability as a concert attraction, which had largely derived from her blindness anyway.

The parents were now alarmed at this prospective threat to the affluence their daughter's affliction had brought them. Even though there had been two public demonstrations, attended by a thousand persons, of her restored sight, Herr and Frau Paradis now suddenly agreed with Professor Barth that she was merely pretending to see. They went to Mesmer and demanded, literally at sword's point, the return of their daughter. When the girl—who had gone into hysterics—refused to go with them, her mother slammed her head against the wall so hard she fell senseless to the floor. Mesmer finally persuaded the parents to leave without her, pointing out that they had made her ill and she now needed his medical care.

This shocking emotional experience caused the blindness to recur. When Fraulein Paradis recovered consciousness, she found herself blind again. It took two weeks for Mesmer to restore her vision, through repeatedly infusing her with—as he believed—animal magnetism, for which he still employed ordinary magnets as conveyers of the "invisible fluid."

The Paradises now came back, profusely apologetic for their intemperate behavior. They expressed deep gratitude to Mesmer for healing their daughter, and promised if he now allowed them to take her home, she would be free to return for follow-up treatment on whatever schedule he wished. He did not believe them, for he was already under confidential notice from the Imperial Court to halt his magnetic treatments, but he had no choice. Reluctantly, he assented. Fraulein Paradis went home, and eventually returned to performing as a concert pianist, billed as being blind. It appears she never fully lost her sight again, but that it soon deteriorated to the point where for all practical purposes she could be regarded as blind. Thus she retained her earning capacity. She did not, of course, ever come back for further treatment by Mesmer.

The full extent of the opposition to Mesmer, and how it made the Paradis case a pretext for driving him out of Vienna altogether, or at least silencing him, remains buried in the Habsburg archives. It is known that Cardinal Magazzi, who largely controlled the Empress's Committee to Sustain Public Morality, had prevailed on Maria Theresa to order Baron von Stoerck to issue a formal order, in the name of the Imperial Court and the Medical Faculty, for Mesmer to "cease this humbug."

This order had been privately conveyed to him during Fraulein Paradis' recovery from her parents' abusive visit. The same high quarters probably advised the parents to go back to Mesmer in a more conciliatory mood, as a way of getting him to let the girl leave with them.

There is also evidence, though not fully authenticated, that the Jesuit Order (which still had great influence in the Austrian Empire at that time) felt it had to sustain Father Hell in his condemnation of Mesmer's animal magnetism. The Jesuits may have worked behind the scenes to orchestrate the outcry against Mesmer that resounded from all sides in the wake of the Paradis incident. By whatever means it was instigated and sustained, this campaign achieved its purpose.

Mesmer left his Landstrasse home, though his wife remained there, and retired to the countryside for a three month stay, during which he tried to sort out his conception of the strange new means of healing he had stumbled upon. What exactly was it? How did it work? Should he proceed any further with it?

He was not able to arrive at a solution that fully satisfied him. He remained uncertain about whether to regard animal magnetism as an independent, outside force he somehow could draw upon and use beneficially. Was it perhaps an additional bodily sense, a sixth one differing from the familiar five natural ones? Was it the creation of his mind, and possibly also of the mind of the person he was treating?

Mesmer wavered between these alternatives. He tended to lean toward the second one, coming close to realizing the psychological nature of animal magnetism, yet again missing it. He concluded that since animal magnetism had demonstrated its effectiveness as a healing force, he should seek a wider audience. There was the possibility of a definitive professional acceptance for it in Paris, which was then the intellectual capital of Europe, where new ideas of all kinds could presumably gain a ready hearing. He decided to go there, and returned to Vienna to plan his departure.

It is probably not quite correct to say Mesmer's departure from Vienna was forced upon him. Having discredited and silenced him, his enemies would probably have been just as happy to have him stay and resume conventional medical practice. He made his preparations carefully and deliberately, with no appearance of haste. He asked for, and readily obtained, a favorable letter of introduction from the Imperial Chancellor, Prince Kaunitz, to the Austrian Ambassador in Paris. Some Viennese physicians who still had confidence in him gave him another letter of introduction to Baron d'Holbach, a prominent French amateur of science with valuable contacts among the medical and scientific fraternities of Paris. He had also hoped to have the endorsement of the Prussian Academy of Sciences, to which he sent a twenty-seven-page summary of his *Animal Magnetism*, written in quite moderate terms and making no vast claims for its efficacy. He was disappointed in the Academy's reply, which concluded tersely that he was making a mistake.

Mesmer appears nevertheless to expected that he would be able to resume magnetic healing in Vienna after he had been vindicated by the French medical establishment. He left two female patients in the care of his wife, and they remained there for sixteen months until compelled to leave by official order.

More than a year had passed after the Paradis episode before Mesmer actually travelled to Paris in 1778. It was about six weeks before young Mozart, in company with his mother, likewise arrived in the French capital to seek his fortune. Although Mesmer and Mozart were both residents of Paris for four months before the composer left with deflated prospects and his mother dead, there is no record of their having met or having sought each other out; probably neither was aware of the other's presence, each being preoccupied with his own concerns. Yet when Mozart took up permanent residence in Vienna in 1781, while Mesmer was still in Paris, his first act was to go to Mesmer's garden, where he wrote to his father in Salzburg, telling of his safe arrival. In the opera *Cosi fan tutte* he composed nine years later, his librettist Lorenzo da Ponte recalled Mesmer in these lines:

This magnet stone
Should give the traveler pause
Once it was used by Mesmer
Who was born in Germany's Green fields
And who won great fame in France.

Great fame indeed, but also heartbreak and disappointment. Mesmer's sojourn in France failed to bring him the
acceptance by the scientific community he hungered for. Yet it
laid the foundation on which the modern science and practice
of hypnotism, psychoanalysis, and other psychotherapeutic
methods of treatment would later be constructed. Although
based on unscientific premises, animal magnetism was, in
effect, a new method of psychotherapy.

III.
THE MESMERIST MOVEMENT IN FRANCE

Mesmer's Place Vendôme Clinic
Créteil, France 1778

CHAPTER 4
Mesmer in the Paris of the Enlightenment

T he Paris in which Franz Anton Mesmer arrived in February 1778 was a city of juxtaposed contrasts of the old and new. Perched astride the divide between a feudalism unwilling to die and a middle-class future still unsure of itself, it was credulous and greedy of wonders with an adolescent eagerness. It prided itself on its salons where a sophisticated intellectualism, flaunting the title of a liberated Enlightenment, held forth with learned and witty conversation, while at the same time it clung to antique notions and outdated impracticalities.

Mesmer found himself upstaged on his arrival, which he had hoped would gain him immediate attention and respect. He was eclipsed by the reception for the supreme idol of the Parisian enlightened establishment—Voltaire. The master of satire, who for over half a century had defied the censures of church and state, and lived in semi-exile on the borders of France, was now, at the age of eighty-four, finally being permitted to enter the national capital. The city gave him tumultuous veneration that went far beyond what Paris had ever accorded to the royalty it still worshipped. "Erase the infamy," was Voltaire's battle-cry against the tyrannical hold of Church clericalism on the French mind. More than anyone else—though many others of mental might, such as Rousseau and Diderot, had also fought the same battle—he had broken that grip. Traditional religion no longer inhibited educated and cultured people from openly expressing free-thinking opinions. A hundred viewpoints about the human spirit and the divine were being circulated, as Mesmer observed while he watched Voltaire being feted and paraded around, to a degree that exhausted the old man and led to his death soon afterward. Even if this ovation for a dying idol had cost Mesmer a week or two of idleness upon his arrival in Paris, he felt he could now turn to his advantage the openness to new ideas which Voltaire had pioneered, and would now be more in fashion among the Parisian elite.

Unfortunately one of those new ideas was atheism, which was a mind-set not receptive to the theory of animal magnetism Mesmer had come to propagate. It was not that he considered it as any sort of religion, but it assumed as a basic premise there was an all-pervading energy, whether one called it divine or anything else, which acted with healing effect on both mind and body. That was a notion which an atheist would find hard to accept—and it so happened that the Baron d'Holbach, to whom Mesmer had the letter of introduction from his Viennese medical friends, and who had responded with an invitation to a dinner with French scientific confreres, was one of the new atheists.

Mesmer became aware of that in the first few moments of conversation at the dinner party, and it chilled his enthusiasm and effectiveness. The Baron set the tone of the conversation with his atheistic views, even though many of the others present did not share them. In the resulting atmosphere, Mesmer's stories of his most recent successes with animal magnetism before leaving Vienna fell flat. (Despite the order from the Imperial Court to desist, he had continued to quietly treat a few patients, and had relieved eye and tubercular ailments.) In addition, he was unable to magnetize those who allowed him to try. Baron d'Holbach quite predictably wrote off the Viennese visitor as a mere dabbler and poseur; and for a short while Mesmer's prospects looked very bleak.

Despite his rather statuesque appearance and imposing presence, which usually enabled him to quickly gain command of any gathering, Mesmer was handicapped by his inability to speak French without a heavy German accent. He also had to compete with yet another rival for the Parisian public's attention once the Voltaire festivities were out of the way. This was Benjamin Franklin, who had been lionized by the French immediately on his arrival, and had now negotiated the formal treaty of alliance between Britain's rebelling thirteen American colonies and the Kingdom of France.

The treaty was revealed about a month after it was signed on February 6, and everybody realized it meant immediate war between France and Britain. There was vast excitement over the prospect of perhaps regaining Canada and other losses suffered by France in its humiliating defeat in the Seven Years War of 1756-63. All of this left little room for interest, despite the Parisian avidity for novelties, in the strange new healing method the Doctor newly arrived from Vienna was trying to promote.

Before very long, even the marvelous Franklin and the coming of war were no longer the topics on everyone's tongue. A fresh sensation was needed. It was provided by the reports of extraordinary results achieved by the new therapy.

Mesmer had decided, after his initial failure to impress the French scientific establishment at Baron d'Holbach's dinner, to pass the word quietly from the lodgings he had taken. He offered treatment to sufferers from all sorts of illness, without charge if they could not afford to pay. Soon he had cured, or greatly relieved, various digestive and liver conditions, cases of partial and total paralysis of the legs, and one of premature senility following on severe frostbite six years earlier. In none, it was attested, had any medicines been administered.

These reports attracted the notice of Jean-Baptiste LeRoux, a qualified surgeon who was the president of the Paris Academy of Sciences, and moved him to visit Mesmer. Favorably impressed by what he heard and saw of the magnetic therapy, LeRoux promised he would report to the Academy that animal magnetism merited a full and impartial examination.

This was of course what Mesmer wanted above all, an opportunity to prove his method had scientific validity. His total honesty, his utter sincerity and frankness made it possible for him to gain the confidence of people he had never met before, whenever they listened to him as LeRoux had done. These qualities, incidentally, are what make an effective hypnotist, as Mesmer certainly was—if only he had known and understood it. His inability however to grasp that not all people had the same concepts of honor he did, led him to repeated disappointment in others when they failed to meet his own high standards of conduct. In the end this soured and embittered him, and made him additional enemies.

But that was still far off in April of 1778, when the approbation of LeRoux gave Mesmer hope for an early favorable judgment by the Academy of Sciences on his animal magnetism. He looked beyond that to its acceptance as a recognized therapy by the Paris Medical Faculty and the Royal Society of Medicine.

As a newcomer to Paris, though, he probably did not realize the factional squabbles in which these two august bodies were then involved, and that stood in the way of their taking any serious interest in his discovery.

The Academy of Sciences had as its preserve the strictly scientific side of all new findings and theories, which it judged in the light of the best knowledge then available. It passed any claims of their healing applications on to the Medical Faculty, which until just two years before had been the sole authority on modes of therapy. Extremely conservative and reluctant to accept any innovations, it was the last medical body in Europe to hold out against inoculation for smallpox, which had been introduced half a century earlier.

When King Louis XV died of smallpox in May 1774 because he had never been inoculated against it, there was a widespread outcry against the obscurantism of the Faculty, which had prevented the monarch from receiving this protection. His grandson Louis XVI, on coming to the throne, at once overruled the old fogies of the Faculty, and had himself and his brother, the Count of Artois, inoculated. (Yet Louis XVI himself still adhered to traditions of high antiquity; at his coronation he touched 2,400 sufferers from scrofula—the "King's Evil," a tubercular skin condition that was supposed to be curable by the mere touch of a monarch. There is no record of how many of the 2,400 were cured, but it would not be surprising if some were, for the healing power of suggestion could work strongly in a setting with the high emotional context of a royal coronation.)

Two years later, on April 9, 1776, the new King went a step further in putting down the pretensions of the Faculty to exclusive medical authority by creating the Royal Society of Medicine, which from then on was to regulate the medical profession in France.

The reaction of the Faculty was one of shocked disbelief, for it had not even been consulted. It watched in horror as the majority of physicians sought membership in the new Society. Finally, in the spring of 1778—just when the Academy of Sciences, through President LeRoux, was taking cognizance of Mesmer and his animal magnetism—the Faculty rallied itself to declare it would banish from its ranks all who did not resign from the new Society by the end of July.

It was in this tense situation that LeRoux, on behalf of the Academy, which was trying to keep on good terms with both of the feuding medical bodies, invited Mesmer to one of its regular meetings, where he would introduce him as an innovative pioneer of a new therapy. Again it was a disappointing affair. LeRoux could not gain or hold the attention of his audience. Some laughed openly at what they said was "sheer quackery." Finally twelve members agreed to stay after the meeting for a private discussion with Mesmer about his method. They then indicated they would like an actual demonstration, and all adjourned to LeRoux's home for this purpose. Mesmer's first try was on a man who suffered from severe chronic asthma. He proved hard to magnetize, and as Mesmer continued his attempts at induction, seven of the twelve Academicians declared they had seen enough of this tomfoolery and left. At that point the patient began to respond and was soon feeling more comfortable. He also tasted water as wine when Mesmer suggested it was an intoxicating beverage.

Two of the remaining five Academy members were sufficiently impressed enough to propose Mesmer conduct further trials before them a few days later, this time with some of the patients he was treating. The demonstration went off well, but one of the two observers, M. de Maillebois, discerningly observed that it seemed to him the phenomena he had witnessed were caused by the patients' imaginations, which Mesmer was stimulating. Whether any cures of their conditions were effected was immaterial; what happened was a reality in itself.

Maillebois unwittingly came close to the truth about hypnosis and its procedure. However, his remarks angered Mesmer, who retorted that if the effects all came out of the minds of the patients, how was he achieving cures of their ailments? The academician only replied he would be interested in hearing of the effect of animal magnetism on a greater number of patients with a wider variety of ailments. On that rather unsatisfactory note the demonstration ended.

Upon reflection, however, Mesmer decided to act on Maillebois' suggestion and begin treating a greater number and variety of the sick, to see whether the beneficial results would continue. In May, three months after his arrival in France, he set up a clinic in the suburban village of Créteil, where he began receiving patients on a regular daily basis. Twelve days after it opened he was visited by a small delegation of physicians from the Royal Society of Medicine, who told him he should allow his new therapy to be examined by the Society, rather than the Academy, which was not concerned with medical treatments.

Mesmer had not yet given up on getting a determination of the scientific validity of animal magnetism from the Academy, and was not quite pleased with the Society's intervention, but he agreed that doctors from the Society should observe his treatments and judge for themselves. The Society indicated the patients should be examined by its doctors to certify the nature of their illness. However, Mesmer stipulated, on the contrary, they should first be examined by physicians from the Faculty.

Though the Society assented, it was a disastrous requirement, and had Mesmer been fully aware that the Faculty and the Society were at daggers drawn, he doubtless would not have made it. He did so in the mistaken belief it would expedite approval of his method by all three bodies—the Academy, the Faculty, and the Society. As it was, the Academy had already lost interest—LeRoux appears to have had no more contact with Mesmer from this time on—and under the unfortunate arrangement Mesmer had specified, only one patient was ever sent to him.

By that time (late June), the King had overruled the Faculty, ordering it to retract its expulsion decree, and stripping it of its power to accredit physicians, which in August he bestowed exclusively on the Society. Victorious in its turf battle, that august body no longer cared about the Viennese visitor and his strange notions about healing with animal magnetism. The package of documentation Mesmer had submitted, detailing his treatment of several patients, along with the results and the opinions of several physicians who had accepted his invitations to observe and examine, was returned unopened by the Secretary of the Society, Felix Vicq de Azyr.

Mesmer then made one more attempt to interest the Society and the Academy. The Society sent a curt four-line note of rejection; the Academy did not even reply. He was now faced with the necessity to decide what his further course should be. Ought he to give up trying to get official recognition in France, and return to Vienna? More and more people were coming to his clinic, where he had devised means—the soon to be famous *baquet*, multiple tubs—for treating a large number of patients at the same time. He felt he had an obligation to all these sick people to continue to give them relief and healing, even if his work was ignored by the learned and powerful. How closed of mind they were, he mused, they seemed to think animal magnetism—if indeed it was real—was something that could be prescribed and administered like a drug. They could not see that animal magnetism involved the interaction of mind and body, and required a thorough understanding of both. Surely he would incur severe blame by posterity if he did not keep on developing and refining his discovery. He was not in financial need, and had come with adequate funds for a lengthy stay. Many patients were paying him well, and he was accumulating money. Yet the lack of official status for what he was doing rankled within him. As the summer ended, he came to a decision to close the clinic in its semi-rural location for the winter, and open another in the heart of Paris. He hoped in that way to attract the notice of influential personages connected with the Royal Court, from which he might obtain the authoritative sanction he so greatly wanted for his work. This time his hopes were in large measure fulfilled.

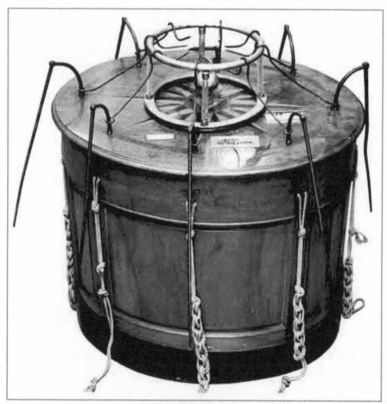

Mesmer's baquet

CHAPTER 5
The Transitory Triumph of Animal Magnetism

A t the Créteil clinic, Mesmer had employed for the first time his *baquet*—a contraption for magnetizing many persons at the same time—though he appears to have already experimented with the idea while still in Vienna. The great numbers of patients who came to him at Créteil made it necessary for him to resort to the *baquet* device, for he could not possibly treat all of them individually. In the new clinic opened in the fall of 1778 at the Place Vendôme, Mesmer further elaborated the *baquet* technique. He continued to modify the device at the still larger premises in the Hôtel Bouillon, in the Rue Montmartre, to which the escalating growth of his practice soon compelled him to move and to set up what was virtually a hospital.

Most of the descriptions we possess of the *baquet*—many written by hostile witnesses, intent on depicting Mesmer as a charlatan—are from a period four to six years later, when Mesmer and animal magnetism had attained their summit of Parisian success. These are dressed up with melodramatic trappings that probably were only gradually added to the basic technique. At this stage, in 1778-79, the *baquet* consisted essentially of a round oak tub and lid, between five to six feet in diameter and eighteen inches high, with about twenty rods of glass or iron of varying lengths and bent at differing angles, protruding through holes in the lid.

The tub itself contained a layer of water covering scattered bits of iron filings and broken glass, over which there floated symmetrical circles of bottles filled with water, the necks of the bottles in each circle being alternately bent toward and away from the center of the tub. As many as twenty people could be treated at a time. The patients sat in circles around the tub each grasping one of the rods. The rods were of varied lengths and angles, so those in the outer circles could also reach out and take hold of one of them.

It was Mesmer's conviction, one that demonstrated the inconsistencies that persisted in his concept of how animal magnetism worked, that by his first magnetizing the water in the tub, the vivifying invisible magnetic fluid would be conveyed into the sick persons grasping the rod. To enhance its effects, a cord was tied to the tub and then passed around the waists of all of those sitting around it. The patients were also instructed to maintain physical contact with each other by taking hold of the left thumb of the one nearest them, between their own right thumb and forefinger.

None of this, of course, would have had the slightest effect had it not been for the expectancy, implanted by Mesmer, that it would help them. Conviction of cure, in many of the cases, resulted in cure. In Vienna Mesmer had concluded that magnets were not necessary for his method to work, but since it was not possible for him to treat each patient individually, he devised these mechanical aids. As he visualized the magnetic force to be some sort of rarefied and invisible fluid, it was natural for him to think water (being also a fluid) would be an effective conveyer of it. Iron of course had magnetic properties, and at that time some thought glass did too. Nevertheless, Mesmer sought to give some personal attention to his patients by walking between the tubs (at the Hôtel Bouillon, he had four in use every day, with eighty to a hundred patients around them) and reaching out with an iron staff, with which he touched each one on the places where they indicated their afflictions were located. He would also look fixedly into their eyes, employing what was to become a standard induction method for hypnosis. Before coming out to the tubs, Mesmer would play his favorite instrument, the glass harmonica. Exotic incense was burned and heavy draperies over the windows put the room in semi-darkness; all calculated to induce a receptiveness to animal magnetism.

Later, but probably not yet in 1778 or the early part of 1779, Mesmer trained assistants to follow through with inducting the patients into what he called the "crisis," which he believed was essential for expelling from them whatever was obstructing the beneficent action of the animal magnetic fluid. At this stage, in the first months of his in-city Paris clinics, he had to select those patients he discerned to be most in need of his personal ministrations. That took time and thus put a limit on the number of patients he could attend.

This personal treatment commenced with applying his hands to the areas of the patients' bodies he had already touched with his rod, and then stroking the lower part of their abdomens. Mesmer would seat himself directly opposite the sufferer, feet and knees of each touching. He moved his hands up and down the afflicted body, over the ribs and above the head, where he joined his fingers in a pyramidal form, and down to the shoulders and finally to the feet. The process would then recommence, and sometimes go on for hours, until the "crisis" was evoked.

Mesmer claimed that about one patient in four went into the total convulsive crisis he believed was necessary for a complete cure. The rest would either experience mild crises while still in the circles around the tubs, without being personally attended to, or could not be induced into convulsive crisis by any effort on the part of the magnetizer. Those having mild crises (usually limited to coughing, spitting, sweating, fleeting sharp pain, etc.) were, Mesmer felt, probably not seriously ill to begin with. The resistant ones were either beyond help — though he was very reluctant ever to admit this — or were held back from the relief they sought by lack of total belief in his treatment. Here again, Mesmer was admitting, unwittingly and unwillingly, his cures were all effected through psychological processes, for if his postulated animal magnetic fluid was real, it should not be hindered by any lack of belief on the part of his patients.

The total convulsive crisis generally began with intensive hiccupping, moaning, complaints of severe pain, uncontrollable weeping, and flinging around of arms and legs. In most cases the convulsed patient was then removed to a separate room (the "crisis-chamber"), specially padded to prevent injury. Mesmer himself would accompany the patient into this chamber, denying access to anyone else. After a while they would emerge, the patient restored to calm and often declaring him or herself completely cured. Sometimes, though, more than one crisis was needed, the patients (usually in these instances, women) often insisting the experience was so pleasurable they wanted to repeat it over and over.

It is obvious from these descriptions of the mode of treatment and the convulsive crisis, that the whole process was susceptible of being viewed as a means of sexual excitation and abuse. In time this became a serious problem and a vehicle of attack for Mesmer's detractors. (Shortly after Mesmer's disciple, Charles d'Eslon, whom we shall soon meet, opened a magnetizing clinic, he received a visit from a man in uniform, who asked, "In my capacity as lieutenant-general of police, I wish to know whether, when a woman is magnetized and passing through the crisis, it would not be easy to outrage her." D'Eslon answered in the affirmative, but explained that only the colleagues of Mesmer, physicians of probity, were entitled and privileged to produce a crisis.) Mesmer continued to deny any imputation of impropriety in his treatments, nor was any specific case ever alleged against him. Yet it can hardly be denied that however honorable he may have been, in thought and act, the importance he attached to the convulsive crisis in his treatments made the whole procedure highly suspect in the eyes of those he was seeking to impress with its seriousness, and therefore hindered its acceptance.

Modern hypnotherapy does not require any convulsive crisis in the patient for the therapy to be effective. Mesmer was misled, by the strangeness and novelty of his method, which evoked such crises in some highly nervous and suggestible patients, into believing they were essential to the process. On the other hand, the notoriety of the crises among the Parisian public at large unquestionably attracted the attention of many who would otherwise have ignored Mesmer and his animal magnetism.

Whatever the particular motivation that brought the Chevalier Charles d'Eslon, a leading member of the Paris Medical Faculty but not in sympathy with its ultra-conservatism, to visit the Place Vendôme clinic soon after Mesmer opened it in September 1778, the Chevalier was fascinated by the whole procedure. As he was the chief physician to the King's brother, the Count of Artois, d'Eslon's immediate conversion to the cause of animal magnetism at one stroke opened up to Mesmer the entrance to the circles of the French royal court he had so eagerly sought.

The Count of Artois, who nearly half a century later would reign as Charles X, the last of the Bourbon line on the French throne, was then a young man of twenty-one, imbued with some of the freethinking notions Jean-Jacques Rousseau had for over two decades been disseminating among the French intelligentsia through his controversial writings. (Rousseau, incidentally, had died in that summer of 1778, in obscurity, in his rural retreat of Ermenonville. It is one of the ironic coincidences of history that both he and Voltaire should have passed from the scene within a few months of the coming to Paris of Mesmer, who equally with them represented a departure from long-established norms.) Having such leanings, it was not surprising the Count had chosen the open-minded d'Eslon to be his personal physician, but though he listened attentively to what the Chevalier eagerly told him of Mesmer's astonishing discovery, he never investigated it himself and later sided with those who denounced the new therapy.

This was typical of the Count's alternations between liberal and repressive thinking. On the outbreak of the French Revolution in 1789, he was one of the earliest of the royalty and nobility to go into exile and form an emigré die-hard opposition; yet on the restoration of the Bourbons after the fall of Napoleon, he advocated a policy of amnesty and oblivion of past offenses for all who had taken part in the Revolution. He gained vast popularity with the French public on coming to the throne as Charles X in 1824, by doing away with press censorship, but then went on to rule in ways so reactionary and authoritarian he brought on himself his overthrow in the July Revolution of 1830.

Nevertheless, in 1778 his relative openness toward Mesmer and his patronage of d'Eslon enabled the former to exploit to the fullest the opening thus provided into the highest levels of French society. Not only that, but d'Eslon's prestige as a medical man meant his endorsement of Mesmer resulted in a huge increase of applicants for treatment by animal magnetism. Indeed, this was the prime reason why the Place Vendôme clinic soon had to be given up for the more spacious quarters in the Hôtel Bouillon. Here there was ample room for four *baquets*, an orchestra to accompany Mesmer's own musical renditions, fountains and even a courtyard with a tree that was magnetized to provide cut-rate treatment for the swarms of poor who could not be accommodated at the *baquets*.

Before long, d'Eslon had acquired sufficient proficiency in magnetizing to set up his own clinic. Relations between him and Mesmer were still highly cordial, and d'Eslon now proposed a new attempt to persuade the Faculty to take a fresh look at animal magnetism; to do that, he told Mesmer, it would be necessary for each to write a book. Mesmer should write about the theoretical basis of the new therapy, and d'Eslon would undertake a clinical study of how it worked in practice.

Mesmer completed his assignment within a few weeks. His *Dissertation on Animal Magnetism* appeared in the late spring of 1779, and was hardly more than a brochure. It briefly detailed how he had made his discovery, the beneficial results he had achieved with it in Vienna, and the abuse and vilification that had been his reward. He concluded with a statement of the twenty-seven basic principles of his art. They amounted to the claim that an extremely rarefied fluid kept everything in the universe, including human bodies, in continuous contact; its ebb and flow, similar to that of the tides, could be controlled and directed by humans through various magnetic conductors, for purposes of healing all manner of ailments, both physical and mental. Further, he asserted, it was possible to store and transport this fluid, when properly magnetized, in concentrations of particular efficacy. "Through this means," he stated, "the physician will be able to determine the state of each individual's health with exactitude, so all maladies can be treated and prevented. The art of healing will thus reach its final stage of perfection."

Had these very large claims, that even today are in their fullness beyond the reach of hypnotherapy, been backed up at least in some degree by the clinical observations of d'Eslon, Mesmer's slim volume might have met with a better reception from the Faculty and the Paris medical fraternity in general. With few exceptions they ignored it. Meanwhile, Chevalier was making only slow progress with the writing of his own promised book; it would not come out until a year after Mesmer's. In the meantime, though, he offered to try to convince individual members of the Faculty, by inviting them to a special lecture by Mesmer followed by a dinner at which the subject could be freely discussed by all.

He persuaded a dozen members to come to the lecture and then to the dinner, which was at his house. All present admitted they had been favorably impressed by Mesmer's presentation, but were reluctant to commit themselves to any public endorsement of him. Some suggested Mesmer work for a while in a hospital, where his method could be better evaluated. Mesmer agreed, but the Faculty doctors then procrastinated about setting a starting date for him. Finally three of them volunteered to work with him in his clinic and closely observe his procedures.

They stayed at the clinic for over seven months, through the summer and into the fall of 1779. Mesmer became increasingly impatient as they kept delaying any final evaluation, and in the end—convinced they would never make any public statement in his favor—he asked them to leave. Only later did he learn that two of the three had become convinced his treatments were genuine, but what they felt was his supercilious attitude toward them had kept them from saying so. Now, offended by his dismissing them, they would keep silent.

Thus another opportunity of getting the formal endorsement Mesmer wanted had been lost. Nor was the majority of the Medical Faculty, still smarting from its loss of prestige and standing to the upstart Royal Society of Medicine, at all inclined to give any recognition to this other upstart— Mesmer's animal magnetism with its trappings of *baquets* and convulsive crises. The heads of the Faculty reviewed the alarming increase of interest in the new therapy, spreading even in the royal circles at Versailles—the Queen herself, Marie Antoinette, was said to be sending ailing intimates to the Hôtel Bouillon—and decided to forestall the already advertised publication of d'Eslon's clinical studies by putting out a contrary book of their own.

It was written in haste by one Jacques de Horne, and was no more than a sixteen-page pamphlet, but with its blatant attack on Mesmer's alleged immorality in his management of the crises, it gained a wide readership. One of the results was that d'Eslon's book, *Observations on Animal Magnetism,* was largely ignored when it came out a few days later. Mesmer was further assaulted by a leading member of the Faculty, Dr. Jean-Jacques Paulet, in an article in its *Medical Gazette,* that accused him of sleeping with some of his female patients. For this accusation Mesmer had, it is true, given some grounds by sometimes sleeping in the same room with a patient requiring more extensive treatment, but all evidence indicates no other improprieties took place.

There now came forward an ambitious young physician, Augustin Roussel de Vauzesmes, recently admitted to the Faculty at the unusually early age of twenty-six. Seeing in the discrediting of both Mesmer and d'Eslon an opportunity for his personal advancement in the medical profession, he proposed to the faculty it should grant d'Eslon's repeated request for a public hearing on the merits of animal magnetism, and turn it into a devastating exposé of its fallacy.

The hearing was convened on September 18, 1780. On arriving, d'Eslon—who had expected to make a presentation of the case for the new therapy—was curtly told to sit in the audience, which included a total of 160 doctors from Paris and its suburbs. It was de Vauzesmes who took the floor to deliver a long and stinging, ridicule-loaded attack on the whole concept of animal magnetism and on d'Eslon's betrayal of his oath as a physician by lending himself to such a charlatanic enterprise. Several of the alleged cures narrated in d'Eslon's book were dismissed as fraudulent or explainable by conventional means.

To his credit, d'Eslon rose from his seat and demanded he be allowed to reply to this diatribe. Though boos from the assembled doctors almost drowned him out as he began speaking, the Chevalier proceeded to make a reasoned response, presenting the facts in numerous cures obtained through the magnetic therapy. When he had finished, the Faculty recessed to deliberate its judgment, which was shortly delivered in the following terms.

The Chevalier d'Eslon was admonished to watch his behavior in the future; he was to lose his voting rights in the Faculty for a year; if by that time he had not repudiated in writing the views expressed in his book, he would be expelled; he was likewise to repudiate all the claims made in Mesmer's book.

Shocked and humiliated, d'Eslon made no response. He did not promise to comply with these demands. He continued to receive and treat patients, and the word started to be quietly passed around that he was even more effective than Mesmer himself.

As yet, however, Mesmer manifested no open jealousy of his pupil. He wrote a new pamphlet, titled *A Precise History of the Facts Relating to Animal Magnetism*, that appeared early in 1781; in it he rebutted the allegations of de Vauzesmes. He also busied himself with an attempt to translate the approbation he had gained in the circles around the Queen into the official endorsement he still pursued.

It proved as elusive a quest as ever. Though eminent courtiers such as the Count de Ségur and the Minister of State, M. de Maurepas, expressed their support of him and recommended his treatments, they shied away from setting up the Royal Commission Mesmer was asking for which would pronounce once and for all a seal of validation on his discovery. Finally, in March 1781, soon after the *Precise History* pamphlet came out, Mesmer decided to force the issue. He announced that since he and his treatments were not being properly appreciated in Paris, he would be leaving the French capital for good on April 15.

There was immediate consternation at Versailles, as well as among the sick who had continued to flock to Mesmer's *baquets*. Marie Antoinette wrote to him, pleading that it was heartless of him to abandon his patients in this way. He replied that although he felt he had amply proved his dedication to the sick, he would reconsider if the court made a serious offer of recognition and support for him. The Count de Ségur was now sent to negotiate with Mesmer, and made the following, seemingly very generous proposal.

The Royal Commission would be set up, consisting of five distinguished men of science. If it determined animal magnetism was useful and beneficial, the King would issue a royal decree to that effect. The King would also make him a grant of property on which to locate a permanent clinic. Mesmer would be granted a life pension of twenty thousand livres annually—equivalent to the salaries of the highest paid government officials—on condition he would never leave France without royal permission.

Mesmer raised two objections. He wanted the property grant to be specifically identified as to its location—he did not want it to be out somewhere in the provinces—and that there be an adequate structure, preferably a castle, already on it, to save him the cost of building one. Also, he wanted the commission to do its investigation and report its decision before the April 15 deadline—only a month away—when he would otherwise leave Paris.

The Court demurred. The stipulations, it felt, were unreasonable. However, after thinking it over, the King modified his terms and sent M. de Maurepas to offer them to Mesmer. Louis XIV was willing to issue the royal decree in favor of animal magnetism without any investigation by a commission, provided Mesmer would teach his method to at least three physicians specified by the Court. As for the grant of land, in place of it the King now offered a life pension of thirty thousand livres annually, which should enable Mesmer to buy any property he desired, and build on it, without feeling any financial hardship.

To the astonishment of everyone, Mesmer rejected this offer also. The King was not a scientist or a physician; what weight would his decree carry among those who were? As for teaching physicians picked by the government, that was in effect making them his judges. He would choose his own pupils. The increase of the pension offer smacked of bribery; if the Court wanted to be truly generous it could easily afford to give him a country estate worth 400,000 or 500,000 francs.

The Chevalier d'Eslon was present when Mesmer spurned this offer. To d'Eslon it seemed sheer folly to turn it down. He began to have doubts of Mesmer's sanity. What he did not understand or appreciate was Mesmer's high sense of personal honor. The Viennese would always insist on being taken at his real value. He would not be bought, nor fawned over by those to whom he was simply a fascinating novelty.

Nevertheless, he did not want to offend Marie Antoinette. He wrote to her, explaining the moral considerations that had prompted his refusal. He added he would defer his departure to September 18, the first anniversary of the Faculty's condemnation of him and d'Eslon.

Exactly why Mesmer set this second date is not clear. In any event, it passed without his leaving Paris. He may have been planning some sort of counterstroke, with d'Eslon, to the Faculty on the anniversary. A growing coolness was now setting in between him and d'Eslon, and if there was any such plan, it was given up. Two new personages had now replaced d'Eslon in close association with Mesmer. Their interests and objectives were more political than medical, and they would be prime factors in the final Parisian downfall of Mesmer and his doctrine. At the moment, though, they were his most fervent disciples.

Their names were Nicholas Bergasse and Guillaume Kornmann; the former was the scion of a prosperous Lyons merchant, a philosopher-playboy with a long array of neurotic ailments, and the latter a wealthy banker from Strasbourg on the Rhine, who shared the visionary idealism that led Bergasse to found what he called the Society of Universal Harmony, having as its goal the remaking of society in a peaceful image. Mesmer became a member of this society soon after the pair started a regular attendance at the *baquets* in the spring of 1781. Later in the year Bergasse circulated a pamphlet he had written, satirizing the opposition to animal magnetism. In it he argued the healthier people are, the more likely they are to demand all sorts of things they would never ask for otherwise. Therefore it is in the interest of the ruling and possessing classes to keep the bulk of the population in a state of perpetual poor health, and so they oppose Mesmer's therapy because it would make everyone healthy.

This was playing around the edges of the widening French social chasm, from which in another seven years would leap up the flames of the Revolution.

As yet, however, readers in the upper classes found such talk merely amusing. The wealthy and titled were not, as a class, opposed to Mesmer. They probably did not take him or his animal magnetism too seriously, but it was a new and fascinating fad with which they liked to play. In fact Mesmer began to complain at this time that all too many who could afford it were setting up their own *baquets*, though without knowing how to use them properly, much as in our time it has become a status-symbol fad to have a hot tub for its supposed benefits of health and togetherness.

There was, though, in the Medical Faculty's embittered hatred and scorn for the Chevalier d'Eslon, an implied accusation that he was betraying the interests of the privileged orders to which he belonged, by promoting a novel and suspect medical treatment capable of being mastered by almost anyone. The medical profession saw itself in danger of being rendered obsolete, with the loss of its age-old high social status and attending perquisites. When the year's probation on which the Faculty had placed d'Eslon expired on September 18, 1781, it was extended for one more year to give him a final chance to redeem himself in their eyes, but this was accompanied by a stern warning to expect no further indulgence.

Indeed, some of the Faculty were determined to ruin the Chevalier's reputation without waiting for the second year of grace to run out. They put out a pamphlet, allegedly written by d'Eslon himself, which in insulting language attacked the Academy for its excessive conservatism and resistance to new ideas. To protect himself d'Eslon had to ask the Paris police to remove the pamphlet from sale and to circulate his statement denying he had written it. Damage had been done, however. Many did not believe his denial, and began to point fingers at him as a charlatan angered by the Faculty's exposure of him.

Among the more temperate criticisms of d'Eslon's practice and defense of animal magnetism was one that, had it been properly looked into further by either him or Mesmer, might have changed the whole course of the development of hypnotism by producing an earlier understanding of its true nature. In his book cited above, d'Eslon had sought to reply to those who objected that the effects of animal magnetism resulted wholly from the imaginations of those being treated. He asked: "If this method is indeed nothing more than a means of using imagination to bring about health, is that not marvelous? If imagination is the best medicine, why not use imaginative medicine?" The Chevalier's critics pointed to this passage as an admission by him that in fact imagination was all there was to animal magnetism.

Instead of taking up this challenge and coming to a realization that it was through the imaging power of the subconscious that animal magnetism worked, d'Eslon insisted the passage was a mere figure of speech, a "momentary conjecture" not intended to be taken seriously. Neither did Mesmer avail himself of this opening to seek a more correct understanding of how his treatments achieved their effects.

He was, in any event, becoming increasingly estranged from d'Eslon. They hardly ever met or consulted with each other anymore. The final break came in the summer of 1782, during a five-week vacation Mesmer took at the eponymous resort of Spa in the independent Bishopric of Liege, now part of Belgium. The Chevalier, noting his second probationary year had only a few weeks left to run, asked the Faculty to permit him to address them in defense of himself and the treatments he was continuing to give. Permission having been granted, he delivered a speech that was notable mainly for the absence of any mention of Mesmer.

What he was doing, d'Eslon emphasized, was to be judged on its own worth, and not in relation to anyone else's methods. This divorcing of himself from Mesmer did not save the Chevalier from final condemnation by the Faculty. It voted to expel him permanently, with no possibility of future re-admission. All he had achieved was the separation of himself from his mentor; a breach that in the end would prove fatal to the interests of both.

However, it was Mesmer who made the first public revelation of the rupture with d'Eslon. On returning from Spa, he received an anonymous package, probably from someone on the Faculty, containing a copy of the Chevalier's speech, with attention drawn to the omission of any mention of the originator of animal magnetism. Mesmer was deeply distressed by what he saw as desertion by his friend. After thorough discussion with his new leading disciples Kornmann and Bergasse he published on October 4, 1782, a letter he had sent to the Faculty, disclaiming any further connection with d'Eslon or his brand of animal magnetism, which he attacked as faulty and at variance with his own.

Two weeks later, d'Eslon replied to Mesmer in a short, curt letter, reminding his former mentor he had always sought to promote the acceptance of his discovery. The Chevalier also returned the gold snuffbox Mesmer had given him at the beginning of their friendship. Mesmer was ungracious enough to make a public response, denying the gift had in any way implied his approval of d'Eslon's practice and promotion of animal magnetism on his own. Such behavior was not typical of Mesmer; it indicated how deeply he felt hurt by d'Eslon.

For the moment, the breach between Mesmer and d'Eslon did no harm to their respective practices; if anything, it redounded to their advantage. The Chevalier's clientele among the upper classes expanded, his separation from Mesmer being seen as a confirmation of his possessing, as befitted his higher social rank, a truer and better knowledge of the new magnetic therapy. Mesmer's unhesitant discarding of his unfaithful pupil attracted many to what they viewed as his stronger and superior character. Moreover, his practice was now being transformed into a regular business enterprise by Kornmann and Bergasse.

They had accompanied Mesmer on the vacation excursion to Spa, and had taken the opportunity to discuss with him the plan, conceived by Bergasse, of making his Society of Universal Harmony, which so far had attracted few members, the vehicle for a wider dissemination of Mesmer's discovery. They also discussed setting up an endowment that would secure

Mesmer an assured income and provide for the training of qualified practitioners to carry on the work. This would free Mesmer from having to depend on royal bounty or official sanction of his doctrine.

Kornmann, whose devotion to Mesmer was unstinted following the cure of his ailing son by the magnetic treatment, put up the initial funding to get the project started. Bergasse, who was also a lawyer, undertook to attend to whatever legal formalities were necessary, and to defend Mesmer against any charges or lawsuits that might be filed against him. In brief, the scheme was based on Mesmer pledging to teach his method to the first hundred subscribers for membership, at 2,400 francs per head, a fee so high it automatically excluded all but persons of wealth and position.

The first twenty subscribers, including Bergasse himself, had paid in by March 10, 1783, when the Society was formally incorporated under French law, with the Masonic-sounding title of the Lodge of Associates of Universal Harmony. It was Mesmer, with his Masonic associations from Vienna, where he and Mozart had been initiates of the Truth and Freedom Lodge of Freemasons, who insisted on this designation, over the objections of Bergasse who was also asked by Mesmer to follow Masonic organizational structure in drawing up the Society's rules and by-laws.

By the end of 1783, a total of forty-eight members had signed up, among them the Marquis de Puységur and his younger brother, the Count de Chastenet, who together with a third brother would be the next great figures of hypnotism. Scions of the great aristocratic families of Montesquieu and Noailles had also joined, as well as the Marquis de Lafayette, who had risen to fame as a fighter for American independence in the Revolution just concluded across the Atlantic. Lawyers, priests, monks, six physicians and surgeons, bankers, and businessmen were enrolled, as too was the Bailli des Barres and one other knight of the Order of Malta which then governed that strategic Mediterranean island.

Fifty more members were swiftly added in the first two weeks of 1784, and though the total of ninety-eight was two short of the stipulated minimum of one hundred, Mesmer and Bergasse decided it was close enough and declared the Society a functioning organization. The designation of it as a "Lodge" had by now been dropped, to satisfy Bergasse, who soon found the teaching of the members was largely devolving on him. Mesmer made it plain he did not see himself as an instructor; rather, he expected the members to learn by imitation, from simply watching him. He did not want them to start magnetizing on their own, nor to teach others in turn. They were to pledge faithfulness to his doctrine, and to spread the word of it, but only he should do the actual therapy.

This limited access to the theory and practice of animal magnetism was not what the subscribers to membership were expecting to get. Bergasse did his best to smooth over the situation, imparting some actual instruction in magnetizing. He also held lecture sessions in which he sought to stress that for animal magnetism to attain its full potential as a cure for all human ills, there had to first be a wholesale transformation of people's thinking, along the lines of Mesmer's principles. This, he said, was of much greater importance for the future redemption of society than just learning the mechanics of magnetizing. For a time, this line—which apparently had Mesmer's approval—went over well.

The Society began to expand with local chapters all over France, and by mid-year of 1784 it had 430 members in all. Seemingly, Mesmer had reached a culmination of success he could hardly have dreamed of when he first came to Paris. He was now making an enormous income—on paper at least, for subscribers were being accepted on pledges to pay, instead of actual cash in full on signing—and animal magnetism was being talked about everywhere, not only in Paris but through-out France. The fame of it was spreading abroad; Lafayette, about to return to America, wrote to General Washington he was bringing with him the news of the greatest medical discovery of all time. In the royal court, the Queen, despite Mesmer's rebuff of her offer in 1781, continued to extol his therapy. The Princess de Lamballe, one of her intimates, became one of his prime advocates, sending him scores of patients from the highest social ranks. The fact that Mesmer was increasingly—at least in Bergasse's presentations—taking a position of criticism of the existing social divisions in France, was not yet hurting him in court circles. Yet it was at this very moment, when Mesmer's glory was at its height, the forces making for his downfall were gathering in a strength soon to prove irresistible. Before the year 1784 had passed into history, Mesmer and animal magnetism had been struck blows that would drive him into obscurity and exile. His discovery would be taken up by others and developed in new, different, and more effective ways.

PRÉCIS

HISTORIQUE

DES FAITS RELATIFS

AU

MAGNÉTISME-ANIMAL

JUSQUES EN AVRIL 1781.

*Par M. MESMER, Docteur en Méde-
cine de la Faculté de Vienne.*

OUVRAGE TRADUIT DE L'ALLEMAND.

A LONDRES.

M. DCC. LXXXI.

Title-page of Mesmer's Précis historique...
which contains the text of his proposals for a trial of his treatment by Animal
Magnetism presented to the Faculté de Médecine de Paris on September 18, 1780

CHAPTER 6
The Fall of Mesmer—But Not of Mesmerism

By March 1784, the vogue of animal magnetism had attained such a pitch the medical and political establishments of France had become seriously alarmed. According to a survey made by order of the Prefect of the Paris police, M. Jean-Pierre LeNoire, at least eight thousand persons in the metropolitan area had been treated in either Mesmer's or d'Eslon's clinics.

Self-appointed magnetizers were springing up in all the leading cities of France. All sorts of radical enthusiasts, such as the crank genius Jean-Louis Carra, who claimed the extreme severity of the winter was due to atmospheric changes caused by the resistance of academic science to magnetizing, were finding in Mesmer's method a panacea for all the ills of society. This dangerous line of thinking was starting to make serious inroads into the wealthy, titled, and educated classes.

Even if there was no other reason to call a halt to the magnetizing mania, its detractors asserted, the grave peril it presented to public morality required its prompt suppression. The scandalous "crises" into which the magnetizers induced their female patients were only a form of sexual orgasm in public, which could no longer be tolerated. It had not escaped the notice of M. LeNoir's investigators there were eight women for every man seeking treatment at the *baquets*.

With arguments of this sort, King Louis XVI—who himself had no particular feeling one way or the other about Mesmer or his therapy, but disliked "all commotions and disturbances to peace and order"—was persuaded to appoint on March 12, 1784, a Royal Commission of Inquiry to determine whether there was anything to the claims made for animal magnetism. The Commission consisted of nine members, some of high distinction in the medical and scientific fields. Four members, including Dr. Joseph Ignance Guillotin (who in a few years would achieve immortal renown for recommending the construction of a machine that would kill all persons condemned to death instantly and humanely), were physicians from the Medical Faculty which had been lobbying intensively in the royal court for a restoration of its status and prestige. Five members were from the Academy of Sciences. These included the noted chemist Antoine Lavoisier and the astronomer Jean-Sylvain Bailly (both of whom would be guillotined nine years later during the Reign of Terror), and Benjamin Franklin, the envoy of the United States to France, famed no less for his practical research into many branches of science than for his diplomatic and political genius in bringing about the independence of the former Thirteen Colonies.

The Royal Society of Medicine, which had displaced the Faculty as the premier body of the medical profession in France, immediately complained about being left off the Royal Commission of Inquiry. Indeed, the Society made such an uproar over it that on April 4 the King named a second Commission, made up of five Society of Medicine members, to conduct a parallel inquiry. Included among the five was a Dr. Poissonnier, whose wife had died of cancer after unavailing treatment by Mesmer, and a botanist, Dr. Larent de Jussieu, who had gained a repute for searching out and using new medications from plants. He was the nephew of three noted botanist brothers who had been among the scientific luminaries of the reigns of Louis XIV and Louis XV.

On the face of it, the commission members appeared reasonably objective. Lavoisier, Bailly, and Franklin were regarded as open-minded, as was de Jussieu. Poissonnier would be prejudiced against Mesmer, but it seemed most of the other members would at least try to examine the evidence fairly.

It did not turn out that way. This was mainly because the royal directives to the commissioners emphasized they were to prove or disprove the existence of animal magnetism and the all-pervading fluid that was supposed to be its vehicle. Since both of these elements were founded on thoroughly unscientific premises by Mesmer and his followers, and had no real existence, it was not difficult for the commissioners to reach negative conclusions about them. The tragedy was that the phenomena they were investigating were real enough, and instead of recognizing them as such and seeking a solid explanation for them, the commissioners dismissed animal magnetism as due merely to the imaginations of the patients. Thus the actuality of hypnotism and its mode of operation were not discerned, and a whole century may have been lost in the utilization of hypnosis for therapy.

Even to this day, there is an astonishing blindness on the part of many writers on scientific and medical subjects in acknowledging Mesmer's concept of animal magnetism as the first step toward the development of scientific hypnotism. Mesmer was the pioneer, from whom an unbroken line of further development extends to the present day. Stephen Jay Gould, the Harvard biologist, geologist, and noted historian of science, famed for his "punctuated evolution" modification of Darwinism, is one of those who has failed to see this. In an article in the July 1989 issue of *Natural History* he represents Mesmer as a fraud and charlatan, and his method as of no consequence or importance.

In Gould's view, the Royal Commission (he ignores the second Commission altogether) performed an admirable work of exposure of an imposition on the public's gullibility. "Never in history had such an extraordinary and luminous group," Gould extols, "been gathered together in the service of rational inquiry." In particular he holds up Franklin and Lavoisier as shining examples of this dedication to pure disinterested search for the truth, crediting them with having devised most of the experiments that supposedly demonstrated the fraudulence of animal magnetism.

A more critical examination of the Commission's procedure and conclusions does not bear out this eulogy. In the first place, Franklin—who was seventy-eight, ill from gout and mainly waiting for Thomas Jefferson to arrive and relieve him of his post so he could finally go home to America after an eight year stay in France—was not a leading participant in the investigation, though he lent his prestige to it. Although he allowed some of the experiments to be carried out at his home in suburban Passy, in a letter to a French scientist friend, LaCondamine, who was on neither Commission, he indicated he was not greatly interested in the debate over animal magnetism, though he suggested that imagination might account for its reported effects. In this, Franklin was on the right track, but he did not pursue it, nor did anyone else. That Franklin was not hostile to the new therapies is evident from the same letter, in which he remarked that good results seemed to have been obtained from the use of electric treatments for nerve and circulation blockages.

As for Lavoisier, his attitude throughout the investigation was one of assertion of his superior intelligence. He was convinced there was nothing to animal magnetism, and anyone who had a contrary opinion was either a fraud, a dupe or a fool. Having made up his mind in advance, he was not going to let himself be confused by the facts. Since animal magnetism had indeed no existence in the mistaken conception both Mesmer and d'Eslon had of it, it was simple for Lavoisier and his colleagues to devise experiments that proved its non-existence. Blindfolded subjects, for example, were unable to discern "magnetized" objects from those which were not.

On that sort of premise—and with Lavoisier brusquely dismissing any attempt to consider any investigation of why, if there was nothing at all to Mesmer's discovery, it was nevertheless curing or relieving a great number and variety of illness—there was total unanimity in the Royal Commission's conclusion. The report released on September 4 stated: "No evidence could be found for the existence of a magnetic fluid and therefore no therapy could be founded on it. All the alleged effects were simply due to the over-excited imaginations of the subjects." Eighty thousand copies of the report were ordered to be immediately printed and distributed to physicians throughout France, to halt the further dissemination and practice of a mode of treatment "both false and dangerous."

A separate report, not made public though filed in the Royal Library where it could be consulted by officials, concluded that the magnetic treatment of women patients incurred grave risks to public morals and decency, and should be discouraged, or even banned. This secret report, "not adapted for general publication," is more curious than the official version.

It has been observed that women are like musical strings stretched in perfect unison; when one is moved, all the others are instantly affected. Thus the commissioners have repeatedly observed that when the crisis occurs in one woman, it occurs almost at once in others. . . . .

Women are always magnetized by men; the established relations are doubtless those of a patient to the physician, but this physician is a man, and whatever the illness may be, it does not deprive us of our sex, it does not entirely withdraw us from the power of the other sex; illness may weaken impressions without destroying them. Moreover, most of the women who present themselves to be magnetized are not really ill; many come out of idleness, or for amusement; others, if not perfectly well, retain their freshness and their force, their senses are unimpaired and they have all the sensitiveness of youth; their charms are such as to affect the physician, and their health is such as to make them liable to be affected by him, so that the danger is reciprocal. . . . .

The magnetizer generally keeps the patient's knees enclosed within his own, and consequently the knees and all the lower parts of the body are in close contact. The hand is applied to the hypochondriac region, and sometimes to that of the ovarium, so that the touch is exerted at once on many parts, and these the most sensitive parts of the body.

The experimenter, after applying his left hand in this manner, passes his right hand behind the woman's body, and they incline towards each other so as to favor this two-fold contact. This causes the closest proximity; the two faces almost touch, the breath is intermingled, all physical impressions are felt in common, and the reciprocal attraction of the sexes must consequently be excited in all its force. It is not surprising that the senses are inflamed. The action of the imagination at the same time produces a certain disorder throughout the machine; it obscures the judgment, distracts the attention; the women in question are unable to take account of their sensations, and are not aware of their condition.

The report nevertheless failed to cite a single actual case of impropriety resulting from the magnetizing of women, nor is there anything in the record of the Commission's investigations that it ever observed a woman patient being brought to a crisis by magnetizing. In other words, the Commission was deciding from impressions and hearsay, not from firsthand observation. Obviously, there was some danger that treatment of women by Mesmer's method could be abused. The Commission made up its collective mind that widespread abuse was happening or was about to happen. It sought no corroborative, factual evidence for its conclusion.

Ten days after the release of the Royal Commission's report, the Royal Society of Medicine issued its own conclusion that also denied the reality of animal magnetism. One member of the Society—the botanist, de Jussieu—dissented, and refused to sign the report. Instead, he wrote a summary of his own determinations, which he released a month later. He argued that instead of simply dismissing animal magnetism as non-existent, without any inquiry into how something that did not exist was nevertheless producing some demonstrable real effects, the Commissions should have considered whether some emanations of the human body might account for them. Perhaps, de Jussieu, suggested, the magnetizer was in some way able to transfer "animal heat" from his own body into a sick person's, which might be deficient in this "heat." In any event, he wrote, all practitioners of the new therapy should be required to carefully observe, record, and publish all aspects of their treatments.

Well thought out and rational though de Jussieu's minority report was, it brought scant comfort to Mesmer, d'Eslon and their followers, who by that time were in disarray and retreat on all fronts. Through the five months of the investigations by the Commissions, the cause of animal magnetism had been struck one damaging blow after another. Even developments that seemed at first to redound to its credit soon turned counterproductive.

One such was the seeming triumph of one of Mesmer's few disciples from clerical ranks, Father Hervier, a popular Paris preacher often invited to appear in pulpits all across France. On April 6, 1784 he had been the guest preacher at the Cathedral of St. Andre in Bordeaux. At the mid-point of his sermon, a young woman of good family, in the pew directly before him, went into what seemed epileptic convulsions. Descending from the pulpit, he "magnetized" her with hand

passes similar to Mesmer's, and in a few moments the convulsions had ended, and she was calm and composed again. The
news of Hervier's success in relieving her accompanied him
back to Paris, where he was hailed as the latest mesmerist
hero. This did not sit well with his superiors in the Church,
who suspended him from preaching and put out pamphlets
suggesting the incident in Bordeaux had not been accurately
reported — the girl's seizure had subsided of itself.

This was followed by the death of the popular writer
Court de Gébelin, while undergoing therapy by Mesmer.
Gébelin's works, largely on esoteric themes appealing to
people's sense of wonder, had gained a wide following for
him all over France, and his turning to Mesmer for treatment
of the illness he was suffering from was seen as a strong
reinforcement of the legitimacy Mesmer continually sought.
Again, it did not turn out that way. Mesmer quickly diagnosed
Gébelin as having an incurable kidney failure, causing severe
pain. He knew he could do nothing for the malady itself, but
the pain might be alleviated by animal magnetism. According-
ly, he took the writer in as a guest, and magnetized him daily
for relief of pain, which Gébelin averred he did receive from
the treatment. When Gébelin died on May 12, Mesmer demanded an autopsy by five physicians to confirm his own
diagnosis of kidney failure as the cause of death, and that his
therapy was never intended by him for such conditions, nor
had he employed it on Gébelin in any hope of curing him.

This precaution on Mesmer's part was, however, unavailing. Soon the word was being widely spread around Paris,
and repeated in scurrilous lampoons, cartoons, and songs, that
Gébelin had been the victim of a charlatan giving him useless

treatments. "Yes, Mesmer relieves pain," these attacks alleged, "by denying his patients proper medical care; soon they die and then of course they don't feel any more pain."

Mesmer was feeling increasingly frustrated in his attempt to make animal magnetism therapy accepted medical treatment. He had been extremely embarrassed when on Good Friday, April 16, at the invitation of the Queen, Marie Antoinette, he attended a concert at the royal palace of the Tuileries, and one of the performers was none other than Fraulein Paradis, very clearly blind. There were varying opinions among the audience of the quality of her piano playing, but little sympathy for Mesmer, who found himself the butt of jeering questions: "Isn't that the young lady whose blindness you said you had cured? How is it that your magnetism didn't take hold? She's still stone-blind!"

He put the best face he could on the situation, and managed to escape from the concert without losing his temper or otherwise lashing out at his accusers, but he was soon painfully aware of a fall-off of patients at his clinic.

On the other hand, d'Eslon seems to have benefited for a while; the public got the impression he, unlike Mesmer, was not making exaggerated and fraudulent claims of cures, and was thus the truer and better practitioner of animal magnetism. The investigating Commissions seem, indeed, to have shared this attitude, and to have regarded d'Eslon as now the prime exponent of the new therapy. Almost all of their experiments were performed at his clinic, or on his patients. Mesmer was virtually ignored, except in reference as the originator. It can be easily guessed that this intensified the antipathy Mesmer had come to have for his former star pupil and friend.

(It might also be guessed that Fraulein Paradis was herself embarrassed by the reaction to her appearance in Paris; she refused to give any more concert performances and from then on supported herself by giving piano lessons at her Vienna home.)

The enmity of Claude Bertholet, a chemist second only to Lavoisier in repute, and who had at first been attracted to Mesmer and spoken in support of him, was another blow in this disastrous year of 1784. Early in April, Bertholet signed up as a member of the Society of Universal Harmony. After a month of attending, he declared he could not see any animal magnetism or magnetic fluid as being the moving factors in the effects he observed, which he acknowledged were real enough. "It is imagination, powerfully stimulated, which produces all these marvelous results," Bertholet stated; "the rest is all a vague and chimeric patter." Mesmer accused him of having broken faith, and the chemist stalked out in a fit of fury. He too had come very close to the real secret of Mesmer's magnetism—the imagination acting on the subconscious—but his defection may have influenced the adverse judgment by the Royal Commission, for he was a close friend of several of its members. Some of Mesmer's partisans were so incensed at Bertholet they physically assaulted him while he was walking near the Palais Royal, though apparently he was not seriously hurt.

Then, at the time the two Commission reports came out, Mesmer had a humiliating failure in attempting to magnetize a royal personage, Prince Heinrich of Prussia, who was visiting France. At an army camp, the military doctors, who had been experimenting with magnetizing, diverted and amused the Prince by magnetizing several soldiers. They then sprang a surprise on him by introducing Mesmer himself, whom they had secretly invited. Unfortunately Mesmer was not at his best; or else the Prince was an unusually refractory subject. Despite repeated attempts, Mesmer could not magnetize him. The story was then put out by some of Mesmer's followers that persons of royal blood had an inborn resistance to being magnetized, a protection instilled by Divine Providence, for the security of the State.

This explanation was seized on by the Princess de Lamballe, mentioned earlier as an intimate of the Queen, to promote her personal vanity. She had been much interested in Mesmer and had sent him patients from her circle, although she herself had never undergone his treatment. But now she asked him to try to magnetize her. If it was true those of royal blood were resistant to animal magnetism, and Mesmer failed with her, she reasoned it would prove her contention she was related to royalty, a claim many had doubted. Mesmer did fail to magnetize her, and she went back to the court in triumph, asserting there was no longer any doubt that she had royal blood in her veins.

It was no triumph for Mesmer, however. He saw all too plainly that he and his therapy were becoming a mere fad and sensation, something with which the rich and mighty could amuse themselves, and not take seriously as an epochal discovery benefiting the mass of mankind. At no time since leaving Vienna had he been as dispirited as he now became. He sought, nevertheless, to make some response to the condemnations by the Commissions, and to several books that appeared either just before their report or immediately afterward. The writers of these books appear to have been in touch with the Commissions, for in large part they echo their conclusions, though at least one, a M. Thouret in his *Researches and Doubts on Animal Magnetism*, concluded there might be something useful in it if it were employed to direct the imagination.

Mesmer had earlier been an effective presenter of his positions in writing, but now he was defensive and his words lacked vitality. Earlier in the year he had published a book that was heavily edited by Bergasse, titled *A Theory of the World and Its Organization*. It tried but failed conspicuously to present animal magnetism as an integral part of a world energy system. Now he aimed his rebuttals not so much at the Commissions' findings, as at the way in which their conclusions had been reached.

They had not really investigated him at all, he insisted in open letters and pamphlets; they had concentrated on the clinic and patients of d'Eslon, who, he said, knew nothing about animal magnetism, being only a clumsy imitator. He proposed that the Royal Commission undertake a new inquiry, but this time limit it to himself and his practice. This was an oblique response, directed more at d'Eslon rather than the Commission, and that body ignored it. At the same time, it widened still more the breach between Mesmer and d'Eslon — a breach that was mostly of Mesmer's making, and served only to weaken the case of each. The response of the Chevalier to the reports of the Commissions was far more straightforward, exposing the distortions, omissions, and often tortured reasoning in them. In the book he published within a month of the publication of the reports, d'Eslon pointed out that contrary to the assertion that none of the Commissioners had felt any effect when magnetized, one (M. Caille of the Society of Medicine) had undergone the typical crisis. He also criticized their dismissal of the numerous cures or partial remissions of many different ailments that had been obtained through magnetizing, especially among the poor who rarely could afford regular medical treatment.

The Chevalier did not agree that the nonexistence of the magnetic fluid had been proven. To him it was simply not believable that imagination alone could produce the astonishing effects he had witnessed, such as the instant relief of pain in severe burns. To ignore evidence of this sort was to d'Eslon a clear proof the Commissions had prejudged their inquiries and had never had any intention of carrying out an objective, impartial examination. They had taken only the most cursory look at Mesmer's clinic, even though Mesmer was the originator of the magnetic treatment and therefore supposed to be the most expert in its use.

This was not mere politeness from d'Eslon toward his mentor and former friend. He was still willing to concede priority to Mesmer and hoping they might join forces to combat the reports. The overture was not heeded by Mesmer, who was now facing fresh humiliations in the satirical attacks on him from the stages of the Paris theaters, always the most influential shapers of opinion in the French capital. On November 26, a play called *The Modern Doctors* commenced a twenty-one-performance run, a sensationally long one for those days, at the Comedie Italienne. It caricatured both d'Eslon and Mesmer as swindlers, and in the closing act featured a chorus of their deluded followers, singing in a circle around a *baquet*. The reviewers hailed it, and the jokes from it passed into the everyday conversation of Parisians. In less than two weeks, animal magnetism was being laughed at everywhere, in homes and on the streets, by high and low alike. Imitation farces and comic skits ridiculing Mesmer became the standard bill of fare at music halls and other places of entertainment. By the mid-winter, animal magnetism had sunk so low in public esteem that Thomas Jefferson, who had now replaced Franklin as the American envoy, in a report dated February 5, 1785 wrote, ". . . the doctrine is now wholly dead, ridiculed to scorn and oblivion."

Mesmer was becoming increasingly withdrawn, as if he felt these slings and arrows of scorn were beneath his dignity to combat or refute. Yet there had been a few persons of note who had attempted to stand up for him amid the rising tempest of rejection. Prominent among these defenders of animal magnetism in its hour of downfall was Jean-Jacques d'Esprémenil, a lawyer and member of the Paris City Council, who before long would play a leading role in the outbreak of the French Revolution. He had joined the Society of Universal Harmony, and was so affronted by the first performances of *The Modern Doctors* he hastily wrote and had printed a pamphlet denouncing the play, and threw a copy of it onto the stage in the midst of the actors. It created a short-lived sensation, but did nothing to halt or even moderate the spreading assault of ridicule and slander on animal magnetism and its promoters.

A writer named Caullet de Veaumorel, who was sympathetic to Mesmer's doctrine, now tried to interject a note of calm appraisal into the agitation. He wrote and published a treatise in which he made the first systematic analysis of what he was among the first to distinctively call "mesmerism." In this treatise, Veaumoral emphasized that the human will was the primary force in magnetizing. What Mesmer had discovered, and successfully applied, was how to focus and direct his will upon the receptivity of his patients. This was yet another very close approach to the reality of hypnotism. Mesmer, in his reply to Veaumoral (in an open letter in one of the leading Paris newspapers) argued the analysis had been based on an incomplete acquaintance with the magnetizing process, since Veaumoral had not attended the clinic but had only studied the notes of those who had.

Veaumorel's response was that those notes were adequate for his purposes, and he had not been attacking Mesmer; quite the contrary, he was trying to elevate his new therapy to a higher level of acceptance. It was high time, he suggested, Mesmer began to appreciate and recognize his supporters, instead of always accusing them of deviating from what he was imposing as unalterable dogma. Those words brought out in the open what Bergasse and Kornmann, and many of the Society of Universal Harmony's membership, had been increasingly feeling but were reluctant to say out loud. Now that Veaumorel had said it, they no longer hesitated.

These dissidents told Mesmer that so many people had now seen the actual practice of animal magnetism, and were capable of doing it themselves, he could not any longer claim to possess the exclusive rights to it. Since he had already received (and they had the account books of the Society to prove it) far more than the 240,000 French livres the Society's original membership had been obligated to pay him, and therefore was not in need of money, the Society should now be open to all applicants, free of any fee. Mesmer was hostile to this proposal. Through the first half of 1785 a bitter dispute, carried on largely in public and further damaging his standing, raged between him and the rebellious faction in the Society. It was finally terminated by the resignation of Bergasse, Kornmann, and the greater part of the Society membership, who joined the pair in founding a new association to promote animal magnetism as a socially redeeming and humanizing method of treatment. Mesmer left Paris in July 1785 and went to London, where he issued a small book he had written attacking his betrayers. From London, where his stay was brief, he traveled to Germany and Italy.

He is said to have attended a grand all-European conference of occultists and faith healers at Wilhelmsbad in the West German principality of Hesse that summer, along with such figures of charlatanic fame as the Count de St. Germain—who by other accounts had supposedly died some months earlier—and Count Alessandro di Cagliostro. In Italy, Mesmer is said to have met with Masonic circles that were going underground as a result of increasing denunciations of them by the Vatican. Beyond the bare facts, however, of his visit to Germany and Italy in the latter half of 1785, none of these stories can be verified. It is known that by winter, Mesmer was back in Paris, and, except for brief visits elsewhere in Europe, continued to live there until 1793. (In 1793, with the coming of the Reign of Terror, he fled France by way of Switzerland to Vienna.)

At the end of June 1785, with the breakup of the Society of Universal Harmony, Mesmer's active career ended. He had been his own worst enemy and had destroyed himself as an effective presenter of his own doctrine. He was so totally convinced of his own integrity he could not understand or accept that animal magnetism had elements that were susceptible to exploitation or abuse. He should have welcomed, rather than rejected, those who tried to find ways to ward off such abuse. Instead of allowing the practice of animal magnetism to develop and expand on its own, he had placed an exaggerated value on official acceptance of his therapy as a proven therapeutic system. He believed that if it had a sound basis — even if that basis turned out to be something other than his postulated magnetic fluid — and was effective, acceptance would follow. But he was too impatient, and too sure of his own rightness, to be willing to wait for this confirmation.

Nevertheless, it cannot be justly said — as some have — that the rest of Mesmer's life, which would extend through four more decades, was a void of inaction and despair. He had been the discoverer, or more correctly the reviver, of a potent healing method. He had seen that discovery pass — by its very vitality — out of his hands and into the hands of others who were spreading it far and wide. After the first, natural reactions of resentment and disappointment had worn off, he was content simply to watch the further development of animal magnetism, and to unhurriedly record his own further interpretations of it.

In particular he continued to be interested by the new phenomenon of "artificial somnambulism" that his pupils, the Puységur brothers, had inadvertently come across in their own experimentations with animal magnetism in the summer of 1784. The Puységurs noted that "magnetized" subjects who entered this trancelike state of "somnambulism," accepted suggestions without question. Their findings had quickly become an issue in the controversies that led to Mesmer's downfall, for they could be used by his opponents as evidence that others could develop his teachings further. Mesmer looked on the Puységurs as upstarts and defectors from the ranks of the true adherents of animal magnetism, and never really forgave them. In his last book, published in 1799, on which he had worked for over ten years, he tried to integrate, though not very successfully, their "artificial somnambulism" concept into the body of his own doctrine.

Induction into somnambulism, with its associated phenomena, was indeed the next great step, beyond Mesmer, in the development of the theory and practice of hypnotism. The Marquis de Puységur, the eldest brother, would succeed Mesmer as one of the World's Greatest Hypnotists. I shall tell his story in the following chapter and also return to Mesmer for the concluding years of his life.

First a few words are needed about the proliferation of radical movements across France, all having at least some connection with Mesmer's doctrine, in the half-decade between the discrediting of its founder in Paris and the outbreak of the French Revolution in July 1789.

Although Mesmer himself may have been held up to scorn and ridicule in the French capital, and his clinic and that of his chief rival the Chevalier d'Elson closed as their clientele shrank to next to nothing, mesmerism was sprouting vigorous new shoots everywhere in the realm of Louis XVI. Most, if not all, of these off-shoots Mesmer would disown as perversions of his original teaching, and many were unquestionably weird and outlandish in their claims. Beside their importance in contributing to the social climate of unrest and expectancy of upheaval, in which the Revolution was engendered and materialized, these movements kept alive the basic tenets of mesmerism and thus provided an essential continuity of connection to the great nineteenth century founders of modern hypnotism.

Some, such as the Mesmerist Society of Lyons, in whose ranks J. H. D. Petetin discovered the applicability of "magnetizing" to induce insensibility to dental and surgical pain, would lay foundations for later advances in scientific hypnotism. Others gave rise to mesmerist groups within occultist and spiritualist circles, such as the Martinists and Swedenborgians, whose transatlantic transplants in the United States would provide fertile ground for the rapid spread of interest in hypnotism there in the second quarter of the nineteenth century. All would have some role to play in the tragic drama of the French Revolution. That is a fascinating story which has yet to be adequately told in its own right, but it is separate from the one told in this book—the lives and achievements of the World's Greatest Hypnotists, the founders and pioneers and developers of the art of hypnotism as a method of healing and constructive growth. Mesmer was the first and in some respects the greatest of them all. His disciple and later rival d'Eslon did not quite attain to the ranks of the greats, but the Chevalier did more than he is often credited with in laying the foundations for later hypnotic exploration. This he did at the cost of his standing in society. When d'Eslon died early in

1786, the vicar of his home parish of St. Eustache would not officiate at his burial, because the Chevalier had adopted and practiced "the irreligious teachings of Mesmer."

IV.
THE DISCOVERY OF ARTIFICIAL
SOMNAMBULISM

Marquis de Puységur
1751 - 1825
Shown in his uniform of General of the French Artillery

The "magnetized" elm of Buzancy. Leaning on Puységur,
Victor Race is falling into magnetic sleep.

CHAPTER 7
Puységur Discovers Artificial Somnambulism

There were three Puységur brothers, born within a few years of each other, who were all interested in Mesmer's animal magnetism, and they all contributed to its further development. They were of an ancient family of the French nobility that for generations had occupied the castle and estate of Buzancy near Soissons, on the high ridge bordering the Aisne valley. Many of their forebears had distinguished themselves in the French military service, and the three also made notable careers in it.

The eldest of the three, Amand Marie Jacques Chastenet, Marquis de Puységur, who became Mesmer's successor as one of the greatest advancers of hypnotherapy, was born in 1751 and served as an officer of artillery in the unsuccessful siege of Gibraltar in 1782. He then accompanied an official mission to Russia before returning to his ancestral home late in 1783. An avid amateur scientist, he experimented with electricity and was attracted to Mesmer by the notoriety then attaching to the latter's reputed cures through his new therapy. However, upon closer examination the Marquis was skeptical and might have lost interest had it not been for the middle brother, Antoine Hyacinthe, known as the Count de Chastenet. Chastenet, as we shall call him for convenience, had a logical and analytical mind. He had joined the Society of Universal Harmony, attended Mesmer's classes, and was cured of an ailment that had bothered him. He convinced his elder brother to look further into the matter. Had he not done so, the Marquis would very likely not have discovered the essence and therapeutic efficacy of animal magnetism.

Chastenet was a naval officer who had been stationed in the Canary Islands, which belonged to France's Spanish ally in the recently concluded War of American Independence. He conducted research into the islands' aboriginal inhabitants, the Guanches, and brought some of their mummies to France for further study. When appointed to take command of a naval vessel at the port of Brest, he trained the officers of the vessel in the art of magnetizing. The entire ship—rigging, masts, sails, and hull—were magnetized by them, so as to make the vessel a huge magnetic *baquet*. During a four month cruise, crew members were magnetized for healing of injuries and illnesses, with a high rate of cures reported.

Still later, Chastenet was sent to Haiti, which was then the wealthiest of the French possessions in the West Indies, its sugar planters reaping enormous gains from the labor of their black slaves. He introduced animal magnetism to this plantation aristocracy and soon *baquets* became all the rage with them. The slaves demanded to have their own *baquets*, and their masters, thinking it a harmless concession, granted their request. It proved to be disastrous, for the blacks quickly adapted the techniques of magnetizing to the voodoo practices they had brought with them from Africa. Together, these forces acted to instill the belief in successful revolt, and inspired the slaves to commence their uprising in 1791 which destroyed the French colonial power in Haiti. Upon hearing of this, Mesmer is said to have declared that the black nation of Haiti owed its freedom to his teachings.

Mesmer had not been happy, though, with Chastenet's observation while still his pupil in 1784, that the phenomena of crisis and curative effects which occurred around the *baquets* were the result of the ability of the magnetizer to impress his will on the people there gathered, suggesting what they would experience. Realizing this undercut his whole doctrine of a mysterious intangible magnetic fluid, Mesmer begged him to keep that opinion to himself, for to make it public prematurely would be very harmful. More than twenty years later the Marquis wrote, "My brother was thus I believe the first to discover the mechanism underlying Mesmer's procedures, and the principal cause of their effects." The Marquis himself came independently to the same conclusion from his own extensive experiments with magnetizing, which he commenced soon after Chastenet had persuaded him to join the Society of Universal Harmony and to receive instruction from Mesmer.

By that time the youngest of the three brothers, Jacques Maxime de Chastenet de Puységur, known as the Viscount Puységur had also become an adherent of animal magnetism. An officer in the French Army, he revived a fellow officer on the parade ground at Bayonne, who had apparently fallen dead from an apoplectic stroke, by magnetizing him. He later successfully treated all the sick in his regiment by the same method.

It was, nevertheless, the Marquis who made the name of Puységur immortal in the annals of hypnotism. Charles Richet, a late nineteenth century French writer on the subject, did not hesitate to place him on a par with Mesmer himself. Richet asserted that while Mesmer was the initiator of hypnotism, Puységur was its true founder. Without him, the method would have been short-lived, merely another in the long series of unusual medical claims that have surfaced through all of history. A very short time after seriously applying himself to the mastery of animal magnetism, Puységur was experimenting on the hundreds of peasants who lived and worked on his vast family estate. He set up a variant of Mesmer's *baquet* around a centuries-old elm tree in the Buzancy town square. Located next to a spring with reputed curative powers, the tree itself had come to be venerated by generations of the peasantry as possessing similar virtues, especially in its bark. Consequently it was easy for Puységur to persuade the peasants that by magnetizing them under its branches he was only continuing a long standing tradition. Seated on stone benches under the tree, Puységur's patients would take hold of the ends of ropes dangling from it, and wrap these around the afflicted areas of their bodies. He then touched them with an iron rod, evoking crises similar to those in Mesmer's treatments, at the same time suggesting they diagnose what was wrong with themselves and prescribe the proper treatment. This early form of self-imaging worked surprisingly well; out of three hundred patients treated in a month's time, sixty-one were cured through treatment prescribed by the patients themselves while in mesmeric trance. When awakened — which was done by having them touch the tree — they remembered nothing of what they had said.

Puységur noted their behavior while magnetized (i.e., in trance) was very similar to that in sleepwalking persons. He further observed that the crises were milder than those he had witnessed in Mesmer's clinics, and in eight of the sixty-one cures the subjects had simply fallen into what looked like natural sleep, though they continued to respond to his verbal commands. He began to think the crisis was unnecessary and that magnetizing could produce all of Mesmer's effects simply by inducing in the subject a condition of artificial somnambulism, so called because it resembled sleepwalking and was descriptive of the state. (In modern hypnotism the term "somnambulism" is used to denote one of the deepest levels of hypnosis.)

This conjecture became a conviction with his treatment of Victor Race, a twenty-three year-old peasant, whom the Marquis had singled out for individual attention. Race was suffering from an infection in his chest, either pneumonia or a severe pleurisy. When the Marquis visited him at his cottage on May 4, 1784 — destined to be one of the landmark dates in the history of hypnotism — he was able to put him into a calm, deep, sleep-like state, with no attending convulsions or other manifestations of the mesmeric crisis. He then suggested to Race that he was enjoying himself at a rural fair, and the young man responded by going through motions of dancing and singing. Within an hour, he broke out into a "good sweat," and Puységur woke him up. He could not remember anything of what had passed, but he was feeling much better; his fever had subsided, he was breathing easily, and the next day he was fully recovered though still a little weak. The young peasant responded to the Marquis' suggestion that he was in good health and having a good time, and gained an immediate upper hand over whatever was making him ill. He also proved to be an ideal subject for additional experiments that further confirmed Puységur's belief he had found the true basis of Mesmer's magnetizing. It was not necessary for the

Marquis to touch him, or even to speak audibly to him. Simply by directing his mind toward Race's, Puységur was able to convey telepathic commands that the peasant carried out unquestioningly while in the sleep-like state. Race could recall none of this after being awakened.

The Marquis did not fully comprehend what he had discovered. He perceived he could make contact with the mind of another person by placing that individual in a trance resembling sleep, but he attributed this to the ability of a proficient magnetizer to communicate his wishes through the magnetic fluid, the existence of which he continued to accept. Though he realized this predicated an exclusivity of communication (i.e., the magnetizer and the subject had to be in rapport with each other only) he did not understand it was suggestion which elicited the response. In Puységur's view, he was simply giving commands to a peasant who would normally be expected to obey him anyway, the only difference being that it was done through an induced sleepwalking condition instead of in the ordinary waking state. But because the commands were given directly into the mind, they produced results, such as swift physical healing, that were not normally possible. When awake, Race would not have been able to throw off his illness simply by being told to do so. However, he was an exceptionally responsive subject. It was not feasible to treat all the sick individually, and even if it were, only a few would respond as fully as Race had done. Thus for large groups of people the most practicable method of magnetizing would still be to employ conduits such as the *baquet* or variants like the elm tree of Buzancy. They would thereby obtain at least some measure of benefits.

These were the limitations Puységur and his followers placed on the advance he had made beyond Mesmer. Until the idea of the actually non-existent magnetic fluid was discarded for good, all further advances would be limited. Even so, what the Marquis had achieved was of real importance. By demonstrating that suggestion, though he did not fully understand it as such, could be exerted without necessarily using such material aids as touching with hands or magnetized objects, he laid the foundation on which modern hypnotism rests.

Puységur's findings were first made public in a book he wrote in the summer of 1784, titled *Details of the Cures Achieved at Buzancy Through Animal Magnetism*. It was published just before the release of the condemnatory findings of the two Royal Commissions of Inquiry. There is no indication that either commission paid any attention to the book. It was followed up in the winter of 1784-85 by an even larger work, in two volumes, in which the Marquis sought to establish a solid basis for magnetizing, using what he himself had discovered. He still advocated the use of touch, stroking, and other tactile stimulation in the induction process; but increasingly asserted "The act of magnetizing is an act of the will, and the awaking from somnambulism is also an act of the will."

The Marquis' brother, Chastenet, also published two books at about the same time, reporting on his own experiments and those of the youngest brother at Bayonne. These publications, coming as they did just when the reaction against Mesmer was mounting to a crescendo of ridicule, helped to counteract the adverse feeling toward animal magnetism by stressing that whatever errors of theory and practice Mesmer might be guilty of, his new therapy was still of value in its own right. But the books also deepened the dislike Mesmer had started to feel toward the Puységurs from the moment he heard of their claims of inducing artificial somnambulism. Early in 1785, a demonstration the Marquis attempted in Mesmer's presence, with Race as the subject, did not go off well. Race apparently resented being used as a guinea pig in Paris. Though no open break ever developed between Mesmer and the Marquis, they did not communicate from this time on.

In August 1785, after the break-up of the Society of Universal Harmony, Mesmer left France to go to England. Puységur was ordered to take command of an artillery regiment at Strasbourg on the Rhine. There, with the local Masonic lodge as a nucleus, he attracted many who had left the original Society, as well as numerous new adherents to the magnetic doctrine. These included about two hundred of the Alsatian Franco-German nobility, who set up centers for magnetic treatment which they offered free of charge to all, and also undertook to train additional magnetizers in the same way they had learned from Puységur. Detailed and accurate records were kept on all treated persons, and these were reviewed at the regular meetings of the new Society. In 1787, eighty-two cures were said to have been effected, and one hundred four in 1788.

At the conclusion of the first course of training in magnetism he gave at Strasbourg, the Marquis proclaimed the principles on which in his judgment the new therapy was based: "There exists within me a power. My belief in this power enables my will to exert it. The whole doctrine of animal magnetism can thus be summed up in two words: *believe* and *want*. I *believe* I have the power to act on the vital principle in all humans. I *want* to make use of this power for their benefit. If you also *believe* and *want*, you can do as much as I."

In the four years before the outbreak of the French Revolution in July 1789, numerous offshoots of the Society of Universal Harmony sprang up in many parts of France and in Belgium which was then under Austrian rule. All more or less followed the principles enunciated by the Marquis. A strong follower was the Harmonious Society of Guyenne which his youngest brother, Viscount Maxime, founded at Bayonne in 1785. In their treatments, the Puységurs and their followers continued to rely considerably on stroking the areas of the body which they believed to be the most receptive to magnetic influence, such as the solar plexus and the eyes. Intermediaries such as magnetized water and objects were also used. Increasingly, however, the emphasis was placed on induction of the sleep-like state of artificial somnambulism. It was here they found cures to be most readily achieved. Therapeutic use was regarded and inculcated by the Puységurs as the sole object of magnetizing. Any other use, such as the performance before audiences of stunts while in trance, they considered to be harmful.

With this rapid and widespread dissemination of the idea of artificial somnambulism as a superior form of animal magnetism — or hypnotism as we would now say — it is not surprising that some claims arose to dispute, in favor of Mesmer, the Marquis' priority of discovery. He himself, as we have seen, credited his brother Chastenet with the first perception of the will, through the exertion of which the sleep-like state is induced, as the principal mechanism and cause of both the process and effects of magnetizing. The three claims that follow are the ones most often cited.

One of Mesmer's Paris disciples, J. L. Picher-Grandchamp, who remained faithful to his master's doctrine, wrote more than forty years later that he had often witnessed somnambulistic effects among Mesmer's patients, and had always believed that Mesmer created them in cases where he judged them to be the best mode of treatment.

The writer of an anonymous pamphlet that appeared late in 1784 criticized the adverse conclusions of the Royal Commissions of Inquiry, and took them to task for not investigating the phenomenon of somnambulism he had observed in magnetized persons.

Another report, published in a Swiss medical journal in December 1784, described the somnambulistic behavior of some of Mesmer's patients, and how after they were awakened they could not recall what they had said or done. Though the last two reports clearly postdate Puységur's experience of May 4, 1784 with Victor Race, which convinced him of the reality of artificial somnambulism, and Picher-Grandchamp's recollections are not fixed to any date, none of these should be interpreted as evidence that it was only after hearing of the Race incident that Mesmer's magnetizing had the effect of producing the sleep-like condition. It would be surprising had it not done so on numerous occasions from the beginning. Whether he sought to deliberately induce this state, or understood its implications, is another question altogether. Mesmer himself does not appear ever to have asserted that he attempted such an induction. In his book published in 1799, he tried to dismiss artificial somnambulism as merely a by-product, and quite possibly a harmful one, of the magnetic crisis. However, he did admit that authentic clairvoyant and telepathic phenomena could occur in the sleep-like trance. He refrained from condemning the Puységurs outright, but he clearly regarded them as strayers from the true path.

There is thus no sound basis on which to deprive the Marquis de Puységur of the credit of originating the first significant step beyond Mesmer in the development of the hypnotic discipline. The Marquis was also more perceptive than Mesmer in not seeking the approbation of official scientific bodies — the search Mesmer so long vainly pursued, and which in the end defeated and embittered him. Puységur took the position that by simply continuing experiments in magnetizing and accumulating a body of evidence supporting the reality of the phenomenon and its mostly beneficial effects, eventual acceptance by orthodox science and medicine was assured. This would probably have followed in due course in France and the rest of Western Europe had not the further development of the magnetic doctrine and therapy been interrupted by the outbreak of the French Revolution. All of the societies founded by the Puységurs and their followers, along with what survived of the original Society of Universal Harmony, had been suppressed before the imposition of the Reign of Terror late in 1792.

It is probable that more than a few of the disciples both of Mesmer and the Puységurs went to the guillotine, since the majority were of the nobility and the upper classes, which were targeted by the extreme revolutionaries. The Marquis' two brothers left France to save themselves; he himself remained, counting on friendships he had formed with some of the radicals to save him. He was, however, accused of corresponding with his brothers abroad, which proved him an "enemy of the people," and was thrown into prison along with his wife and children. After two years they were released by order of the more moderate regime, the Directory, that had succeeded the Reign of Terror. His properties were restored, and the esteem in which he had always been held by the people of his area was manifested by their electing him Mayor of Soissons.

Puységur also continued his experiments with magnetizing, becoming more convinced it was the mind and will which produced the effects. Perhaps there was no magnetic fluid, as Mesmer had thought, but only some electromagnetic current that could be activated by the human will, and by nothing else. In 1807 he published a detailed exposition of his understanding of the phenomenon in a book titled simply *Animal Magnetism*. As time went on, the Marquis also relaxed his earlier opposition to public demonstrations of magnetic trance, or somnambulism, and gave several exhibitions of it, entitling him to be called the first stage hypnotist. After inducing the sleep-like state in a variety of subjects, he observed that while in the condition of artificial somnambulism they were able to see and hear with eyes and ears closed, they often anticipated the commands given them, their memory was much better than when awake, and they manifested clairvoyant abilities, though not always accurately. As had been the experience of Mesmer and d'Eslon, Puységur came under attack from critics who charged that his stroking of female patients verged on immorality and that they could be seduced while mesmerized. However, he fought back with demonstrations of magnetized persons rejecting commands that were against their moral principles.

The Marquis was a pioneer in the psychotherapeutic application of the sleep-like state. About the year 1810, he undertook the magnetizing treatment of a twelve-year-old boy, Alexandre Hebert, who was suffering from a severe psychosis characterized by terrible fits of unrestrainable fury.

For six months Puységur devoted himself to this case, staying with the boy night and day, repeatedly inducting him into the somnambulistic state, in which suggestions were implanted that he would be restored to a normal calmness. Though a "certain irritability" persisted in the boy after this intensive course of treatment, Puységur felt he could claim a cure, for the frenzied fits did not recur. This case made the Marquis a figure of national attention and he was even summoned to an audience with the Emperor Napoleon, who hoped to get from him a prediction of the outcome of his upcoming campaigns. When Puységur disclaimed any ability to foresee the future, Napoleon cut short the audience and dismissed him as "just another country healer."

Still, Puységur's fame had crossed the battle lines of war-convulsed Europe to the receptive ears of Czar Alexander I, who had a liking for mystical things. When the Czar's forces, pursuing Napoleon's retreat from his failed invasion of Russia, entered northern France early in 1814, they were under orders to do no harm to the Marquis or his properties. An aide of a Cossack general named Czernichev called on him and assured him of the Czar's protection. Puységur wrote a letter of thanks to Czernichev, which was intercepted by Napoleon's patrols. Furious, the French Emperor ordered the Marquis to be shot for treason and dispatched a squad of troops to carry out the execution. However, they were in turn intercepted by the Cossacks who burnt the order, which Napoleon's forthcoming abdication would have rendered invalid anyway.

When Napoleon returned from Elba a year later to regain power briefly, Puységur seems to have absented himself from his estate, perhaps in disguise, for fear he would still be hunted down. He did not return until April 1818, nearly three years after Napoleon's final defeat and banishment to St. Helena. He found Victor Race, now nearly sixty, seriously ill and calling for him. The Marquis magnetized him and restored him to health for a while, noting that while in the somnambulistic state Race was able to recall what he had said when in that condition more than thirty years ago. He died later in the year and Puységur erected a tombstone for him with an inscription stating that he had contributed much to the advancement of animal magnetism.

The Marquis continued his magnetizing activities into his seventies, though he was being overshadowed by a new generation of followers of the doctrine that Mesmer had propounded and the Puységur brothers had expanded and made more widely known. On May 29, 1825, the Marquis went to Rheims to attend the coronation of Charles X, the last to be performed according to the medieval ritual that included the monarch touching sufferers from the "King's Evil," or scrofula. It was a hot, humid day with the discomfort increased by the crowding of the thousands who were present. Puységur became ill and was rushed to his ancestral home. He died a few days later at the age of seventy-four.

For generations his memory continued to be cherished by the peasantry of the Soissonnais. The Puységur family moved away from the area, and the ancient elm-tree of Buzancy continued to be venerated and utilized for its healing qualities. It survived unscathed through the battles that were fought in the vicinity for four years in World War I, and was unharmed in the German armored sweep through the Aisne valley in the spring of 1940. But that summer, just before the tree was to be featured in a film on Mesmer's life, a storm uprooted it. The peasants rushed to procure pieces of its bark, which are still preserved in homes there because of the belief in its curative powers. The nearby healing spring still draws crowds.

The Marquis' brother, Chastenet, had died in 1809 after returning to France. The youngest of the three brothers, Viscount Maxime, outlived both, dying in 1848 at the age of ninety-three. He does not appear to have played any important role in magnetizing in the post-Revolutionary period.

We return now to Mesmer to sketch the remainder of his life after he fled Paris in 1793 to escape the Reign of Terror, in which all his wealth. had been confiscated. He went first to Constance, on the Alpine lake on whose further shore he had been born. Then, hearing that his wife was dead and presuming that he would inherit the beautiful estate in Vienna where he had lived with her, he journeyed to the Austrian capital to claim it. Arriving on September 14, 1793, he was treated with suspicion by the Imperial police, who looked on anyone coming from France as a possible Revolutionary spy. They allowed him to resume residence in his old house, but within two months he had been denounced to the police and briefly imprisoned for incautious remarks made to acquaintances that suggested he was not wholly opposed to the Revolution. Upon his promise to leave Vienna and not return, Mesmer was freed. He crossed into Switzerland where he settled in the town of Frauenfeld, near Zurich. There he supported himself by practicing medicine for a clientele mainly of the poor—peasants, small tradesmen, artisans—and came to be greatly loved by them. He did not do any magnetizing, for he had abandoned the hope of converting the world to his method as he understood it. For the record and for posterity, however, he worked on the book in which he defended the reality of the magnetic fluid and the way in which he had employed it.

Published in Paris in 1799 under the modest title of *Memoir of Franz Anton Mesmer, M.D., on his Discoveries*, it generated a brief revival of his fame. The mere fact he was still alive — he was now sixty-five — came as a surprise to most, it having been generally thought that he had died.

Some of his surviving pupils and old friends in the French capital sought to persuade him to return and re-open his clinic. They assured him that magnetizing was now much more favorably looked upon by the public at large and even by the medical men. They petitioned the Government — now the Consulate, with Napoleon Bonaparte as First Consul for life — to grant Mesmer an annuity in compensation for the loss of his possessions during the Terror, and Napoleon approved it. It was a generous one, five thousand florins a year for life, ensuring that Mesmer would never again be in financial need. Nevertheless, he rejected all pleas that he return to Paris. All he now wished for, he said, was to be allowed to live out his remaining years in peace, and in the service of his fellow townspeople of Frauenfeld. So his friends desisted, and for another decade the world heard nothing more of Mesmer. Again it came to be supposed by many that he had died. Meanwhile, the French Empire extended its sway over all of Germany, and along with it there spread the doctrine and practice of mesmerism, as magnetizing was increasingly being called. Particularly in Prussia, whose Academy of Sciences at Berlin had in 1775 told Mesmer that he was mistaken, there was an arousal of scientific and professional interest.

The Prussian court physician, the learned Dr. Friedrich Hufeland, proposed that the Academy set up a commission for the study of animal magnetism, and invite Mesmer to expound his teachings to them in person. It took more than a little searching to locate him, so forgotten had his existence again become. He declined the invitation, saying he was now in his late seventies and lacked the strength for such a journey. Besides, he did not want to re-open old controversies. The Academy was insistent. If Mesmer would not come to the Academy, the Academy would go to Mesmer by sending an emissary to interview him. They chose Karl Christian Wolfart, one of the younger and brighter members of their faculty, and the holder of a medical degree. In September 1812, while the Russians were burning Moscow to make it untenable for Napoleon, Wolfart came to Frauenfeld. He found Mesmer still alert and clear in his mind, and willing to explain at length what he believed animal magnetism to be, and how to utilize it. The visit revived in Mesmer the desire to demonstrate the practical applications of magnetizing. For the first time at his Swiss retreat, he selected subjects from among his medical patients and duly impressed Wolfart with the curative results. Mesmer also turned over to him many records of his magnetizing activities in Vienna and Paris. But he would do no more than that. He said he did not expect to live much longer and it was fitting that he use what time was left in quietly elaborating what he had already found, rather than again risking his reputation in the outside world.

Soon after Wolfart ended his lengthy visit, Mesmer gave up his medical practice and moved to the village of Meersburg, on the shores of his natal Lake Constance. A gypsy he once encountered on a Paris street had read his palm and foretold that he would die near his birthplace in his eighty-first year. Meersburg was as close as he could get without re-entering Austria, where he was still unsure of his reception. April 24, 1815 would be the end of his eighty-first year, hence the necessity for his moving to the shores of Lake Constance while there was yet time. But he did not sit idly, awaiting death. Though no longer practicing medicine, he would inquire from the local doctors about their difficult cases and sometimes visit and magnetize those patients, relieving or curing them. He developed interests in modelling and sketching. A lover of music, he attended the weekly chamber music concerts at a nearby prince's home. He had a new glass harmonica — again a popular musical novelty — in his own home, on which he would play or ask visitors to play for him. The local people noted with awe that flocks of birds would gather around him on his daily walk. They let him touch and speak to them, and were not frightened. Everybody knew about the pet canary he kept in an open cage. It was his breakfast companion, dropping small lumps of sugar into his teacup.

Mesmer had a bladder tumor, which he knew about, but sought no surgical aid. He felt it would not prevent the fulfillment of the gypsy's prediction. On February 26, 1815, his condition suddenly worsened. A week later, on March 5, he died quietly in his sleep, in his eighty-first year. The canary, refusing to eat, followed him in death a few days later. Mesmer was buried at Meersburg, under a three-sided marble monument the Berlin Medical Faculty erected in his memory, bearing a carved sundial and mariner's compass symbolic of Mesmer having charted a new course for humankind. Defaced by nineteenth century vandals, it was later restored.

A few months before Mesmer's death, Wolfart published in Berlin a German translation of Mesmer's 1799 book, along with transcripts of their conversations in 1812. These were lacking in clarity, probably because Wolfart was not fluent in

French, in which Mesmer insisted on speaking. They add little to our knowledge of Mesmer's system, rambling as they do into unrelated subjects such as education, taxes, and prison reform. Wolfart also seems to have lost most of the records Mesmer had entrusted to him.

Whether Mesmer knew of Wolfart's book is not certain. In any event he does not appear to have commented on it or sought to correct its many inaccuracies, such as naming him Friedrich instead of Franz. Mesmer may have felt it no longer mattered. He was aware that the eighteenth century world which he personified was passing from the scene. New approaches to his discovery, by figures from a new century, were coming to the forefront. A Portuguese churchman, the Abbé Faria, was attracting notice for his findings on the post-awakening continuation of the effectiveness of verbal commands given in the somnambulistic state. He would become the next on the roll of the world's greatest hypnotists.

Monument to Abbé Faria

CHAPTER 8
The Abbé Faria Does Away With Magnetic Fluid

The Marquis Puységur's long life-span overlapped the new and rising generation of researchers and practitioners of animal magnetism in France, which still remained the focus of the spreading interest in the new therapy. (There were developments of some importance to its growth at this time in England and Germany, which we shall glance at further on, but they were not as yet in the mainstream of direct evolution from Mesmer's pioneering beginnings.) Increasingly, from the time of the final fall of Napoleon in 1815 and the return of the Bourbon dynasty to the French throne, Puységur was out of touch with this new generation of magnetizers, who drew on his work but advanced considerably beyond it.

There was indeed an entire constellation of shining lights in the magnetism field in the France of the second to fourth decades of the nineteenth century, all of whom contributed significantly to the emergence of scientific hypnotism in the sense in which it came to be accepted and understood. Most prominent in their ranks were Joseph Philip Frances Deleuze,

Alexandre Jacques François Bertrand, Alphonse Teste, Jules Dennis de Sennevoy (known as Baron du Potet), General F. J. Noizet of the French Army, and Charles Lafontaine. I shall sketch their lives and accomplishments, all of which were indebted, in varying degree, to the remarkable investigations into the processes of the mind by the Hindu-Portuguese Abbé Jose Custodio de Faria, whose insights were at least a century ahead of his time. He was the greatest hypnotist of the period that followed the active careers of Mesmer and Puységur.

Faria was born May 31, 1756, in the village of Candolim in the Portuguese colony of Goa on the west coast of India. "Golden Goa," as it was known in the era of Portugal's great age of discovery and conquest in the East in the sixteenth century, was sadly fallen from its former wealth and glory. However, it continued to maintain an active cultural milieu based on a foundation of militant and mystical Roman Catholicism, deriving from the still vividly remembered missionary exploits of St. Francis Xavier. The Faria family was descended from a priestly clan of the Brahmin Saraswati caste that had converted to the Catholic faith. When young Faria was still a boy of only eight or nine years of age, his father, Caetano Victorino de Faria, who had taken minor orders in the Church before his marriage, decided to seek admission to the priesthood. He separated from his wife, who then entered a convent.

In 1771, when Faria was fifteen, he voyaged with his father—now a priest—to the Portuguese capital of Lisbon, and there commenced his own studies for the priesthood. After transferring to the College for the Propagation of the Faith in

Rome, he was there ordained a priest in 1780 and returned to Lisbon where he was assigned a parish. However, he felt the stirrings of worldly ambition, and decided he wanted advancement. The Church in Portugal was torpid and sleepy, lost in dreams of the past. Paris, where churchmen were getting caught up in the intellectual fervor of the Enlightenment, seemed to offer wider opportunities. Faria pushed himself to acquire some competency in French, though he never learned correct pronunciation, and obtained a transfer to Paris. He arrived there in 1788, three years after Mesmer had left under a cloud.

A year later, the French Revolution broke out with the fall of the Bastille, and Faria became involved in political activities to the exclusion of his priestly functions, though the Church does not appear to have unfrocked him. He was a leading figure in the setting up of the Directory on October 5, 1795, after the young Napoleon Bonaparte's "whiff of grapeshot" had helped to topple the First Republic. When Bonaparte's return from Egypt four years later brought about the fall of the Directory and the establishment of the Consulate, Faria retired from the political scene and devoted himself to the study of animal magnetism, to which he had been attracted by reading the books of Puységur and Chastenet.

About two or three years later, Faria (by then called the Abbé, a term loosely used for a churchman—whether a priest or not—who is primarily a scholar) began to give public demonstrations of magnetizing on a limited scale. He was handicapped by his poor French and by his obvious uncertainty as to just what animal magnetism was. That it was not really magnetic or any sort of a fluid soon became clear to him—but what then was it? An abnormal control of the will of others by the magnetizer, as Puységur appeared to imply? That did not seem to be correct either, at least not as a general explanation.

Feeling his way along, Faria attempted all sorts of experiments, some rather bizarre, as for instance one that was recorded by the popular writer François René Châteaubriand in his journal in 1802: "At dinner at Madame Custine's the Abbé Faria attempted to impose his will magnetically on a canary, commanding it to die, but soon had the tables turned on himself by going into a self-induced trance in which it seemed the canary was willing him to die instead. Faria recovered without any apparent ill-effects."

Very little is known of his activities for the next eight or nine years. He must have however, continued the experiments that eventually enabled him to present a coherent explanation that did away completely with the erroneous concepts of magnetism or some sort of impalpable fluid being involved in the observed results. In 1811 he accepted a position as professor of philosophy at the Lyceum Academy in Marseilles in southern France, and the following year he filled a similar post at Nimes in that area. Then in 1813 he returned to Paris and on August 13 commenced giving regular weekly lectures and demonstrations of what he called "concentratism" rather than magnetism. For presenting these he had a formal permit from the prefect of the Paris police. Though charging a rather stiff fee of five francs for each session—about a month's wages for an average workingman—he usually had his large salon on the Rue de Clichy filled with people eager to find out about mesmerism in the new guise he was providing for it. Faria started the sessions with an hour-long lecture attacking the notions of a magnetic fluid and artificial somnambulism as unreal and inconsistent. The latter, he asserted, was a form of waking sleep—"lucid sleep," he called it (not to be confused with "lucid dreaming," in which one attempts to control the content of one's dreams) and was the product of suggestion from the subject's own mind, with some stimulative help from outside. He then proceeded to demonstrate what he had said with experiments on volunteers from the audience.

General Noizet, a veteran of Waterloo, was drawn by curiosity to Faria's presentations in the late summer of 1815, two years after Faria had begun them. "The audience was a cross-section of Parisian high society," Noizet wrote in his memoirs, "with ladies outnumbering the men. After what seemed an interminable hour-long lecture in very bad French of which I could understand nothing, the Abbé, a tall bronzed-complexioned man with a strange-looking face, commenced his experiments that were actually quite exciting."

They followed the usual run of hypnotic phenomena, and while doubtless fascinating to someone like Noizet who had never seen them before, their real importance, however, was in Faria's explanations of them. These were a considerable advance over any previous interpretation of what others were still calling animal magnetism, and are substantially in line with the latest modern understanding of hypnotism. That Faria should have reached such sophisticated conclusions solely from his observations and without discussing and testing them with other experimenters indicates he possessed a mind of very high analytical capability.

Though he found some listeners, especially among those French pioneers of transitional hypnotism listed at the beginning of this chapter, Faria was so far ahead of his time he soon became an object of satire and ridicule. Only a few months after he commenced his public sessions in 1813, a Parisian stage play, *Mesmeromance*, attacked him obliquely, and he also appears to have come under criticism from his superiors in the Catholic Church, which continued to regard animal magnetism with deep suspicion. Then early in 1816 an actor named Potier appeared as a volunteer at one of Faria's sessions and proved resistant to all of the Abbé's attempts to induce trance. Potier then spread the word around Paris that the sessions were a farce that only the gullible swallowed as involving real phenomena. He persuaded a minor playwright, Jules Vernet, to write a play titled *Magnetismania*, in which Potier would be the star. Staged for the first time on September 5, 1816, it was an instant hit with the theater-going public and soon destroyed Faria's credibility.

The Abbé discontinued his presentations and retired into obscurity as the chaplain of a girl's boarding school. He saw this semi-seclusion as an opportunity to write what he projected as a four-volume exposition of his findings and conclusions. He was able to complete only the first volume, *On the Causes of Lucid Sleep*, before he died suddenly on September 20, 1819, at the age of sixty-three. This single book is nevertheless a tremendous step forward in the understanding and application of hypnotism as a clinical therapy. The

Nancy school of clinical practice of hypnotism, which became so prominent in the second half of the nineteenth century, was largely based on the principles Faria first enunciated in his book.

The first of those principles dismissed the notion of a magnetic fluid or any sort of magnetism being a cause of the observed phenomena that he grouped under the general category of waking or "lucid" sleep. The next was a refusal to admit the will of one person as being capable of exerting total control over that of another person. Control could be effected, he said, only to the extent the subject was receptive and prepared to accept it. From this premise there followed logically his third principle, what Mesmer and his successors called "magnetizing" was only the exertion of an ability to concentrate one's powers of suggestion upon another person, and to help that individual to develop an enhanced concentration upon what was being suggested.

The degree to which the "concentrationist"—who we now would call the hypnotist—succeeded in eliciting this response in the subject, or "concentratee" in Faria's initial vocabulary, determined how deep a "lucid sleep" (hypnosis) was induced. Relatively few persons, he thought, could concentrate with sufficient intensity to bring about the abstraction and muscular relaxation that he believed was essential to the process. He stated that in the course of his career he had attempted induction on over five thousand individuals, and in less that twenty percent was he able to obtain the full range of phenomena described by Mesmer and others.

The convulsive crisis, upon which the mesmerists placed such emphasis, was in Faria's opinion, the result of deeply buried memories the subject had either consciously or unconsciously repressed. These were brought up in the trance or "lucid sleep" state. The revival of these unwelcome recollections, he theorized, activated a crisis that manifested itself in physical convulsions and thrashings around. He felt, however, that the process was therapeutic; by bringing up these unpleasant memories and getting rid of them in the crisis, the subject would obtain relief from illnesses that may have been caused by the momories.

All of this is so close to modern psychoanalytic conceptions and practice as to make Faria an unsung predecessor to Freud. He was, clearly, so far ahead of what either the medical establishment or the adherents of "magnetizing" were prepared to understand or accept, that he stood no chance of gaining a hearing. His one book was soon forgotten and was rediscovered only some sixty years later by Hippolyte Bernheim and his pioneering school of modern hypnotherapy at Nancy in eastern France.

But in a subtler way, Faria had been a catalyst of the next stage of the discipline and practice of hypnotism, beyond what it had attained to in the hands of Puységur and lesser figures at the beginning of the nineteenth century. Two who had met him in person and watched his demonstrations, General Noizet, whom we have already mentioned, and Alexandre Bertrand, gathered enough of what Faria was teaching to apply some of it to their own experimentations. They also influenced the many others who were attracted in the 1820s and 1830s to "magnetizing," as it still continued to be called.

Faria's greatest effect on hypnotic usage among his immediate contemporaries was in the primacy he placed on the ability of a skilled "concentrationist" to evoke in a cooperative "concentratee," all sorts of auditory, visual, and tactile hallucinations (such as believing a glass of water to be a powerful medicine, with resulting dramatic effects and side-effects) along with limb paralysis and insensibility to pain. Moreover, these phenomena could be carried on into the normal state of waking awareness through suggesting to the subject that they continue beyond the "lucid sleeping" or trance state.

Continued development of these capabilities along the lines indicated by Faria led, by the end of the first decade after his death in 1819, to the first attested use of hypnosis for surgical anesthesia. Other therapeutic applications of the trance state flowed from the wide expansion of interest in the topic after the end of the Napoleonic Wars.

Though Faria had played a significant role in arousing this interest (and in the long run his influence would be the most far-reaching) in the eyes of the general French public at the time he was far overshadowed by Joseph Deleuze, whose connection with "magnetizing" went all the way back to Mesmer's days of fame in Paris. Faria would nevertheless live on as a mysterious and romantic figure whose name would be appropriated two decades later by Alexandre Dumas the Elder—himself an amateur hypnotist and dabbler in mysticism—for a key character in his melodramatic novel, *The Count of Monte Cristo*. The fictional Abbé Faria is a state

prisoner in the cell next to that of the story's unjustly imprisoned hero, Edmond Dantes, in the infamous Chateau d'If in
Marseilles harbor. Dying in a cataleptic trance, he enables
Dantes to escape wrapped up in his shroud. The accomplishments of the real Faria were thus lost sight of, until
resurrected by the Nancy School of Hypnotism.

While in his thirties, Deleuze became interested in the
work of Mesmer and d'Eslon, and attended some of their
sessions. He long remained skeptical of much of what they
asserted, and did not become publicly involved in any of the
controversies that arose, though he did some experimentation privately and among friends that in time made him an
adherent of magnetizing. Eventually attaining a position of
trust and respect as a professional naturalist, he was assured
of a receptive audience for the book he published in 1813, *A
Critical History of Animal Magnetism*. In it he made the case for
Puységur's more restrained version of magnetizing as a
verifiable phenomenon and, under proper safeguards, an
effective therapeutic tool.

The book was treated well by critics and reviewers, but it
made little or no impression on the medical profession,
which Deleuze had been principally addressing. He decided
to try to convince the public to demand a greater use of
magnetizing by doctors. The best way to effect this, he felt,
was to write a manual of *Practical Instruction in Animal
Magnetism*. This was published in 1825, and told the intelli-
gent lay reader, step-by-step, how the magnetizing process
was carried out, what results could be expected, and what
precautions needed to be taken.

Though in a sense a do-it-yourself manual, Deleuze's handbook—which he spent a dozen years in rewriting before finally committing it to the press emphasized that while magnetizing was basically simple and almost anyone could do it, there were dangers and pitfalls, and these could best be avoided by qualified practitioners of the art, in the medical profession. This approach failed at first to soften the hardened opposition of doctors to magnetism. Most reacted with alarm to Deleuze's advise to his readers that if their physician refused to treat them magnetically without giving adequate reasons, they should get another doctor. Even less welcome to the medical establishment were the examples he cited of laymen who performed minor surgery, such as lancing boils, on magnetized subjects without the subjects feeling any pain. Within a few months, however, as the book circulated more widely among doctors whose patients were increasingly demanding that magnetizing be tried for their ailments, the medical attitude slowly began to change. Doctors found Deleuze had addressed many of the reservations they still had about the therapy that Mesmer had introduced a half-century earlier. In particular, Deleuze offered some common-sense precautions—such as having another woman present—with regard to the magnetizing of female patients, the moral aspect of which had continued to trouble many.

Further, his case histories of the numerous healings and alleviations of widely differing illnesses that had been achieved through magnetizing, were described in medical terms which enhanced their credibility. The clear evidence Deleuze presented that it was possible to achieve insensibility to pain, promised an escape from the terrors of the surgeon's knife. More than a few doctors found themselves being attracted toward at least a wider trial of magnetizing, even if they were not yet ready to accept it as a recognized part of their practice.

Before the year 1825 was out, the new edition of the *French Medical Encyclopedia,* which was consulted by almost every doctor in France at that time, was published. Its article on *Animal Magnetism* had been totally rewritten by L. L. Rostan, a widely known and highly reputed physician. In the previous edition, in 1818, animal magnetism had been dismissed as having no verifiable medical merit. Now, it was declared to be a real method of therapy, of proven value in treating many conditions, though still requiring great caution and needing much further investigation to determine more exactly its limitations and its further possibilities. These possibilities included preventing memory loss and aiding in memory recovery, helping restore mobility to paralyzed limbs, and accomplishing anesthesia sufficiently deep for major surgery.

Even though Rostan expressed many doubts about whether any assured protection could be devised to prevent undue influence over the free will of subjects, especially women, his article was a major step toward the general acceptance of magnetizing as an element of standard medical practice. Deleuze's handbook had, in less than a year, effected a larger shift in professional opinion than any of its predecessors over the span of a half century beginning with Mesmer.

Another doctor of the younger generation, Pierre Foissac, was moved by his reading of Deleuze and Rostan to propose that a new Commission of Inquiry be appointed to investigate the entire field of magnetizing and the claims for it, and to issue an authoritative judgment that would replace the flawed and biased ones of the two pre-Revolutionary Commissions. The Academy of Medicine acted favorably on Foissac's motion for a new Commission, setting up a committee to recommend its form and functions. In its report, the committee stated the former Commissions had made their conclusions in advance, without any thorough evaluation of the facts. A new Commission should therefore sift all the evidence, pro and con, keeping also in mind that, since Mesmer's time, much had changed in how animal magnetism was understood and applied. The report concluded with an appeal to national pride, calling attention to the fact that, between 1815 and 1817, magnetizing had received governmental sanction, with official sets of rules for its practice, in Russia, Denmark, Sweden, and Prussia. France could not afford to be far behind the times in its approach to the matter.

Even so, the new Commission won a slim majority, thirty-five to twenty-eight, in the Academy's formal vote establishing it on February 28, 1826. It was given four years to carry out its work of investigation, and a further year to prepare a final report and conclusions. During that interval it encountered numerous obstacles, including the refusal of the Council General of Hospitals — a body to which most French hospitals belonged — to permit magnetizing of patients in any of its member institutions. This severely restricted the Commission's ability to set up and monitor the experiments necessary to determine the efficacy of magnetizing as a therapy. Deleuze, already in his mid-seventies and in poor health, was not up to providing the Commission with the further input of valuable data they hoped to have from him. His appointment in 1828 to the post he had long coveted, of Librarian of the French Museum of Natural History, removed him from the magnetizing scene altogether. (In 1826, the disabling illness of Bertrand, whose work we are about to discuss, deprived the Commission of another valuable collaborator.)

Nevertheless, in spite of these and other difficulties, the Commission's report of June 21, 1831 was, on the whole, a fair and comprehensive one, and in its main points favorable to magnetizing. We shall return to the report and its contrary aftermath, but first we shall examine what others besides Deleuze were achieving in this key decade of the 1820s.

Although he had performed a labor of inestimable worth to the cause of hypnotism in compiling and publishing his handbook of practical instruction in magnetizing, while at the same time making his own name a household word among the French public, Deleuze had not advanced beyond the generation of Mesmer and Puységur in the theoretical understanding of the nature of animal magnetism. To him, it was still the impalpable, all-pervading fluid imagined by Mesmer that could be directed by the magnetizer to produce curative effects in the subject. He did not, to be sure, lay stress on the *baquet* or on magnetized water or rods as means of conveying the fluid, apparently regarding these as mostly unnecessary complications of an essentially simple procedure. Still, he included instructions for using them if desired. Deleuze must have at least heard of Faria and probably had read his book, in which the Abbé expressed his astonishment that anyone could think that tubs of water or any other material contrivance could either originate or convey a wholly mental phenomenon. However, Deleuze's convictions about the fluid had not been shaken.

It was Alexandre Bertrand's growing skepticism about the reality of any magnetic fluid, reinforced by what he gathered from Faria both directly and through General Noizet that was the opening wedge to the abandonment of the concept of the fluid over the next quarter-century. Trained both as an engineer and a physician, Bertrand brought a keenly analytical mind to the study of animal magnetism, which he began to investigate in his early twenties, around 1816. He had met Faria and by 1819 became a close friend of Noizet; together they read Faria's book and sought to apply its insights to their own observations. Bertrand however did not immediately accept Faria's denial of any magnetic fluid. Offended by the hostile article on animal magnetism in the 1818 edition of the *Medical Encyclopedia*, he persuaded a leading Paris hospital, the Hôtel Dieu, to allow him to experiment on its patients. The generally positive results led him to offer a public lecture course in 1820, in which he still extoled the merits of magnetizing as an exertion of the human will through a universal fluid.

Three years later, Bertrand published a treatise in which he began to retreat from his original position, proposing that it was through the magnetizer's suggestions that the subjects reacted to the fluid in different ways. The fluid itself was not redistributed in any way by the magnetizing procedure, contrary to what had been previously asserted. Noizet's influence is evident in this revision of Bertrand's earlier views; the General had been insistently arguing with him, in a friendly way, in support of Faria's explanation.

A further three years effected a complete change of standpoint in Bertrand. His second book, published in 1826 under the innocuous title of *Animal Magnetism in France*, attacked the whole notion of magnetic fluid as a figment of the imaginations of magnetizers and subjects alike. In terms that are surprisingly modern, Bertrand asserted that people never had any difficulty in seeing or believing whatever they had been conditioned to see or believe. He described how some patients said they could see the fluid emanating from his finger-tips when he was making his magnetizing passes, and how others said magnetized water had a different taste from ordinary water. All purely imaginary, Bertrand stated, because that was what they were expecting. All indicative of how the mind can create convincing simulations of reality under the stimulus of suggestion. Not all people, as Faria had pointed out, were equally open to suggestion. Some, he asserted, were excessively open, and from among such came religious enthusiasts, ecstatics, and prophets. This last statement outraged the Roman Catholic clergy, who were still powerful opinion-shapers in France at that time, and they vociferously condemned the whole book. Bertrand was taken aback by this reaction, as he had not intended to offend religious sensitivities. The clerical attack on him may have contributed to the illness he complained of soon afterward, and which led to his death in 1831, at the age of thirty-six.

Despite the clerical outcry, Bertrand's book was widely read and shook the, until then, prevailing belief in a magnetic fluid. It took another generation or so for it to be finally and totally discarded, but after Bertrand, that demise became inevitable. General Noizet, though he waited until he was an aged man to publish in 1854 the book he had written in 1820 on the nature of "magnetizing" in the light of Faria's findings, continued to be quietly influential through his occasional lectures and frequent conversations with magnetizers. He lived to see the virtual abandonment of the magnetic fluid fallacy, though it continued to be propagated by some of his noted magnetizing contemporaries, even if they no longer made much of it in their practice.

Among these, the most outstanding was the Baron du Potet, also called Jules de Sennevoy. Born in 1796, he lived to the age of eighty-five, and until less than a year before his death, was continuing to treat patients in the conviction that he was helping them by directing the magnetic fluid. He conceded, however, that it was only the exertion of his own will and that of the subject, in assenting to what he suggested, which made this of any practical effect.

The Baron was indeed a flamboyant and remarkable personality, a bridge over three generations of advances in hypnotherapy. As a young man he had met Puységur and Faria, and had worked with Bertrand at the Hôtel Dieu. He was closely associated with Deleuze while the latter was preparing his handbook. He performed many of the experiments for the new Commission of Inquiry during its first two years of investigation. In 1828 he moved to London where, as we shall see, he was a potent influence on the emergence of the great British hypnotists of the mid-century.

The innovation in practice for which du Potet is most widely remembered was his "Magnetic Mirror," a circle about five inches in diameter, drawn on the floor with deep black charcoal. The subject was told to stare fixedly at this. Within a short time, he or she would begin to hallucinate images within the black circle. Through employing this variant of the age-old fortune-tellers' method of "scrying" in crystal balls or other objects on which the attention could be focused, the Baron was able to draw out suppressed emotions and memories from the subjects, producing relief for psychosomatic ailments.

Another prominent magnetizer who never totally gave up the premise of the magnetic fluid was Charles Lafontaine. Born in 1801, he was at first an actor who became interested in magnetizing for stage performances. He later became principally a therapist, employing the methods prescribed in Deleuze's handbook, with an outstanding record of success. His demonstrations in England in 1841 were to be of crucial importance for the future of hypnotherapy, for it was at one of them that James Braid, to whom we owe the first correct explanation and naming of hypnotism, had his initial encounter with it.

This seminal episode will be fully treated in our chapter on Braid. However, at this point we have to digress briefly to catch up with the significant developments that had been taking place in Germany during the first third of the century, and then to tell of the unfortunate sequel in France to the investigations and reports of the Third and Fourth Commissions of Inquiry, which closed off further progress in that country for forty years. Across the ocean, magnetizing was at this very time—the decade of the 1830s—making its first important impressions upon the American public, to whom it was introduced by French practitioners seeking a fresh audience for their efforts. This too requires a chapter of its own, setting it in the context of what had been already achieved in Europe, and was about to be more lastingly achieved in Britain.

Justinus Kerner
1786 - 1862

CHAPTER 9
The German Sidepaths

A t the same time as the new and innovative generation of magnetizers was emerging in France in
the years immediately following the end of the
Napoleonic Wars in 1815, what appeared to be an equally
impressive array of practitioners of the art was arising in
Germany. However, there was not yet a German nation. The
Kingdom of Prussia had, by virtue of having led the German
"liberation struggle" against Napoleon, become the leader of
the conglomeration of small independent states that were
collectively known as Germany. Prussia had more territory
and a bigger population than the rest of them put together,
and it counted for something in the power politics of Europe.
But a German national culture and ethos were still in the
process of creation, and the lack of them in any finished form
weighed against the development of a national body of
magnetizers such as evolved in France and later in Britain,
even though individually the Germans were probably as
advanced as any in those countries.

We have already seen that in 1812, the Prussian Academy
of Sciences became avidly interested in the teachings
of Mesmer and sent Karl Wolfart to interview him at his

retreat in Switzerland. Wolfart then translated and published in German the book Mesmer had written in French in 1799 summarizing his doctrine. Though Wolfart's version abounded in errors, it reinforced the already surging fascination with magnetizing, both in Prussia and in the smaller German states. In 1816 the Universities of Berlin and Bonn, under the auspices of the Prussian Government, established chairs of Mesmerism, and the journal founded by Wolfart, *Asklapeion* (named for the ancient Hellenic sleep temples described in our first chapter), was for several years influential in maintaining the prestige of magnetizing among the medical profession in Germany.

Numerous reshapings of the theoretical basis of magnetizing were worked out by these German pioneers. Friedrich Hufeland, the Prussian court physician, regarded the relationship of magnetizer and patient as comparable to that of a pregnant woman and the fetus in her womb. The cure at the end of a course of treatment, with the practitioner letting go of the patient, corresponded to the mother letting the child go from her body.

Carl A. F. Kluge, who wrote a text book on mesmerism that had a popularity in Germany rivalling that of Deleuze's in France, saw the magnetizer and patient as locked in a closed world from which all other individuals were excluded. Intrusive light, noise and other extraneous disturbances were all to be strictly avoided during treatment. Kluge proceeded further to construct a system of six stages of the magnetic trance, the last of which assumed the attainment of a clairvoyant ability to transcend time and space. This was taking magnetizing into a metaphysical sphere Mesmer had never sought or advocated, and reflected the degree to which the growing Romantic Movement in the arts was starting to take over mesmerism from the medical field to which it properly belonged.

In a few years this accelerating trend would cause the German scientific and medical communities to drop their interest in and support of magnetizing. Popular attention shifted to a handful of highly publicized mystical visionaries, most notably Anne Catherine Emmerich and Frederica Hauffe, who tended to cast doubt on the morality and validity of magnetizing, though it had a role in their lives. Medical experimentation, advances in magnetizing practice, and a creditable record of cures of both physical and psychological illnesses, were increasingly ignored in both the professional and lay press. By mid-century, when the newly named hypnotism was making its great forward strides in Britain, the practice of the art had come to a virtual dead end in Germany.

There were some vigorous attempts to forestall that demise by those who sought to link the scientific and medical aspects of magnetizing with the religious and metaphysical speculations of the Romantics. Two of these attempts should be mentioned, those by Kurt J. H. Windischmann, who proposed magnetizing be made into a "Christian healing art" which only priests could practice in conjunction with the sacraments of the Church, and by Johann von Ringseis, who advocated a "Christian Germanic science of magnetic medicine." More unconventional was the plan of Johann Ennemoser for magnetizing fetuses to assure their proper development before and after birth, and for magnetizing trees to promote the bearing of fruit. All of these, and other proposals now long forgotten, continued to be based on the erroneous notion of the magnetic fluid, and were thus foredoomed to failure. The German divergence into the sidepaths of mysticism and romanticism delayed for almost two generations the acceptance in Central Europe of the understanding of the true nature of hypnotism that Faria, Bertrand and Braid had achieved in the West.

In another sense, however, the interest of the German philosophers of the Romantic period (roughly 1800 to 1840) in mesmerism and related mental phenomena, was the seedbed of modern psychiatry, which has its roots in the work of Friedrich Schelling, Arthur Schopenhauer, and many others who at that time in Germany began to investigate mental processes. Though they saw magnetizing as peripheral to their main work, they derived several of their insights from observing the reactions of magnetized subjects.

We are concerned here mainly with the setback to the evolution of modern hypnotism in Germany, which was in large part the result of the general preoccupation of the public with the two visionaries, Emmerich and Hauffe, whom we noted above. How this situation came about can be seen from the involvement of mesmerists in their lives.

Anne Catherine Emmerich (1774-1824) was a peasant from the Westphalian plain, in the northern Rhineland, who experienced in her childhood and adolescence a recurring series of visions of divine personages. Becoming a nun, she expanded these visions into lengthy excursions out of her physical body, into times and places other than her own. The stigmata of the crucifixion appeared on her flesh, and she subsisted for more than a decade on virtually no nourishment other than the Eucharist. She was bed-ridden and in severe physical distress much of the time, and it was in the hope of relieving this that those who looked after her resorted, against her wishes, to mesmeric treatment.

The sufferings and visions of Emmerich belong to the province of Roman Catholic hagiography, and we are not passing any judgment on them. Our interest is in the attempt of Dr. Wilhelm Wesener, a Westphalian physician who had successfully magnetized several patients with a variety of ailments, to alleviate the physical torment she was undergoing. This consisted primarily of agonizing and convulsive pains in her chest, and persistent retching and vomiting of a watery fluid. Over a period of eight years, from 1813 to 1821, Dr. Wesener repeatedly sought to magnetize her, but while he was usually able to induce mesmeric trance, he could not get her to follow the instructions given while she was in that state.

Gradually a dialogue developed between them. Dr. Wesener persistently attempted to convince Emmerich that mesmerism was not contrary to the doctrines of the Church, that properly employed by responsible persons, it had brought and was continuing to bring great relief to many who had been needlessly suffering. Emmerich's contrary argument was that while she did not deny the power exerted through magnetizing was real and that the claimed effects were also real, it was a power that could not be safely entrusted into human hands. The mesmerist would inevitably be drawn into using it for improper purposes, no matter how pure his original intentions. She would therefore not permit the power to have any effect on her beyond the mere induction into mesmeric trance, which she admitted she did not have the strength to resist. Her suffering was from God and was for a purpose the world could not understand. She was not asking for relief.

Wesener would rehearse these dialogues from memory in his discussions with his medical colleagues, and parts of them thus came to be circulated by letter and word of mouth, and eventually by the press. The public found Emmerich's views more convincing than Wesener's defenses, and mesmerism now started to sink in general esteem. Wesener himself finally abandoned magnetizing as a part of his medical practice. Emmerich had shown him, he said, "magnetizing was an intrusion into the innermost consciousness of the patient," as he phrased it, and he was unable to justify that penetration into the human psyche. Modern hypnotherapy does, of course, justify it, because there is now a much better understanding of psychodynamic concepts than was available to the German doctors of the decade after Waterloo.

As it was, the pain-wracked Anne Catherine Emmerich, alternating between two disparate states of reality had by her opposition dealt a severe blow to the progress of hypnotism in Germany for a long time to come. An even heavier blow was soon to be dealt by another and quite different sort of visionary, Frederica Hauffe.

She was the protege of Justinus Kerner, a small-town physician in the Swabian Alps foothills in Wurttemberg, then an independent kingdom in southwest Germany. Kerner had been healed of a nervous ailment at the age of twelve by a mesmerist named Gmelin. He was a firm believer in magnetizing and employed it in his own practice. Possessed of an outgoing, friendly personality and an insatiable curiosity and interest in almost everything, he soon attracted — in spite of his out-of-the-way location—a wide circle of learned and literary friends. He wrote quite good poetry and carried out medical and chemical experiments, one of which led to his identifying the form of food poisoning known as botulism.

Kerner was at the age of forty in his flourishing prime when in 1826 he was called to treat Hauffe, a young woman of twenty-five. Hauffe had been forced into an unwanted marriage at nineteen and since then had fallen into a state of more or less spontaneous trance, suffering also from convulsions, hemorrhaging and high fevers. Finding that his magnetizing of her alleviated these symptoms, after a few months Kerner took her as a live-in patient into his home, where she lived the two years that remained of her life.

During this period Hauffe was magnetized several times a day by Kerner, and while in the trance state she became a visionary, making detailed statements on the nature of the universe and on the composition of many substances. She did so in a flawless High German instead of the Swabian peasant dialect she normally spoke. (She had received only the most elementary schooling, though she could read and write.) She also spoke on occasion, while in mesmeric trance, in language she claimed was the original pre-Babel tongue of humankind, which she taught Kerner to understand and translate, though he failed to record its vocabulary and grammar.

He did however keep transcripts of all her statements while in trance, and published them in a book called *The Seeress of Prevorst* (the name of her native village) soon after her death in 1829. For a while it was very popular, and is still valued as one of the most comprehensive first-hand testimonials to the mythopoetic (myth-creating) function and capability of the human subconscious. Soon, however, there was a backlash of public feeling against Kerner in particular and mesmerism in general. Had not a holy woman—Emmerich—already witnessed against them? Now here was a poor witless peasant woman being made to talk all sorts of nonsense by this fool Kerner with his magnetizing.

Kerner struggled against this adverse reaction for over two decades. He published two periodicals in which he asked readers to report similar phenomena, and provided analyses by himself and other doctors. But in spite of these efforts, Kerner finally became melancholic and succumbed to a severe depressive disorder, in the grip of which he died in 1862 at the age of seventy-six. It is believed that his dismay at the widespread rejection of mesmerism and hypnotism by the German scientific community from the 1820s on, a rejection to which his own study and publicizing of the trance experiences of Frederica Hauffe had unwittingly contributed, had much to do with the onset of Kerner's depression psychosis.

Even under its influence, he retained some of his creative faculty. He became intrigued by the meanings that could be read into the images created by ink-blots, and wrote a small book on the subject that was published after his death. It eventually became the foundation of a standard tool of psychiatry, the Rorschach inkblot test, used as a method of personality analysis.

One further figure from the twilight of the original mesmerism in the German-speaking lands needs to be mentioned: Baron von Reichenbach in Vienna, who in the 1830s and 1840s sought to gain acceptance for a new version of the discredited magnetic fluid. He called it the Odic (or Odylic) force, and

even today it has some adherents. Reichenbach's story, however, will best be told in conjunction with that of James Braid
of Britain, who was his leading opponent and the propounder
of a wholly psychological basis for mesmeric phenomena,
attributing nothing to magnetic or any other fluid or force.

Mesmer et ses disciples.

Franz Anton Mesmer and his disciples Joseph Philippe François Deleuze and Armand Marie Jacques de Chastenet de Puységur

CHAPTER 10
The Mid-Century Eclipse in France

I n the 1820s and early 1830s, something similar to the
retreat of the German pioneers into sidepaths and blind
alleys of romanticism befell what had appeared to be
rapid progress in France toward a scientific understanding
and clinical application of hypnotism. It was not as total an
eclipse as in Germany, and from a world standpoint was offset
by the great advances that were soon to be made in Britain and
America, largely through the efforts of French missionaries of
magnetizing. Moreover, this temporary halt to French
progress in the discipline would be followed by the tremendous achievements of the master French hypnotists of the
latter third of the century.

Nevertheless, the French eclipse cannot be glossed over as
insignificant. It was a definite setback to the scientific development of hypnotism, from which in some respects it did not
fully recover for decades. Some familiarity with how this came
about, when the trend was running strongly in favor of greater
acceptance of hypnotism is necessary for grasping the severity
of the longer-term effects.

As was stated in Chapter Eight, the report of the French
Academy of Medicine's Third Commission of Inquiry into

Animal Magnetism, released on June 21, 1831, after five years of study, was favorable. Yet a majority of the Academy voted not to have the report printed, because, in the words of one of the faculty, "It tends to destroy half our knowledge of physiology." This did not prevent the report's conclusions and premises from becoming known to the public, for they were widely covered in the Paris newspapers. A careful reading of them soon disclosed that only a dozen subjects had actually been experimented upon, because of the refusal of the Paris hospitals to make their facilities or patients available. Far too much emphasis was placed on attempting to refute extreme claims such as clairvoyance and psychic diagnosis in the mesmeric trance, and too little on demonstrated practical effects. A notable success was Dr. Jean Cloquet's painless excision in 1829 of a large cancerous breast tumor from a sixty-four-year-old woman who had been mesmerized by a magnetizer named Chapelain. One would think such an unprecedented event—the first attested case of painless major surgery—would have riveted the attention of the investigating commission and caused it to seek additional instances of so radical an advance in surgical practice. Instead it is barely mentioned in the report, along with a cautious recommendation that the alleviation of surgical pain by animal magnetism be further analyzed. (The fact that the patient died three weeks after the surgery from severe pleurisy as a result of going outside in freezing weather may have had something to do with the commission's scanting of the incident.)

The faint praise of the report had an echo in the approval the Academy gave at about the same time for lay persons to magnetize for medical purposes, under the supervision of a physician. These lay magnetizers were to keep a diary of their proceedings and turn it over to a doctor once a month. This injunction was widely disregarded and there seems to have been no serious attempt to enforce it. It merely widened the renewed split that was again developing between the adherents of mesmerism and the majority of the medical profession.

Two years later, in 1833, two imprudent magnetizers publicized what they claimed was startlingly accurate clairvoyance they had elicited in mesmeric trance from two of their subjects. However, one of the subjects revealed that the magnetizers' assistants had made known to them beforehand what they would be asked. They had pretended to be mesmerized and gave the answers the experimenters wanted.

The result was a stiffening of the official attitude toward mesmerism. It had become totally hostile by 1836 when a dentist named Oudet attested to having extracted a tooth painlessly from a mesmerized patient. The Academy of Medicine officially denounced the dentist for claiming a "known impossibility," but then was challenged by a young magnetizer named Berna to investigate the results of the procedure on patients he had treated. A Fourth Commission of Inquiry, composed of ten of the Academy's faculty (including two of its most fervent detractors of mesmerism), was thereupon formed to take up Berna's challenge. Six months later, in the fall of 1837, it issued its conclusions. They were totally negative. Magnetizing was declared to be an illusion and a fraud, and its claimed effects wholly imaginary. One of the members of the commission, a Dr. Burdin, offered to pay three thousand francs out of his own pocket to anyone who could read while blindfolded and in the magnetized state. A claim this could be done had been made at some point during the investigation. Several came forward to try to win the offered prize, but all failed, and some were found to have attempted fraud.

Animal magnetism was now in very bad standing with the French medical and scientific establishment. Most physicians were again refusing to have anything to do with it. The few who still did so, risking their professional standing, dropped to virtually none after the publication in 1841 by Burdin and his colleague Dubois of their book, *Academic History of Animal Magnetism*. A caustic attack on magnetizing in all its forms from Mesmer on, the book had the effect of imposing an almost total ban on the use of hypnotism in French medical practice for almost three decades.

This was particularly unfortunate in that it had been preceded in 1840 by the publication of Dr. Alphonse Teste's *Practical Manual of Animal Magnetism*, which superseded Deleuze's handbook. A young physician who had commenced practice at the age of twenty-three in 1837, Teste discarded altogether the notion of any magnetic fluid, offering instead a wholly practical and effective induction procedure with which he had atained positive results. In several respects his approach foreshadowed the employment of indirect suggestions that would characterize the work of Milton Erickson in the United States a century later.

Had Teste come on the scene a decade earlier, before the French medical profession closed its collective mind to hypnotherapy, it is probable he would have been ranked among its greatest practitioners. His practical common-sense approach, which had in it nothing of the spectacular and made no extravagant claims, might well have become the standard among French physicians. As it happened, though, he quickly perceived there was no future for him in the medical environment of France in the wake of the Fourth Commission of Inquiry and the Burdin-Dubois book. He went to England, where the greatest creative epoch of hypnotism since Mesmer had just commenced, and had an English version of his book published in 1843. This had a wide circulation and influence on British hypnotism. Teste was, however, unable to establish a remunerative practice in that country, even though that other and much more flamboyant Frenchman, the Baron du Potet, had done so as early as 1828.

Having been pushed beyond the pale of respectability by the French medical establishment, animal magnetism, or hypnotism as it would soon be called, became vulnerable to legal attack. Several cases were tried in the French courts during the 1840s and 1850s. Magnetizers and their clairvoyant aides—usually women, and called "somnambulists"—were accused of various malfeasances and frauds. However, the judges appear to have acted with great circumspection. Acquittals were more common than convictions, and sentences where imposed were nominal. The conclusion seems inescapable. French public opinion, due in large part to the favorable prominence of magnetizing in the hugely popular novels of Honoré de Balzac and others, did not share the condemnatory attitude of French official medicine and science. The courts reflected this feeling among the populace by refusing to either initiate or take part in any substantive restraint on magnetizing.

A look at two of the most significant cases will bear out this impression. In 1842 a lay magnetizer named Ricard was charged with extortion of money under false pretenses for having treated a man suffering from epileptic seizures. Ricard was found guilty, but sentenced to only fifteen days in jail and a fine of fifty francs. The patient came forward saying it was absurd to punish Ricard for having helped him, for he now felt better than he had ever felt in his whole life. Since this was not the only instance of mesmerism being of benefit in epileptic cases, Ricard decided to appeal. The appellate judge took a more severe view of the offense and raised the jail sentence to six months. Ricard then appealed to the Court of Cassation in Paris, which had the final say, and in 1843 won a complete exoneration. The Court declared he had employed no fraudulent means and had used a treatment that had been recognized at various times as legitimate. As a result of this decision, several other prosecutions pending in the courts were dropped. Also, the initiation of additional prosecutions was hindered after 1846 by the wide distribution of a pamphlet written by the well-known journalist and author Aubin Gauthier pointing out the loopholes in the laws through which magnetizers could avoid or thwart legal actions against them.

Following the revolution of 1848 which brought to power Louis Napoleon Bonaparte—who would shortly declare himself the Emperor Napoleon III—the official standpoint hardened again. A decree issued on July 9-10, 1850, stated that magnetizers, their assistants, and physicians making use of their services or of their methods, would be liable to prosecution for fraud. The first to be arrested were a married couple named Mongruel, lay practitioners of mesmerism, and a doctor and pharmacist who had collaborated with them. The charge against the pharmacist was dropped, but the doctor was fined five francs and the Mongruels sentenced to five days in jail and a fine of fifteen francs. The doctor paid his five francs and disappeared from the case, but the Mongruels appealed, and their appeal retraced the course of the Ricard case. The appellate judge upheld the medical establishment, increasing the fine to five hundred francs and the jail sentence to thirteen months. These far more serious penalties were appealed by the Mongruels to the Court of Cassation, which threw them out. In the end, the couple had to spend three days in jail for having practiced medicine illegally and to pay the original token fine of fifteen francs for trying to "tell fortunes from dreams." It would seem that this charge came from their interpreting what their subjects said in trance as foretelling the future.

In its ruling, the Court of Cassation made a sharp distinction between animal magnetism as such, and the incompetent or illegal practice of it. The mental and physical states induced by magnetizing, the Court declared, were not false or imaginary; they were capable of causing severe harm or even death, if invoked by those not qualified to deal safely with them. This finding largely took away the power of official medicine to prosecute doctors for practicing animal magnetism, except where it could be proved that they had not been properly trained in it. Lay magnetizers did become more exposed to prosecution for illegal practice of medicine, but the slap-on-the-wrist penalties they incurred in most cases meant a vast amount of magnetizing was continuing at the rural village and urban street level in France through the mid-century decades when it was under a cloud of official disapproval. It was a situation the opposite of that in Germany, where the public had joined in the hostility of the medical, scientific, and legal establishments to both the doctrine and the practice of magnetizing.

The reason why the French public was so much more receptive to animal magnetism, to the point of sheltering and nurturing it through the mid-century period of official eclipse, has to be sought in the favorable light in which it was cast by the French novelists of that period. With the rapid growth of literacy, the novel was exploding into an unprecedented influential force for shaping popular opinion. And one relatively obscure man emerges as the prime mover in gaining the support of the literary and intellectual levels of French society, for both the doctrine and practice of animal magnetism in the confused years after the fall of Napoleon when there was a searching for new directions and new anchors. He was D. F. Koreff, of rather mysterious antecedents and linkages, who first became known in the Prussian national revival after the kingdom's crushing defeat by Napoleon in 1806.

Koreff treated Prince Hardenberg, who, along with Baron vom Stein, was the principal architect of the reforms that brought about the rapid renascence in Prussia of animal magnetism for various ailments. Koreff was rewarded with the chair of physiology at the University of Berlin, and a seat in the Prussian State Council. Next he was appointed to organize the new University of Bonn. After this, however, Hardenberg's relationship with him seems to have cooled, perhaps because he came to see Koreff as annoyingly persistent and demanding. Whatever the reason, Koreff left Prussia after the overthrow of Napoleon and made himself at home in the salons of Paris, where his ingratiating personality won him an instant following among intellectuals. He was constantly praising magnetizing as the answer to the world's ills, and was listened to avidly by such rising masters of the novel as Balzac, Victor Hugo and Stendhal. Through them he would influence the Alexandre Dumases, father and son, and Theophile Gautier, as well as those visionaries of social reform Charles Fourier and Claude de Saint-Simon. All of these were more or less ardent converts to animal magnetism, and advocated it in their writings. These writings reached a broad cross-section of the French public, which also relished the mesmerism-laden poetry of Heinrich Heine and the even more mesmerist dramas of E. T. A. Hoffmann, both of whom were introduced to it by the ever-proselytizing Koreff.

Honoré de Balzac more than any other French novelist was a missionary of the magnetizing gospel. Among the ninety-four novels that comprise his enormous masterpiece of satire on the French society of his time, *The Human Comedy*, all written within the scarcely credible span of only twenty years, four stand out for their emphasis on magnetizing as a key to how people behave, five others have their plots keyed to the same theme, and it appears at least briefly in almost all the rest.

Louis Lambert, the earliest (1832) of Balzac's four pre-eminently "magnetizing" novels, is actually a lengthy statement of his own conceptions of the phenomenon. It is about a young man who lives in a state of suspension between the physical and spiritual worlds. The Balzacian notion of animal magnetism went far beyond what either Mesmer or Faria or any present-day hypnotist would subscribe to, but as a novelist he was not bound by limitations of practicality and possibility. Balzac continued to believe implicitly in the reality of magnetic fluid even while it was being discarded by Faria and Bertrand, and attributed truly remarkable powers to it. He conceived of it as being directed outwardly from the eyes and being able to traverse both space and time, endowing those who had learned how to control it with a clairvoyance able to discern events in the past or at great distances, and to effect virtually any kind of healing.

Serafita, which followed in 1834, argued that Emmanuel Swedenborg, the mid-18th century Swedish scientist-mystic, was a forerunner of Mesmer. It too was more an exposition of a thesis than a novel in the ordinary sense. (Few have agreed with Balzac on his ideas about Swedenborg, who never proposed or experimented with anything resembling Mesmer's magnetism.)

Ursule Mirouet (1842) is a well-plotted novel, in which the attempt of greedy relatives to defraud a young heiress out of her inheritance is defeated by her uncle-guardian's conversion to magnetizing, through which the evil schemes are brought to light. Yet this is more a display of miraculous clairvoyance than of therapeutic magnetism.

Finally in *Cousin Pons* (1848, two years before Balzac's death from overwork and stress, at the age of fifty), the principal character's life is saved, briefly, by his close friend exerting on him an outflow of the "vital fluid" about which Mesmer had theorized and in which Balzac continued to believe.

Balzac's friend and fellow novelist Theophile Gautier also believed in the existence of the magnetic fluid and that it could be projected outward from the eyes. "Balzac wanted to be a great man," Gautier wrote, "and he became one by incessantly projecting that fluid which is more powerful than electricity." Gautier theorized that the invisible fluid could be drained out of someone by an enemy who knew how to do it. This is the way a character is killed in his novel, *Jettatura*.

Victor Hugo, considered by some an even greater novelist than Balzac, was another believer in the existence of the vital fluid permeating the entire universe. Hugo did not employ magnetizing themes in his novels to anywhere near the extent Balzac did. His *Philosophical Preface* to *Les Misérables*, often omitted in English translations of that book, is, along with Balzac's preface to the collected edition of his *Human Comedy* and Chapter 13 of *Cousin Pons* (*A Treatise on the Occult Sciences*), the definitive statement of the mid-19th century French literary embrace of animal magnetism. "Science," Hugo wrote, echoing Balzac, "has under the pretext of having become miraculous, abandoned its duty which is to get at the root of things." Obsessed with weighing and measuring exteriors, science was forgetting the greater problem of understanding the inner being.

While the general public was thus being conditioned by these writers to accept the reality of the powers of the mind and the unconscious (though the latter concept was still hidden under the erroneous one of the "vital fluid"), the more serious adherents of magnetizing had access to the latest developments in the field through the monthly *Journal du Magnetisme*. This had been founded in 1845 largely through the efforts of the irrepressible Baron du Potet who had returned from Britain. Published for seventeen years until finally suppressed by the Second Empire's thought police, its twenty volumes remain an invaluable source for this critical period when the dawning science of hypnotism was struggling to stay alive in France until the coming of a more favorable era. It finally arrived in the 1880s when France again leaped to the forefront in hypnotic research and application.

In the interval, leadership had shifted to Britain, through the discoveries and achievements of our next three of the World's Greatest Hypnotists, James Braid, John Elliotson, and James Esdaile. Significant developments were also taking place in America. It is to these English-speaking areas we now turn.

V.

THE MESMERIST MOVEMENT IN BRITAIN

John Elliotson
1791 - 1868

CHAPTER 11
John Elliotson Introduces Mesmerism to Britain

There were three distinguished pioneers who properly share the honor of having introduced the art and practice of mesmerism to the British public and medical profession: John Elliotson, James Braid and James Esdaile. All three were contemporaries, born within less than twenty years of each other. Elliotson is generally ranked at the head of the trio. He was the eldest and the one who made the first and widest impression on both the public and the medical mind. His close friendship with Charles Dickens resulted in the great novelist's conversion to the mesmerist doctrine, and through its sympathetic treatment in Dickens' books—though never as overtly as in those of Balzac—his vast reading audience was brought to look at it with at least an interested curiosity.

That it took a little over half a century for mesmerism to have anything other than a fleeting influence in Britain can be ascribed to the general antipathy in the island kingdom to all things French. This attitude, born of a century of more or less constant war against France for the mastery of the oceans and of overseas empires, and heightened by the twenty-three years' death grapple with Revolutionary and Napoleonic France, was overcome only very slowly in the decades of peace following Waterloo.

There had been some attempts at mesmerist penetration of British insularity in the immediate wake of Mesmer's own notoriety in the Paris of the last years of the Ancienne Regime. Mesmer's brief visit to London in the summer of 1785, after his final discomfiture in the French capital, was followed by the appearance of a Dr. Bell, of whom little is known, offering a course of lectures on mesmerism to English audiences. These attracted only a handful, but three years later, in 1788, one of the Chevalier d'Eslon's pupils, named de Mainauduc, gave public demonstrations of mesmerism in London with considerable success. So much so, the ever vigilant moralist Hannah More was moved to complain to her long-time pen-friend, the essayist Horace Walpole, about "the demoniacal mummery now acting in this country . . . Mesmer gained a hundred thousand pounds by it in Paris, and de Mainauduc is making as much here." This, of course, was a wildly exaggerated figure.

The English, however, saw mesmerism more as a form of public entertainment than a medical therapy or serious advance in science. People were paying one to three guineas for tickets — sometimes even more to "scalpers," who were already an extant breed — to see pretty women, in the throes of the magnetic crisis, flinging themselves about on the stage. The mesmerism-as-a-spectacle craze in England reached its height in 1790 when a talented artist and showman, Philippe-Jacques de Loutherbourg, staged great outdoor exhibitions of it, complete with fireworks, at Hammersmith on the Thames. Thousands flocked to these performances.

Loutherbourg was from Strasbourg in Alsace, where the Marquis de Puységur had founded a thriving call of mesmerist activity in 1785. He became a British citizen and later attained prominence as a painter, especially of fiery night scenes at the forges and factories of the dawning Industrial Revolution. He claimed to be a proficient magnetizer, as did his wife, and between them they were reputed to have effected two thousand cures. Had the short lived English fascination with the mesmeric spectacle developed into a more sustained interest, it is conceivable Loutherbourg could have become a true pioneer of the art in Britain. As it was, though, the public tired of it once the novelty wore off. The authorities also took a condemnatory attitude after numerous complaints that the exhibitions were harmful to public morals. The growing excesses of the French Revolution further contributed to a general abhorrence of anything French. The above mentioned Dr. Bell reappeared in 1792 to write the first handbook in English on *The General and Practical Principles of Animal Magnetism*, but it was never published.

For the next forty years the subject was totally ignored in Britain except for two poems of Percy Shelley, and a little-noticed treatise by a Dr. John Hygarth of Bath, in 1800, on *The Imagination As A Cause And Cure Of Illnesses Of The Body*. Shelley's brief involvement with mesmerism is an interesting episode, despite having to rely for its attestation—outside of the two poems—on the memoirs of his cousin Tom Medwin, written a quarter-century after the fact and in a time when mesmerism had come far more widely into public acceptance.

Medwin was four years older than the precocious Shelley, and had been his companion and protector from rough hazings and pranks while they were schoolmates. Medwin asserted in his memoirs that the poet had been wholly ignorant of Mesmer and of magnetizing until he told him about them in 1821, when Medwin returned from India after a ten-year absence. This assertion is difficult to accept.

Through the entire course of their long youthful association, lasting until Shelley was nineteen and about to marry Harriet Westbrook, and Medwin was leaving to seek his fortune in the service of the East India Company's armed forces, there is ample evidence for the poet's intense interest in every form of what are now termed "borderline sciences." He devoured vast numbers of obscure publications on alchemy, water-witching, experimentation with gases and explosives, communication with the dead, and so on. It is hardly believable that he could have been completely unaware of mesmerism, or of Loutherbourg's widely publicized demonstrations of magnetizing in England.

Shelley was still interested in these subjects when Medwin next met him a decade later at Pisa in Italy, where the poet was staying with his wife, Mary Wollstonecraft Godwin, whom he had married after Harriet's suicide. Mary's stepsister Claire Clairmont was also with them, in an uneasy ménage à trois; into which the arrival of Medwin, full of anecdotes about his experiences in India, may have come as a welcome diversion from thinking only about themselves and each other. Shelley was suffering from a painful recurrence of a kidney condition, and was glad of anything that would take his mind off its agonizing spasms.

Medwin appears to have had his own first encounter with hypnotism in India, where he saw it used by fakirs and yogis; and he had amused himself by compiling a treatise on what he had found out about Mesmer and magnetizing after his return to Europe. Whether the information was as new to Shelley as Medwin later claimed it was, the poet was soon eager for a trial of it to ease his nephritic pain. Medwin successfully induced Shelley into trance by touching his forehead, and in Medwin's words the poet "Slept for a space with his eyes open, then awoke refreshed and with his pain eased."

Mary and Claire had both been present, and were duly impressed. Claire recorded in her diary, "To be a magnetizer requires profound belief, a capacity of intense application to the act, and purity of motive; for without this the experiment will fail." (An observation that no present-day hypnotist would dispute.) Claire however was tiring of being one-third of a triangle, and shortly departed to Florence; the more readily as she saw herself being replaced by Emilia Viviani, a teen-age *femme fatale* who was being romantically incarcerated — as Shelley imagined it — in a convent while her family arranged a marriage for her.

Actually this was quite common procedure among upper-class Italians at that period, and no restrictions were placed on her being visited by Shelley and Mary, who tagged along for propriety's sake. (The wives of geniuses often have to put up with a lot.) Emilia next came to figure, in Shelley's remarkable poem *Epipsychidion*, as the sun, in a planetary configuration in which Mary was the moon, Shelley the earth and Claire a comet that darted in and out of sight. Employing Mesmerist verbiage, Shelley described how the sun and moon ". . . dart Magnetic might into its heart" i.e., the heart of Shelley, the earth.

After Emilia had been safely married off, and Medwin after several weeks as house guest departed to England, Mary tried her hand at magnetizing Shelley, whose kidney condition was again worse. She succeeded beyond her expectations, Shelley being an easily hypnotizable subject, but had to give it up after a while, as in trance the poet reverted to his earlier habit of sleepwalking and one night almost walked out the window into the Arno river.

Medwin was now replaced in the Shelley circle by Edward Williams, who had served with Medwin in India; and Williams' common-law wife Jane. A statuesque and attractive brunette, it was not long before she became a new third in Shelley's continual triangle. He taught her the art of magnetizing, which she practiced on his recurring kidney pains with rather better results than Mary. At least he did not sleepwalk as frequently when put in trance by Jane; whom he rewarded by dedicating to her the poem he wrote descriptive of her efforts, *The Magnetic Lady to Her Patient*.

Shelley seems nevertheless to have desisted from being a magnetic subject early in 1822, a few months before he and Williams were both drowned in the wreck of their sailboat off the Italian coast. Physically he was improved, perhaps due to living more of an outdoor life than hitherto, and maybe felt less need to continue the magnetic treatment. At the same time Shelley was falling with increasing frequency into hypnagogic states that suggest he experienced self-hypnosis—without conscious intent—and was unable to cope with the psychic depths he thus dredged. There is more than a hint of suicide in the fatal shipwreck.

The first revival of general interest came in 1828 through the work of an Irish physician, Richard Chenevix. He had practiced in the Netherlands and Germany, and been a profound skeptic of mesmerism until convinced otherwise by attending the Abbé Faria's lectures. He gave a series of demonstrations of the medical uses of magnetizing at St. Thomas' hospital in London. They attracted wide though largely hostile interest among members of the medical profession in the city. This hostility was heightened when the *London Medical and Physiological Journal*—the mouthpiece of the establishment— opened its columns in October 1828 and for the following year, to articles by Chenevix explaining more thoroughly the Farian doctrine of magnetizing. The articles were immediately satirized and ridiculed in succeeding issues, but Chenevix was no longer in London to respond to them, having returned to Dublin to test the effectiveness of magnetizing on patients at a hospital for incurables. Soon the brief flurry of controversy aroused by him had subsided. He died suddenly in the following year (1830), and mesmerism might have had to wait still longer for its real British discovery had there not been one doctor at St. Thomas who had a deeply perceptive curiosity about the phenomenon that Chenevix had presented there.

That doctor was John Elliotson, then in his late thirties, and one of the most noted physicians in the British capital because of his innovativeness and his criticism of the medical establishment's obdurate resistance to new and more effective modes of treatment. Born in 1791, the son of a pharmacist in the London suburb of Southwark, he received his medical education at the University of Edinburgh, then and for long afterward the premier medical school of Britain. With the opening up of the European continent to British intercourse after Napoleon's fall, he pursued graduate research at several of the leading European universities. After returning to England he studied further at Cambridge and on the staffs of Guy's and St. Thomas' hospitals in London. In 1817, at twenty-six, he was appointed Assistant Physician at St. Thomas, and a full physician in 1823. This customarily conveyed the privilege of giving clinical lectures. Elliotson, however, had to fight for this right, for he was making enemies by insisting on introducing new procedures. He was the first in Britain to use the stethoscope, soon after Laennec's invention of it in France. It would take a generation for it to be accepted by British doctors in general, who long scorned it as "that useless piece of wood Elliotson raves about."

Similar resistance and discredit greeted his success in treating malarial ague with large doses of quinine instead of the ineffectual driblets that had been the standard; and also to his employment of various hitherto neglected substances (iodide of potassium, prussic acid, sulphate of copper) as effective drugs. However, he had the support of a powerful ally, Thomas Wakley, who had been his classmate at Edinburgh, and had gone into the field of medical reporting and journalism. Although he had a medical degree, Wakley practiced only briefly, his interest being principally in fighting and exposing what he saw as the corrupt, inbred, nepotic and favoritism-ridden world of the London medical establishment. After failing to make much headway with his articles in the lay press, Wakley, who was wealthy, decided in 1823 to found his own weekly journal, *The Lancet*, which became, and is today, one of the world's foremost medical publications.

Wakley's pugnacious and caustic editorials, his publication of the jealously guarded clinical lectures of the medical schools, and his championing of Elliotson's innovations, soon made *The Lancet* a force to be reckoned with. When Elliotson was finally allowed to start giving lectures in 1828, Wakley's publication of them made a wide medical audience aware of his careful and detailed case descriptions, the diagnosis and the treatment, the outcome, and the inferences—often daring—drawn from what had been learned in each instance.

Those who were able to attend the lectures in person were enthralled by the obvious personal involvement of Elliotson in what he was describing. He saw himself as responsible, not only for the relief or cure of the patient he had treated, but for extracting the maximum amount of useful information from the case. Short and lithe, dark-haired and dark-complexioned, with piercing black eyes, he gave an impression of being imbued with electric energy as he strode with agility around the lecture stage, emphasizing his points with passion and sincerity.

Elliotson was already a person of rising renown and prestige in the medical world when his attention was captured by Chenevix's demonstrations of mesmerism at St. Thomas in the summer of 1829. He had not been unaware of mesmerism up to that time, but had not considered it as having any significance as a medical therapy. He regarded with favor, verging on acceptance, the rival Continental European theory of phrenology that had been making steady progress since it was propounded by Franz-Joseph Gall at Vienna in 1796, and at Paris from 1807 on. At times embraced by some of the leading Continental magnetizers, and more or less tolerated by most of them as an adjunct to their own doctrine, phrenology claimed to be able to locate the seats of human emotions and traits in various portions of the brain and to identify the outward minute cranial protrusions—"bumps on the head" in popular parlance—that supposedly corresponded to these. Elliotson had attended with fascination the course of eighteen lectures on phrenology delivered by Gall's disciple Spurzheim in 1825 at the Crown and Anchor Tavern in London's Strand. He had followed up by founding the London Phrenological Society with himself as chairman. For over a decade until he became seriously involved in mesmerism, he would call the Society's meetings to order at the Tavern every Saturday evening at 8 o'clock.

Phrenology was, however, destined to fade from serious medical acceptance, much as its predecessor physiognomy (the eighteenth century doctrine of reading people's character-istics from their physical features) had done after a brief spurt of acclaim. Elliotson, even if he still viewed phrenology as credible, may have sensed its coming demise as he watched and listened to Chenevix. He did not, to be sure, immediately commit himself to support mesmerism; at this stage he only took careful notes and filed them away for future reflection.

He was, in any case, deeply engrossed by two major projects at that time, demanding all of the time and energy left over from his professional duties. The first was the founding of a teaching hospital at the University of London, where he was appointed Professor of Medical Practice in 1831. He had long felt it was a serious shortcoming of British medical schools not to have their own teaching hospitals. Lacking these, they had to rely on access to regular hospitals for case studies, and often were denied full control of them. Strongly backed by Wakley and *The Lancet*, Elliotson succeeded in 1834 in getting the University Hospital established as an institution where medical research and physician training could be carried on in conjunction with care of the sick, with full control maintained over all experiments.

The second undertaking that preoccupied Elliotson in the half-dozen years after Chenevix's mesmerism exhibits was the completion of his textbook *Human Physiology*, a truly landmark volume that went through five editions at annual intervals after it first came out in 1835. He had started it in 1815, while studying in Germany, as a paraphrased translation of the noted German physician J. F. Blumembach's *Institutes of Psychology*. (A title that recalls Jean Calvin's monumental *Institutes of the Christian Religion*.) As time went on, Elliotson's version became more and more his own book, with Blumenbach's material relegated to footnotes. When the first edition finally appeared, it was at once a medical textbook and an encyclopedia of human physiology in its historical, medical and humanistic aspects through the centuries. Mesmerism was mentioned only briefly and neutrally, while phrenology had a lengthy description and defense.

Bracketing the initial publication of *Human Physiology* were the appearances of two other books that, coming out when they did, were strongly influential in preparing the British public mind for the mesmerist onslaught that began in 1837. The German philosopher Heinrich Jung-Stilling's *Theory of Pneumatology*, published in an English translation in 1834, was a compendium of theories of spirituality, apparitions, and non-material existences, all based on the foundation of the Christian revelation. It was immensely popular and helped to refute the notion that mesmerism was somehow anti-religious. This was a fatal objection in the minds of Britons in the first half of the ninteenth century, who were still clinging fiercely to the literal truth of the Biblical account of the Creation, the Flood and the Dispersal of the Nations from Babel.

Three years later, in 1837, the British dilettante writer John C. Colquhoun published his *Isis Reveleta: An Inquiry Into Animal Magnetism*. A leisurely, chatty account of what Mesmer and his successors had discovered and practiced, it was non-critical and indeed naive to a degree, for which reasons it was attacked by Elliotson, Esdaile, and Braid, who felt it reduced a significant new scientific advance to the level of an interesting fad. However, the easy comprehensibility and down-to-earth vocabulary of Colquhoun's book opened the minds of tens of thousands to the reality of mesmerism, which hitherto had been seen as an obscure concept smacking of trickery and charlatanry.

Isis Reveleta had just made its appearance in British book-shops, when in July 1837 there appeared at the University Hospital a "small, pale, plain-looking and unassuming Fren-chman" who, through an interpreter, requested the permission of Dr. Elliotson to carry out demonstrations of magnetizing therapy on the hospital's patients. The Frenchman was none other than the Baron du Potet, otherwise Jules de Sennevoy. Du Potet was regarded in his native France as a flamboyant personality, but was doubtless somewhat subdued by being among strangers of a culture and language so different from his own. According to some accounts this was not his first visit to England. He is said to have accompanied Chenevix to London in 1828 and to have watched the Irishman's magnetiz-ing experiments at St. Thomas, but returned to France after concluding the time was not yet right for introducing mesmer-ism to Britain.

Exactly where du Potet was during the next several years is somewhat of a mystery. He seems to have made no public comment on the partly favorable report of the French Third Commission of Inquiry in 1831. A French critic in the 1850s alleged that twenty years earlier du Potet had been making a living by magnetizing patients at the Provencal Brothers restaurant, not far from the royal palace. However that may be, du Potet appears to have decided early in 1837—when the Fourth Commission of Inquiry was preparing its negative report on magnetizing—that there was no future for the art in France for a long time to come, and that he should once again try the prospects in England.

Elliotson received du Potet warmly, and assigned him several epileptic women patients for experimentation. Attention and controversy were immediately aroused. To forestall premature and harmful publicity, du Potet and Elliotson insisted on admitting only "gentlemen of culture" as observers. Wakley of *The Lancet* was unenthusiastic about the whole thing, but agreed to have his sub-editor, George Mills, cover the experiments, which were carried on almost daily from the middle of July to the beginning of September. By the end of August, Elliotson believed that positive, beneficial and genuine results were being obtained, and said so in a clinical lecture in which he strongly recommended the continuation of the demonstrations.

The lecture was published in full by *The Lancet* in its issue of September 9, by which date Elliotson had left for a vacation trip to the European continent. He returned at the beginning of October to find that the popular press had picked up the story and was giving it wide publicity. This displeased the

Hospital's faculty, which was now besieged by requests from all sorts of people wanting to witness the experiments, so it put a stop to them and denied du Potet access to the hospital.

Elliotson stepped in and smoothed things over. He persuaded the reluctant faculty that the experiments should be resumed. It was necessary in the interests of science, he told them, that the question be fully resolved as to which of the observed effects were indeed artificially produced and which were natural and fortuitous. To lessen undesirable publicity, he decided to conduct all further experiments himself, with the assistance of William Wood, his principal and trusted understudy. The Baron du Potet would no longer be a principal actor, though he would be allowed to observe the proceedings on pledge of taking no active part in them.

On these conditions the experiments were resumed and continued into the following year. Though Elliotson did his utmost to restrict access to them, he was under continuous pressure from persons prominent in public life to be allowed to see what was being done. Among these were Charles Dickens and his illustrator, George Cruikshank. Dickens was then in the early stages of being lionized by the British public as the nation's foremost novelist. His first masterpiece, *Pickwick Papers* had just been published, and *Oliver Twist* was appearing serially. Together they visited the wards of London Hospital on January 14, 1838, with Elliotson's full permission, and guided by his aide William Wood.

Dickens' fascination with mesmerism, its influence on his work, and his own remarkable experiences as an unprofessional but competent mesmerist are so remarkable a story they require a separate chapter. So intertwined however were the activities of Dickens and Elliotson—they became the closest of friends—the novelist will inevitably enter into our account of the doctor's career. This first inspection by Dickens of mesmeric therapy in the wards involved one Hannah Hunter, a girl in her early teens. She suffered for many years from a painful left ear, had frequent asthmatic attacks, and for half of 1837 had convulsive fits ending with rigidity of various parts of her body. As a result her feet and lower legs had become totally paralyzed. She was admitted to the hospital for treatment two weeks before Dickens and Cruikshank saw her. William Wood mesmerizing her daily with simple motions of his hands, directing into her the "magnetic fluid" Elliotson and his pupils continued to believe in.

The girl was not allowed to remain in the mesmeric state more than a few minutes on account of her generally weak condition, but she was starting to show an improvement that Wood attributed to the mesmerizing. Dickens was enthralled by what he saw, even though he still had some suspicions that some form of hocus-pocus was involved. He returned several times through the early months of 1838 to watch Elliotson and Wood mesmerize patients with varying ailments, and became convinced that both the method and its results were genuine. His friend, the noted actor William Macready, who had made Elliotson his family doctor two years before, was also a frequent but rather skeptical visitor. Another was the historical novelist William Harrison Ainsworth, whose genius for writing tales of witches and hauntings made him keenly receptive to the reality of unusual phenomena.

Even before the coming of du Potet that launched him on what seemed a dizzying upward climb of publicity about mesmerism, Elliotson's private practice and income had grown tenfold over the previous decade. *The Lancet* reported on September 2, 1837, that he was then earning five thousand pounds a year compared to five hundred in 1827. No doctor in all Britain was as much in demand, especially by those in the upper ranks of society. He decided to expand the fame and fortune that the mesmeric experiments were bringing him by proposing public demonstrations to which notables of all kinds would be invited.

Baron du Potet was also profiting from the public's interest in mesmerism, that mounted with each new story in the press about the wonders being performed in Elliotson's hospital wards. Apparently able to command the services of competent English-speaking helpers, du Potet was already placing advertisements that offered "treatment of acute and chronic diseases and nervous affections by animal magnetism at No. 20 Wigmore Street, Cavendish Square ... seances conducted by Baron du Potet every day except Sunday from 1:30 to 3 o'clock ... fee, 2 shillings 6 pence." At that low price (less than an American dollar), which made his ministrations accessible to all but the very poorest, it was likely du Potet could give only cursory attention to the ailments of all who came, and could not follow through with any prescribed course of treatment. He was, in short, simply milking a favorable situation while it lasted. On a more responsible level, however, he was also writing, and would publish in English before the year was out, his *Introduction to the Study of Animal Magnetism*. Although this was based on the erroneous notion of a magnetic fluid, it did provide useful guidance for mesmeric induction. For two or three years it would be the standard handbook in English on the subject.

Meantime, Elliotson considered himself fortunate in having for the subjects of his planned public demonstrations a remarkable pair of sisters who could be relied on to hold the attention of the audience. They were Elizabeth and Jane O'Key, who had both been in the hospital for about a year receiving treatment for recurrent epileptic episodes. Elizabeth, sixteen years of age and the younger of the two, was the one who immediately drew the attention of onlookers. Very small of stature, pale and downcast in appearance, the back of her right hand covered with ugly warts, she was nonetheless skillful and clever in repartee.

She and her sister had previously appeared speaking in tongues at the revival meetings held on Islington Green in north London by the Scottish evangelist Edward Irving. They had also played roles in pseudo-spiritualistic performances staged by him before large audiences, and were adept at acting a part. In the hospital, Elizabeth had, during her twelve-month stay, been mesmerized over one hundred times. Being one who sought out other patients and exchanged experiences with them, it might be fair to guess that she had formed a substantial set of ideas as to what was expected of her in the mesmerized state. Elliotson thus allowed his eagerness for attention-catching publicity to get the better of his judgment; he did not adequately take into account that the O'Key sisters were accomplished manipulators as well as pliable subjects for manipulation. He would have been wiser to select other, less self-dramatizing subjects with which to make his first direct impression on the public.

He scheduled two demonstrations with the O'Keys in 1838, one on May 10, and the other on June 2. Over two hundred distinguished guests were in attendance at the first session. Among them were Dickens and Cruikshank, along with other figures from the world of literature and the arts, as well as several Members of Parliament. William Mosesworth, the famed expositor of the philosophy of Hobbes, who had donated the substantial sum of thirty guineas to the hospital for the furtherance of mesmeric experimentation, was there to see the practical results of his gift.

Elliotson opened the proceedings with a speech declaring his sole object to be the determination of facts and the exposure of fallacies. Elizabeth O'Key, with William Wood waiting beside her, listened impassively with no expression of interest on her face. Then, inducted into light mesmeric trance, she moved across the stage as a sleepwalker does, initially not fixing her attention on any object or person. Finally she pointed to a worn chair on the stage, saying it was "dirty," and staring at the Marquis of Anglesey in the audience, saluted him with "Hello there, white trousers." She followed that up by offering to relieve Sir Charles Paget of his hat, whereupon Elliotson, with a wave of his hand, seemingly unseen by her, placed her in deep mesmeric trance. She then toppled over backward, sound asleep, and was barely caught before hitting the floor. He demonstrated how her resistance to mesmeric commands ("don't be silly, Dr. Ellisson, my hands won't move the way you want") was overcome by deepening her mesmeric state. After about two hours of variations on this and similar themes, she was replaced on the stage by her sister Jane. The audience was becoming restless, and Elliotson cut short the remainder of the demonstration, showing only how in mesmeric trance Jane could lift weights heavier than she was capable of doing in her normal state, and was able to predict to the minute when she would awake from the "magnetic sleep."

In his concluding remarks, Elliotson claimed he had shown animal magnetism to be a natural phenomenon, somewhat akin to electricity, which could be directed and controlled. The effects on the mesmeric subject were in direct proportion to the area and mass of the application; i.e., one finger lightly touching would produce brief, shallow mesmeric sleep; a whole hand pressing heavily would cause a longer and deeper "sleep"; and so on.

Unfortunately, he was seeing correlations that simply were not really there. Most who were present, though conceding that the phenomena they had seen were genuine (although enhanced by the O'Keys' obvious role-playing capability), were skeptical that anything had been proven about animal magnetism being reducible to a set of fixed principles similar to those applicable to gravity and other natural laws. Nevertheless, when opening the second public demonstration on June 2, Elliotson reiterated that his experiments were continuing to confirm that the proportion of mass and area operated in mesmerism according to undeviating rules, making it possible to apply it scientifically.

The second demonstration had more than a little flavor of a spiritualist seance. Jane O'Key claimed to be controlled by a Negro spirit, under whose direction she lifted a weight of seventy pounds, though unable to budge a four pound weight when not in mesmeric trance. Both sisters also made clairvoyant statements it was not possible to verify on the spot, since they related to things concerning themselves in the following days. Elliotson later insisted they had been borne out, but satisfactory independent confirmation was lacking. The demonstration lasted three hours and much of what passed between Elliotson, Wood, and the O'Keys on the stage was not heard by the audience because of a heavy rain drumming on the roof skylight; but again there was a general feeling that what had been shown was real enough, even if Elliotson's explanations of it failed to carry much conviction.

The Hospital faculty, or Committee as it was called, was even less convinced of the propriety of the public demonstrations, which it felt were taking on the harmful atmosphere of theatrical performances. A few days after the second one, it requested Elliotson not to present any more, and rejected his proposal they be continued with smaller, more restricted audiences. The Committee could not however prevent him from allowing visitors to come and watch the mesmeric treatments in the wards.

The sub-editor of *The Lancet*, George Mills, was an eyewitness to most of Elliotson's experiments, both in public demonstrations and in the wards, and continued to report favorably on them. There were no grounds, he stated, for thinking the O'Keys were fraudulent subjects. Actors they might be, and probably were, but not imposters any more than the scores of other patients who were being regularly and systematically magnetized in the hospital, with some benefit in most cases, and very substantial improvement in a few.

However, Mills' chief, Dr. Wakley, was becoming deeply suspicious of the whole episode. To him it seemed his old friend Elliotson had most regrettably become the dupe of charlatanry and was irresponsibly propagating it. He requested that a private demonstration be held for him at his home in London's Bedford Square. Elliotson assented, and it took place in the first week of August 1838, two months after the second and last demonstration. Wakley watched in silence; he was unable to come to a conclusion. He asked that the session be repeated the following week. Elliotson did so, but again Wakley indicated neither acceptance nor rejection of what he saw. He requested a third session, and Elliotson agreed to it. It was this third session which turned Wakley into an open opponent of mesmerism.

Elliotson had come to believe certain metals would—as in the case of electricity—act as receptacles and conductors of the postulated magnetic fluid. In attempting to demonstrate this on Elizabeth O'Key with a piece of nickel that was supposed to be a magnetic conductor, and another of lead which was non-conducting, he found to his confusion that she responded according to what she was told, rather than the asserted qualities of the metals. Wakley thereupon told him he was wholly mistaken and that there was no such thing as a magnetic fluid; the girl was merely responding to what was being suggested to her.

Shaken and dismayed, Elliotson insisted there had to be some explanation he could not immediately supply. He asked to be allowed to come back the next day to repeat the experiment, to which Wakley agreed. It turned out to be a very long day indeed. After the metals test results were the same as the day before, Wakley demanded that all twenty-nine experiments of the previous three sessions be gone through again.

By the time the exhausted participants had finished — after thirteen hours of induction, experimenting, and waking — Wakley was convinced that to the extent that there was any reality at all to the mesmeric phenomena, it was purely mental and the result of an ability to work on a person's suggestibility.

Any modern hypnotist would largely agree with that conclusion. Had Elliotson been able to give up his adherence to the concept of the magnetic fluid, *The Lancet* would have continued to cover his investigations objectively. That, however, he could not do, smarting as he was at having been put in the wrong by a man who had been his close friend and ally. Wakley on his part was equally unreasonable, believing that Elliotson had abandoned his commitment to scientific medicine for the pursuit of illusion. From that time on, *The Lancet* pilloried Elliotson unmercifully, and gave copious free publicity to every rumor, no matter how unfounded, that he and his aides abused the "trusting females" they treated in their mesmeric experiments.

Elliotson, anticipating he might soon be driven from the hospital by these attacks, now began magnetizing patients at his home on 37 Conduit Street, a splendid and spacious mansion that he had acquired with his new-found affluence earlier in the decade of the 1830s. In late November he started giving mesmeric demonstrations in the house, to which he invited prominent individuals, including Dickens and Cruikshank, who continued to believe in his version of the art. The O'Key sisters, shuttled back and forth between Elliotson's home and the University Hospital, were the star performers in these exhibitions.

As the year of 1838 drew to a close, the O'Keys became the center of a new furor at the hospital. They professed to be able to foretell clairvoyantly the recovery or death of patients whose beds they approached. Their forecasts proved to be uncannily correct, much to the consternation of patients who shuddered in fear of a death prediction by them. Cornered by his necessity to defend the sisters, Elliotson sought to explain away this ability as a physiological one, by asserting that persons near death exuded a "peculiar effluvium" that only those as sensitive as the O'Keys could detect.

The Hospital Committee and staff now became split into two fiercely hostile factions. One was headed by Elliotson and the other by his former close colleague and friend, Dr. Richard Liston, now a bitter enemy who avoided speaking to him after some inflammatory exchanges between them. Liston moved to have the Committee require Elliotson to discharge Elizabeth O'Key, who had already stayed two months beyond the statutory eighteen-month limit for any one patient, and if Elliotson refused, to forthwith ban him or anyone else from practicing animal magnetism, under whatever designation, in the hospital. The Committee having so moved, Elliotson resigned from the hospital's staff, as well as from the University, on December 28, 1839, and celebrated by having Dickens to dinner that evening.

That was on a Friday. When the medical students came back to the hospital from their Christmas-New Year's vacation on Wednesday, January 2, 1839, many were up in arms over the resignation of Elliotson, who had been very popular. They rallied behind William Wood, who had remained loyal to him, and at a mass meeting in the anatomical theater on Friday,

January 4, demanded that the Committee refuse to accept Elliotson's resignation. About an equal number, however, were there in support of Liston, and there were also some who tried to act as peacemakers. It was finally decided to have all the students vote the next day, Saturday, between 1:00 p.m. and 3:00 p.m.. The choice was between two resolutions—one to accept Elliotson's resignation, the other simply to express regret that circumstances had made it necessary. The vote was 124 to 113 in favor of the second motion, which also conveyed the appreciation of its supporters for Elliotson's teaching and dedication to the healing profession. While the balloting was taking place, the Committee was accepting his resignation.

Elliotson, now in his late forties, had to adjust to the new lifestyle of a professional practice from a home office only, a much lowered income, and ostracism and snubbing by many who had previously held him in such high esteem. He had a final humiliation to endure from the hospital that had been so central a part of his life. It refused to let one of his former pupils read aloud in class a thirty-six page letter of farewell he had written. Perhaps fortunately, Ellliotson was not married and thus did not have the additional burden of seeing his family hurt and shamed by the loss of his university and hospital connections.

One thing Elliotson did not lose was the friendship and acclaim of those prominent in British cultural life who had hailed him as the pioneer of a new science and a new therapy, and who continued to honor him even though not always agreeing with all of his views. Dickens, whose family physician he became in 1839 shortly after leaving the hospital, spoke for many in a letter written in 1842: "I have the utmost reliance in Dr. Elliotson's honor, character and ability, and would trust my life in his hands at any time. After what I have seen with my own eyes and observed with my own senses, I should be untrue to myself if I shrank from saying I am a believer [in mesmerism] and became so against all my previous conceptions and opinions."

The third edition of Elliotson's *Human Physiology* textbook had come out shortly before his break with Wakley, and contained much stronger statements in favor of mesmerism than any in the first two. Those in the fourth edition, in 1839, were even stronger; and in the fifth and final edition, that of 1840, which remained for a generation the often-consulted, definitive work in its line, he added a lengthy chapter on the usefulness of magnetizing in the treatment of nervous disorders and epilepsy. He included an account of his own involvement in the introduction of the new therapy to Britain, and instructions for its use. The wide readership of the book in medical circles meant that henceforth the profession could no longer dodge the issue; mesmerism had to be confronted and its claims fairly judged.

There soon followed the entry of James Braid into the mesmerism field (which Braid subsequently named "hypnotism"); and the achievements of James Esdaile with surgical anesthesia. As *The Lancet* was now closed to any objective reporting of these historic developments, and the other medical journals followed its example, Elliotson decided to launch his own publication under the name of *The Zoist*, a Greek term roughly translatable as "life-giving." In so doing he may have set the example for du Potet, who returned to

France about this time and started publishing his valuable *Journal of Magnetism* in 1845.

The Zoist preceded the *Journal of Magnetism* by two years, the first of its quarterly numbers appearing in April 1843. It would continue to be published for almost thirteen years, the final number appearing on December 31, 1855. The annual volumes have an average of five hundred pages each, about 6,500 pages in all. They are a priceless repository of first-hand, contemporary information on the critical formative period of modern hypnotism as it evolved in the hands of its three great British pioneers, and several lesser ones including W. J. Tubbs of Cambridgeshire. He was ahead of his time in his eye-fixation technique of inducing hypnosis, and in training lay assistants such as his elderly housekeeper to serve as what would now be called hypnotic technicians.

Another significant advance made possible by the advocacy of *The Zoist* was the founding of mesmeric infirmaries at London, Edinburgh, Dublin and several lesser cities of the British Isles. These provided centers of practical application of the techniques of painless surgery James Esdaile had developed, as we shall see, in his practice in India. At one mesmeric infirmary in Exeter, in southwest England, a surgeon named Parker was said to have performed two hundred painless operations on patients in mesmeric coma. In 1842 another surgeon, a Dr. Ward of Nottingham, amputated a mesmerized patient's leg at the thigh without any discomfort or pain. These and similar reports, all published in *The Zoist*, regularly sent *The Lancet* into paroxysms of wrath. It called them "infamous" and cited establishment surgeons as saying that the patients had to have been trained not to give expression to the pain they must have felt. Even if mesmeric anesthesia were possible, these doctors argued, it would be wrong; it was good for the patients to feel pain, and the severer the pain, the more rapidly they recovered.

By 1847, however, the whole controversy over mesmeric anesthesia had been shunted aside by the multiplying evidence that ether and chloroform provided anesthesia with dependable regularity. There seemed little point in pursuing the further development of hypnosis for this purpose, since the practitioner needed special aptitude and training, and there were always patients resistant to induction into a depth necessary for total anesthesia. Elliotson's inveterate foe at the University Hospital, Richard Liston, hailed the advent of chemical anesthesia as heralding the total demise of mesmerism, an expectation that would not be fulfilled, since hypnotism would be found to have many other applications besides anesthesia. (Today, however, the use of hypnosis to induce anesthesia is being re-examined and revived for the poor surgical risk where there is a contraindication to chemical anesthesia; for severe burns; and in the fields of obstetrics and dentistry. Hypnosis is also a valuable adjunct in combination with chemical anesthesia for the debilitated and geriatric patient undergoing major surgery.)

John Elliotson was a supporter and advocate of many other social and medical advances, and made *The Zoist* a forum for them that they could not find elsewhere, at least not as unrestrainedly. He attacked the overcrowded and unsanitary conditions in which the urban poor had to live, as well as the harshness and insensitivity with which the children of the early Victorian era were often treated. Medical fads and fashionable diseases were among his favorite targets, and also the lack of a national system of education with adequate minimum standards. His stands on these issues, shared by great numbers among the more literate and affluent, ensured that he retained the favor and friendship of many who did not fully agree with his views on mesmerism, and heightened his esteem among those who did. This broad spectrum of favor won him an invitation in 1846 to deliver the prestigious Harveian Lecture (named for William Harvey, the seventeenth century discoverer of the blood-circulatory system) at the Royal College of Surgeons, despite savage opposition from *The Lancet* and most of the medical establishment.

Not only did Elliotson defy threats of physical harm if he were to accept the invitation, he broke precedent by delivering the lecture in English instead of Latin as had been the rule for two centuries. (For the printed version, he did provide a matching Latin text.) And instead of responding in kind to the vilifications of him by his adversaries, he spoke in calm and measured phrases, reviewing the results of his own and other researches into mesmerism, and urging its further dispassionate study. He reminded his audience that virtually every great scientific and medical discovery—including Harvey's—had been violently attacked and accepted only after long debate and contention.

Though the lecture did little to soften the criticism to which he continued to be subjected, it was influential in gaining a wider medical acceptance of hypnotism, as it was now starting to be called. Elliotson remained active through the 1850s both as an advocate and practitioner, never giving up his belief in the magnetic fluid though no longer placing emphasis on it. About 1861, as he entered his seventies, his health began to fail and he had to sell the Conduit Road mansion. One of his old pupils at the University Hospital, Edmond Symes, who had become noted both as a physician and hypnotherapist, took him into his home in London's Berkeley Square, enabling him to live out his last years in comfort. It was there Elliotson died on July 29, 1868, at the age of seventy-seven, having lived to see hypnotism accepted into at least a limited use in regular medical practice in Britain.

Charles Dickens
The Creative Mesmerist

CHAPTER 12
Charles Dickens Heads the Creative Mesmerists

W e have seen how in France the enthusiasm of highly popular novelists, such as Balzac and Hugo, for the doctrine of animal magnetism was influential in arousing and sustaining a public interest and support that kept it alive through the mid-nineteenth century period of official disapproval. And we have also noted how the awakening of the British public to Mesmer's discovery, through the efforts of Elliotson and others from 1837 on, was furthered by the ardor with which Charles Dickens, and indeed a whole array of noted figures of the English literary firmament of that period, took up the cause.

Though Dickens, possessing as he did the greatest talent and the greatest reputation, was the undoubted head of this band of creative literary mesmerists, Sir Edward Bulwer-Lytton and Harriet Martineau were also in the forefront of promoting both popular and scientific acceptance of mesmerism. Even more energetic and active, though less well known, were the poet Richard Monckton Milnes and the learned clergyman Chauncy Hare Townshend.

Essential differences are clearly evident in the French and English literary approaches to mesmerism. In the French fictional works, mesmerism frequently has an essential role in the plot; in the English ones, it has a much more peripheral function. To even the casual reader with at least some general knowledge of mesmerism (and in the 1840s and 1850s almost anyone in England who could read knew something about it), it was readily apparent that the novels of Dickens, Bulwer-Lytton, Wilkie Collins, and many others, were penetratingly accurate regarding character and motivation. This was because of the mesmeric capabilities of their authors. Yet these capabilities were mostly inferred and guessed at, for the social customs of that early Victorian era did not permit much public disclosure of the sometimes very advanced hypnotic experiments that several of its literary greats either performed or subjected themselves to. Not during his lifetime, nor for more than half a century afterward, was it known that Dickens had become a proficient mesmerist and even thought of setting up a professional practice. In common with many other possessors of great imaginative mental gifts, he was an egocentric, seeing everything in reference to himself. He had a constant need to dominate and manipulate others.

This inherent characteristic had been hardened by Dickens' difficult childhood. The slights and humiliations he had suffered were still recalled with bitterness forty years later in *David Copperfield*. When, under Elliotson's coaching, he discovered that he could affect the minds of others through mesmerizing them and issuing commands they obeyed, he felt it was compensation for what he had been forced to do at the behest of others. At the same time he justified it to himself as an act of benevolence; he was helping the person he mesmerized.

Again in common with others of strong imaginative power, Dickens had the capacity to visualize himself outside of his own person. In one of his travel sketches collected under the title of *The Uncommercial Traveller*, he tells an odd anecdote about observing, from his seat in a stagecoach going to the Kentish town of Rochester, "A very queer small boy" by the roadside. He called to the boy and asked where he lived. The boy replied "At Chatham, where I go to school." Dickens stopped the coach and picked up the boy. As they proceeded on their way, the boy remarked that they were coming to Gadshill, "where Falstaff went out to rob the travelers." "So you know about Falstaff?" Dickens asked. "Yes, I'm all of nine years old and I read all sorts of books," said the boy. Then, pointing to a high house on the hill, the boy said he had been admiring it since he was only half as old as nine, and dreaming of living in it. His father had told him that if he were very persevering and worked hard, he might some day do just that, "though that's impossible," said the boy. Unnerved, Dickens dropped the boy from the coach, for the house on the hill was his own house, the house he had dreamed of owning and had finally bought with the earnings from his writings.

It is obvious that this was not a real boy, but a product of Dickens' powerful imagination, recreating himself in the impoverished childhood he still resented and fought against; the childhood in which he read books far beyond his years, and despaired of ever having his superior mental capacity recognized. Success had finally come to him, but not before he had come to believe that he could achieve and sustain it only by dominating others. For their own good, of course, he would maintain, if pressed on the point. A personality of that sort could exert a strong influence. In different circumstances, there is little question that Dickens could have become a very effective hypnotist, perhaps even one of the greatest. Even as it was, the record of Dickens' mesmeric achievements is impressive.

Dickens was still only a fascinated bystander in 1839, after Elliotson's resignation from the University Hospital. Though he continued to attend the mesmeric demonstrations at Elliotson's home whenever he could, it was not often, for he was writing *Nicholas Nicklby* in biweekly installments, attempting to finish *Barnaby Rudge*, and trying to start a new magazine—*Master Humphrey's Clock*. Because of these activities he was not able to attend a dinner party that the actor William Macready (who could never overcome a basic skepticism about mesmerism even while remaining deeply interested) held for Elliotson in late March, and to which Harriet Martineau, Thomas Carlyle and Charles Darwin were also invited. Carlyle and Darwin would remain outside the mesmeric camp though examining it from time to time; Martineau was to be an advocate of it. Soon afterward, Richard Monckton Milnes, then still young and showing signs of greatness as a poet that he never quite fulfilled, became an adherent and his convivial breakfast parties became forums for discussion of every aspect of mesmerism.

Dickens finally completed *Nicklby* in the fall of 1839 and gave Elliotson a presentation copy. He then plunged into writing for the *Clock* a serial that was to become *The Old Curiosity Shop*. He was so busy working on it during the first half of 1840 that he overlooked the publication, early in the year, of the Rev. Chauncy Hare Townshend's *Facts in Mesmerism,* which was soon a best-seller. It bore a dedication to Elliotson, and Elliotson succeeded in calling Dickens' attention to it six months after it appeared by inviting him to dinner along with the author. The fifth and final edition of Elliotson's own *Human Physiology* had just come out and furnished an additional reason for a celebratory gathering.

It was the first meeting of what was to become a congenial trio. Townshend, fourteen years older than Dickens but three years younger than Elliotson, was a Cambridge graduate, sensitive and fine-mannered, an intimate of poets like Southey and Wordsworth, and a minor poet himself. Though he had taken holy orders in the Anglican Church, he possessed private wealth that made it unnecessary for him to be a parish priest. Spending much of his time on the European continent (he would later buy a villa, Mon Lorici near Lausanne on Lake Geneva, where Dickens would be a frequent guest) Townshend had become acquainted with mesmerism well before du Potet introduced the art to England. He soon discovered that he had the gift of magnetizing, and staged both public and private demonstrations.

Dickens and Townshend took to each other immediately, and met once more before the latter returned to Europe in the spring of 1841 to begin a series of public mesmerism demonstrations in London that drew large audiences. It had been a sad winter for the circle forming around Elliotson and Dickens. Macready's daughter died, and his young son remained seriously ill, despite all that Elliotson's medical skill could do for them (he did not attempt mesmerism), and Dickens almost worked himself into a state of emotional collapse over killing Little Nell in the final installment of *The Old Curiosity Shop*. Thus it came as a welcome relief to have new mesmeric sensations to divert them—first, Townshend's series of demonstrations, then a star attraction he brought from Belgium.

This was a fifteen-year-old boy named Alexis who could play the flute and read sheet music in the dark while mesmerized. For years he would puzzle those who sought to discover how he performed these and other feats including clairvoyance. He was suspected of trickery. The famous actress Fanny Kemble was convinced he was cheating, but the charge was never proved. Dickens, though, was enthusiastic over the boy, and watching him perform whetted his own growing desire to attempt to magnetize. He felt sure he could do it, though he repeatedly fought off Townshend's suggestion that he first be a subject himself. Dickens, the manipulator and dominator of others, could not endure being placed into what he believed would be the control of another, even in trance.

He took training from both Elliotson and Townshend before he sailed with his wife, Kate, in January 1842 on their long-planned visit to America, where his books were already as popular as they were in England. In Boston he was invited by the local mesmerists to witness their demonstrations. He may have made a first cautious trial of his own ability on one of these occasions. In any event, by the time he reached Pittsburgh in March, he felt confident enough to try magnetizing Kate before two acquaintances he had met there and to whom he had held forth at length on the wonders of mesmerism. Considering that he dominated her thoroughly (though silently she rebelled), he had every reason to expect that he could quickly mesmerize her. He started by making hand passes around her head. At first there was no apparent effect; then after six minutes of these passes, she became hysterical. Dickens thereupon resorted to more vigorous passes, and within two more minutes she was in mesmeric trance, seemingly asleep. He had no trouble arousing her, using Elliotson's and Townshend's technique of stroking the subject's eyebrows with thumbtips and blowing softly on her face.

Encouraged by this first test of his mesmeric powers — though admitting afterward that he had been alarmed by the rapidity with which he transformed Kate's paroxysm of hysterics into mesmeric trance — on his return to England Dickens began experimenting widely with his family and friends. He was able to avoid inducing hysterics in further sessions with Kate, but found he could not get his sister-in-law Mary Hogarth beyond the hysterical phase. He was also unable to magnetize Macready at all; the actor was apparently one of the minority who are resistant to hypnotic susceptibility.

With numerous other subjects among his ever expanding circle of acquaintances, he was invariably successful and his confidence grew steadily. He claimed to have relieved several cases of illness through his mesmeric ministrations, but did not keep precise records of these cures.

Ample documentation, however, does exist for his protracted treatment of a woman named Madame de la Rue for a nervous breakdown, in which he went beyond his expertise and was unable to achieve a complete remission of her symptoms. It is, nevertheless, a highly instructive and illuminating instance of what Dickens, three generations before Freud, intuitively understood of the unconscious, and how he sought to apply that understanding for therapeutic purposes. At the same time it vividly highlights his egocentricity and compulsive drive to dominate.

The year 1843, which led up to this episode with Mme. de la Rue, was for Dickens another period of exhausting toil. In addition to writing short pieces for periodicals, he was working on two books at the same time. One was *Martin Chuzzlewit*, a novel, and the other the non-fictional *American Notes*. He was also struggling to keep up with the rising costs of living that his celebrity status increasingly demanded. In everything he did, he had to be the leader and in charge. Whether as reformer and critic, novelist and editor and essayist, amateur actor and mesmerist, lecturer and public reader from his own works, he was jealous of any rival and intolerant of advice or criticism. He had to have his own way and he usually got it.

Eventually this frenetic activity, and his unwavering insistence upon continually being in charge of everything, would destroy his health and peace of mind, killing him with a massive stroke at the still relatively young age of fifty-eight. In 1843, at thirty-one, he still retained some sense of balance, and before the end of the year realized that he needed to get away to some less expensive place where he would be free of the daily demands on his time and energies, and where his family would have more peace and quiet.

Continental Europe in those days offered many opportunities for extended low-cost family vacations. After considering and rejecting several locations in France, Dickens chose Italy, which he had long wanted to visit. There was then no such political entity as Italy. The peninsula was divided up between several small kingdoms, principalities, and duchies, along with a sizable chunk of the Austrian Habsburg Empire, and the Papal States where the Roman Catholic Church still held political sovereignty. Genoa, where the Dickens family went at the beginning of July 1844, was the principal seaport of the Kingdom of Piedmont. Emile de la Rue, a Swiss banker with a London office and a family home in Genoa, who had become a friend of Dickens, made the arrangements, and the two families became close Genoese neighbors. The Dickenses occupied the late-medieval Palazzo Peschiere, while the de la Rues lived in the top floor of the Palazzo Rosso, across from and a little higher than the Peschiere.

As workaholics often do when freed from immediate stress, Dickens soon became very restless after settling down in his Genoese palace. He went for long walks in its scenic surroundings; he continually smoked large cigarettes; he had a bothersome pain in his side; he did not sleep well; and he was worried over not having any inspiration for a new novel, though he did write his annual Christmas story. In short, he needed some new activity to keep him busy, something that would be a change from writing, to which he had given so much of his energy.

He found that new interest in the health complaints of his neighbor, the small dark long-haired Mme. de la Rue, an Englishwoman by birth though perhaps not by ancestry. She had constant recurrences of nervous headaches, an annoying tic in a facial nerve, and occasional convulsions with twisting of her limbs and cataleptic loss of consciousness, along with sleeplessness and moods of depression. In between these spells she was talkative, cheerful and hospitable. By December

1844, she agreed to have Dickens mesmerize her with a view to alleviating or curing her ailments, which he believed had a mental origin. He explained to her husband what he proposed to do, and Emile de la Rue assented fully, saying he had the utmost trust in Dickens' sincerity.

By this time Dickens had perfected his induction technique and had no difficulty placing Mme. de la Rue in a trance. She was a willing subject, and obeyed all the commands he gave her. During the trance she began to experience relief from her symptoms, but when out of the trance the symptoms started recurring with increasing frequency. Dickens had to be summoned to her bedside at all hours of the day and night to put her into the mesmeric trance that brought immediate relief from her afflictions.

This was bringing the practitioner and patient into a situation of intimacy that went far beyond what was permitted by early Victorian customs. Madame. de la Rue had a separate bedroom from her husband's, and Kate Dickens grew ever more uneasy about what was happening. Dickens himself could see nothing even remotely improper in his privately attending his female patient; was that not a traditional privilege of the doctor? He saw the matter only through his own eyes and not those of others.

Dickens concluded that to bring more lasting relief to Mme. de la Rue, the root cause of her illness had to be searched out and overcome. On January 15, 1845, he placed her in a deeper trance than heretofore and commanded her to give an account of what she was seeing. Prodded with leading questions, she gave a rambling narration about a sad and neglected brother named Charles, who was very different from her real-life brother, and a sinister male figure who threatened her with harm. She also begged Dickens not to leave her, as he was planning to do a few days later to go with his family to Naples and Rome. He could not cancel these plans without risking an immediate break-up with Kate, but arranged to have Emile de la Rue write to him daily with full details of his wife's condition. In return, Dickens promised he would try to exert his mesmeric influence from whatever place he happened to be in, between eleven o'clock in the morning and noon each day. He cautioned that it was essential that she not fall into the grip of the "Phantom," which was the name he gave to the sinister man in her trance.

As the Dickenses made their way slowly by stage coach down the Italian west coast, with Emile de la Rue's letters — often copiously added to by Madame herself — usually waiting at each nightly stop (when at times they weren't, Dickens was beside himself with anxiety), the psychic drama intensified. Leaving Sienna, on the way to La Scala, Dickens altered his custom of riding on top of the stage coach and sat inside it. Kate said she wanted to ride on top to take advantage of the sun and fresh air. Noting that it was then eleven o'clock, Dickens began projecting, as he imagined it, the magnetic fluid across the distance of more than a hundred miles to Mme. de la Rue in Genoa. Suddenly he noticed his wife's muff falling past the window. Shouting to the coachman to stop, he jumped out and looked up to see Kate in mesmeric sleep and in danger of falling off the coach. He climbed up to her side as quickly as he could, and had unusual difficulty in awaking her. When he asked her what had happened, she said she had been magnetized.

This revelation of how a person could unintentionally be put in the mesmeric state by getting in the way of a projection of the magnetic force or fluid—whatever it was—astonished and somewhat frightened Dickens. He had seen instances in the University Hospital experiments of people becoming magnetized by simply walking into a ward where an induction was in progress. But Kate had been on the other side of the heavy wooden roof of the coach, and Dickens had been, or thought he was, projecting outward rather than upward. The force, it now seemed, not only penetrated material barriers with ease, but could not always be controlled in its direction or objective.

Dickens now focused all the energy of his powerful and imaginative mind upon the struggle with the evil Phantom in Mme. de la Rue's psyche. He made that fight a personal one, identifying himself with the "sad brother Charles" of her vision. She became the battleground for this titanic conflict, which Dickens waged without any regard for what was being inflicted on her. Each day's letters told of the suffering she was enduring and of being trampled under by the combatants. She had terrifying dreams in which she saw hideous figures attempting to seize her. The only relief came from the twice-daily inductions by long-distance. (Dickens had added a second one, between one o'clock and two o'clock in the morning, as Madame usually stayed up past midnight feverishly wagering at the Genoa casino.)

As the Dickenses journeyed on through Rome to Naples in February, planning to return to Rome for Holy Week in March, Mme. de la Rue grew calmer. She was sleeping better at night. Dickens was not reassured. The Phantom, he felt, was only staging a strategic retreat, preparatory to an assault that could kill her or drive her insane. It was vital that he be near when that attack came. He pleaded in letter after letter for her husband to arrange matters with his banking partners, so as to be able to come to Rome with her in March. Finally Emile de la Rue succeeded in getting leave from his partners, and the two families found themselves under one roof, in the Meloni Hotel at Rome, about the middle of March.

Madame's condition worsened immediately. The moment she lay down to sleep, she was besieged by bloody-faced specters. Dickens was constantly with her, totally neglecting his own family. He was getting no sleep himself, for the attacks of the Phantom were now incessant and could be repelled only by the instant exertion of all his mental powers. The crisis reached its peak on the night of March 19. Assaulted with sharp and piercing stabs by the Phantom inside her brain, Mme. de la Rue rolled herself into a ball on the bed, encircled by her long hair that normally hung down to the small of her back. Dickens recorded, in the journal he kept of all these proceedings, that he could find her head only by tracing the hair to its roots in her scalp. He did not know what to do and could only await developments. To his great relief, after about half an hour she gradually unrolled herself and then fell peacefully asleep. In the morning she declared herself well.

Once again, Dickens was not convinced of final victory. The Phantom had been defeated, but not destroyed. He did feel, however, that its power had been broken. It could still annoy her, perhaps even make her ill again, but was no longer able to put her in mortal peril of life or sanity. All the more reason, then, for him to continue in the closest possible "magnetic rapport" with her, to forestall the Phantom's renewed harassments.

Dickens insisted on the two families traveling together on their return from Rome to Genoa. At every roadside stop of their carriages — at olive grove, vineyards, wayside taverns, or wherever a halt seemed desirable — he inducted her into a trance, commanding the Phantom to desist from approaching her. This continued throughout their stay in Genoa, and almost until the Dickenses left in June to return to England.

For Kate Dickens it was a time of deepening humiliation and rejection. She became increasingly convinced that she had lost her husband's love and affection. Toward the de la Rues she could hardly behave with ordinary politeness any more. Dickens finally had to take Emile into his confidence and explain Kate's state of mind. He also gave her a lecture in which he berated her for thinking that he could be unfaithful to her, or that his ministrations to Madame were anything other than those of a doctor to a patient.

This cleared the air briefly. Emile de la Rue tactfully conveyed to his wife that she no longer needed as much attention from her therapist, and she agreed. Kate did her best to be friendly when they parted. Nevertheless, Dickens was profuse in his promises to write often to guide Madame in her further recovery, and of continuing to exert his mesmeric influence on her from a distance. Inwardly Kate had not, and never would, forgive him for what she saw as his desertion of her; their estrangement would keep on growing until thirteen years later what remained of their marriage would dissolve.

With his supreme egotism, Dickens could neither perceive nor understand what his preoccupation with proving his mesmeric capability on so worthy a subject was doing to Kate's self-esteem and the integrity of their marriage. After returning to London, where he became immersed in the writing of *Dombey and Son*, a novel that he had more difficulty with than any that preceded it, he continued to write every few days to the de la Rues and to inquire closely into Madame's condition. She reported that though she had again glimpsed the Phantom, she had not been harassed by it. Dickens thought this was a very favorable development and attributed it to the beneficent influence of the magnetizing he was still directing toward her at stated intervals.

Gradually, however, the mesmeric liaison between the two began to fade. The de la Rues were constantly finding reasons why they could not come to London, as Dickens repeatedly urged them to do. He started to wonder whether Emile was keeping him as fully informed as he should about her condition. As the winter of 1845-46 passed, and contact with them grew steadily more infrequent, Dickens found his creativity at a low ebb. He was making hardly any progress on *Dombey and Son*. If only he could see the de la Rues again, he felt, he would regain his lost energy. He decided to vacation in Switzerland, from where he could readily arrange a private meeting with them — private, for he could not risk Kate's knowing about it.

One thing after another delayed the Swiss vacation until August of 1846. The Dickenses stayed at Rosemont on Lake Geneva, near Rev. Townshend's villa. Elliotson was there also, and seeing them both again helped to restore Dickens' vitality. He gave a highly successful demonstration of his mesmeric powers at a party in Lausanne, placing a man in deep trance. It was not until late October, however, that he finally saw the de la Rues at breakfast in a secluded restaurant in Vevey. Kate knew nothing of it at the time.

Immediately thereafter, Dickens moved to Paris where he settled down to a winter of solid work, finally completing *Dombey and Son*. The correspondence with the de la Rues also became more frequent again. Madame de la Rue, though subject to some passing recurrences of her affliction, appeared to be doing well. Dickens grew more immersed in his creative work and thought of her less often. He found new subjects for his mesmerizing, most notably his friend the artist John Leech, who in September 1848 was seriously injured in a fall. Dickens treated him for relief of pain and for hastening the healing of his injuries, and Leech recovered with a rapidity that astonished his doctors.

This success had Dickens seriously considering giving up his literary career to become a practicing mesmerist. But the financial aspects of the matter soon made him decide against it. To maintain the opulent lifestyle he and his still multiplying family had become accustomed to, he would have to charge something like twenty-five guineas a treatment—the equivalent of about $130 in today's U.S. currency—and it was not very likely that he would have a continuing supply of patients able to afford such fees.

So Dickens continued to turn out a steady stream of novels that sold as no books had ever sold before. He also kept in touch with the de la Rues, who finally came to London to see the great Crystal Palace exhibition in 1851, and Dickens was able to meet them at a private dinner. By 1853, the stresses of overwork and of increasing unhappiness in his home life were again weighing on Dickens, and he told Kate he would have to take an extended vacation on the European continent with his literary protégé, the rising young novelist Wilkie Collins. On this holiday, though, much of Dickens' time was taken up with negotiations for European translations and reprintings of his novels. He did not get to see the de la Rues until late October in Genoa and then the meeting was a bitter let-down.

Madame confessed that her affliction had continued to reassert itself more strongly than she had admitted. When Dickens offered to resume his treatments of her on the same basis as before, she declined. It was not that she doubted it would again bring relief, she said, but she could not bear the pain of having that relief disappear once more, little by little, as it had over the intervening years. Something also seems to have been said, by her or Emile, or both, to the effect that the previous course of treatment had offended Dickens' wife.

Although their parting was friendly, and Dickens wrote to reassure Madame that if she kept up her courage the old Phantom could never regain its domination over her, it was clear that the former closeness between them was gone and could not be restored. The more Dickens realized this, the angrier he became with Kate. It was her petty, childish jealousy that had disrupted the wonderful but wholly innocent relationship between him and Madame. Even worse, it had prevented him from completing what would have been one of the most marvelous of all mesmeric cures, establishing his reputation for all time as one of the foremost practitioners of the art.

Finally, in December, Dickens gave vent to this resentment against Kate in an extraordinary letter of accusation. He commanded her to apologize to Mme. de la Rue, for all her suspicions and meanness toward her. Mesmerism, he wrote, had become his guiding principle, and the key to the ability which enabled him to create his endless galleries of true-to-life fictional characters. Kate had no right to dispute his mesmeric commitment or object to his exercising it for the benefit of others.

That Kate's response was a lightly worded apology disguised in the form of a letter to Madame asking for an Italian recipe says something about her own discretion and common sense. For the time being, it served to smooth things over between her and Dickens, but it could not slow down the inexorable breaking apart of their marriage. Four years later, they separated—divorce was something that no one in Dickens' public position could resort to.

As for the de la Rues, though they still met with Dickens on several more occasions, they were now somewhat distant friends. Madame appears to have sought treatment from Elliotson, on Dickens' recommendation, but there is no record of the result. It there was any benefit, it was not lasting, for in a letter to Dickens in 1869, a few months before his death, Madame wrote that "at times her sufferings are still unspeakable."

The extent of the crumbling of Dickens' private life and health over the last sixteen years of his career, and how he was at last pulling himself together through a deepened understanding of the subconscious processes of the mind (as evidenced by the character studies in his last, unfinished masterpiece, *The Mystery of Edwin Drood*) are beyond the scope of this book. Here we have been primarily concerned with how Dickens' interest in mesmerism related to the great British awakening to hypnosis in the mid-nineteenth century.

Two other British literary notables of the Victorian era need to be looked at briefly, in terms of their relationship to that awakening from which modern hypnotism and hypnotherapy were to spring. They are Harriet Martineau and Sir Edward Bulwer-Lytton. Martineau was a total convert to the Mesmerist doctrine, on the strength of its having cured, she believed, a painful physical affliction. In this she was mistaken, yet she never retracted her belief in magnetizing, and her public endorsement of it was influential in securing a wider hearing and acceptance for the work of Elliotson and his two great successors, Braid and Esdaile. Bulwer-Lytton, on the other hand, had a deep intellectual interest not only in mesmeric phenomena, but in all aspects of the paranormal. However, he also had a highly developed critical faculty, and this ensured that his attitude to mesmerism fluctuated between enthusiastic acceptance and skeptical dismissal. He could have been Balzac's peer in popularizing mesmerism in Britain through his novels in which it is a more or less principal theme. However, all his novels strongly emphasize doubt as to whether humanity has yet evolved to a level where it can effectively handle the forces underlying the mind, and this made them cautionary rather than proselytizing works.

There is both contrast and similarity in how Martineau and Bulwer-Lytton came to encounter and deal with mesmerism after having first established themselves as popular writers on subjects wholly unrelated to it. Martineau had struggled through her adolescence under serious physical handicaps. From birth she had been unable to taste or smell, and serious hearing loss began when she was sixteen. She nevertheless aspired to a literary career. Despite being under the influence of a domineering and disapproving mother, and living in the provincial town of Norwich in East Anglia, away from the centers of culture and publishing, she was by her late twenties a recognized writer on social issues. Traveling to America in her thirties, she gained a reputation as a critical observer of the Jacksonian republic across the ocean.

She then turned her hand to fiction, but in this she was less successful, primarily because she continued to be psychically crippled by her overbearing mother, which prevented her from creating fictional characters of real independence. Her health deteriorated still further and she became bed-ridden. Her doctor, T.M. Greenhow, who was also her brother-in-law, diagnosed an ovarian cyst, which was not in itself serious enough to make her an invalid. Guessing correctly that she was making herself ill, he suggested mesmeric treatment. This was early in 1844, when she was forty-two, and some months before Dickens would be treating Mme. de la Rue in Italy.

The treatment of Martineau, highly beneficial though it turned out, was hardly any more professional than that of Mme. de la Rue at the hands of Dickens. Martineau resorted first to a touring stage-mesmerist, Spencer Hall. She saw him only once, but that was enough to get her out of bed. The follow-up was carried out by her housemaid, who had read a book on mesmerism, and a clergyman's widow residing nearby, whose qualifications seem to have been even slimmer. Nevertheless, within a few weeks they had Martineau up and walking five miles a day. She wrote a letter to the widely read literary weekly, *The Athenaeum*, which appeared in its November 23, 1844 issue, declaring that mesmerism was a true fact and had restored her from invalidism to full health in a short time.

Had she let the matter rest there, little more might have been heard about it. But for several months she went on to wage a war of words in the letter columns of *The Athenaeum* in which she defended some of the more questionable forms of mesmerism, such as clairvoyance, in which she claimed another of her maids was proficient. Skeptical readers fired broadsides at her. Regretting now that he had ever recommended mesmerism to her, her brother-in-law issued a pamphlet in which he claimed she had been getting better anyway under his conventional medical treatment, and any benefit she got from magnetizing was mental and not physical. The pamphlet, which sold extremely well at the price of a shilling, identified its subject only as "Miss H.M.," but everyone knew who was meant. In the pamphlet she was called "a stubborn hypochondriac," which greatly outraged her.

The Athenaeum's editor finally ended the letters by refusing to print any more. The episode had probably raised the level of public skepticism of mesmerism, which had been falling for three or four years, but this effect did not last. Martineau, unrepentant, lived on into her seventies, dying in 1877, by which time the public had long since ceased to talk of mesmerism or magnetizing, and had begun to call them hypnotism. Autopsy revealed that Martineau's death was the result of heart and lung complications caused by the continuing growth of the ovarian cyst. Mesmerism, rather crudely done, had neither reversed nor halted the progress of the cyst, though it may have slowed it. Imaging techniques that are available to the modern hypnotherapist for tumor reduction and remission were as yet unknown. Still, hypnosis, in the guise of mesmerism, had restored to Harriet Martineau her self-esteem and self-confidence, enabling her to return to an active life for over three decades.

Sir Edward Bulwer-Lytton's personality was very different. He was assertive and outgoing. His early novels, of which *The Last Days of Pompeii* still has a following, are filled with action and incident, and have little of the mystical and reflective in them. The change in his writing that was first evident in his *Eugene Aram*, in which the motivations that make people turn to crime are searchingly analyzed, foreshadowed his great novel of the occult, *Zanoni*, which was rooted in his close acquaintanceship with Elliotson and Braid in the early 1840s. Though it has been called the world's first mesmerist novel (a distinction that properly belongs to Balzac's *Louis Lambert*, a decade earlier) *Zanoni* is not really about mesmerism, but explores the much wider field of the unseen reality beyond the visible world. Into that broader area, mesmerism fitted, but only as one of many avenues to the deeper layers of the mind.

Zanoni attracted a wide readership and has been credited with having had an influence on the founding of the Theosophist movement. It was followed by a wide array of works, both fictional and factual, on paranormal themes from Bulwer-Lytton's pen over the remaining three decades of his life. But as already indicated, his keen sense of limitations kept him from becoming an outright advocate of mesmerism. His position, as stated to Elliotson, was that he had no reason to doubt that many remarkable cures and other marvels had been performed by mesmeric means, but they meant little. There was as yet no corpus of disciplined practice that could ensure the certainty of the results, and no generally accepted picture of the processes of the mind beneath its conscious surface. Only when that understanding was attained, Bulwer-Lytton asserted, could hypnotic practice become a scientific therapy.

VI.
ON THE THRESHOLD OF A NEW SCIENCE

Dr. James Braid
1795 - 1860

CHAPTER 13
James Braid Coins a Name that Sticks

The second and third of the trio of Britain's great mid-nineteenth century pioneers of hypnotism, including the one who bestowed on the discipline the name it has since borne, were both products of that tremendous flowering of genius and talent in Scotland between 1775 and 1825, which made Edinburgh known as the Athens of the North. Robert Burns and Sir Walter Scott were the most widely known figures of this late-blooming Scottish Renaissance. There were also many others, including historians, poets, artists, engineers, and men of science, who made their mark on the world of their time, some with lasting effect on succeeding generations.

Though the achievements of James Braid and James Esdaile came later than the time of the Scottish Flowering, they were born around its mid-point, and their personalities were in keeping with its innovative outlook. Braid was born in 1795, the son of a Fifeshire landowner who had the means to send him to Edinburgh University to be educated for the medical profession. Esdaile, born in 1808 at Perth, was the son of a clergyman of the Church of Scotland, a person of some modest wealth and cultural attainments. For young Esdaile too, medicine offered a path to social standing and money, and conveniently located Edinburgh University was a place to get the necessary training.

The deaths of Braid and Esdaile occurred within a little more than a year of each other, in 1859 and 1860, respectively, and less than a decade before Elliotson's, whose longer life (1791-1868) spanned both of theirs. Yet curiously, their careers, though parallel in time and in their objectives, were on diverging tracks. It is not even firmly on record that any of the three ever met each other. If indeed they did not, this was partly due to a streak of jealousy in Elliotson, with his resulting inability to see that Braid had gone beyond him in establishing the true nature of what had until then been only partly understood under the names of mesmerism and magnetizing. On the other hand, Elliotson's mouthpiece of the movement, the *Zoist*, gave full publicity to Esdaile's equally epochal work with mesmeric induced surgical anesthesia.

All of Esdaile's major work was accomplished in India, where he was out of touch with developments in England. After his return in 1851 he became practically a recluse, partly because of a temperament that shunned publicity and partly because of serious physical ailments that led to his death in 1859 at the age of fifty. He did publish some of his experiences and conclusions, and these writings were fully noted and hailed by both Elliotson and Braid. But there was never any collaboration between these three great British pioneers. Had there been, it is unlikely hypnotism would have declined so severely in British medical practice after their deaths, even while the practice of it was reviving and scaling new heights in France.

It was from France that the original stimulus for Elliotson's conversion to mesmerism came, through the personal influence of the Baron du Potet. And likewise it was from France that the motivation came, a little more than four years after du Potet's appearance at Elliotson's hospital, for James Braid's acceptance of what until then he had scorned as trickery and fakery. This time the responsible person was the noted stage mesmerist Charles Lafontaine, whose itinerary through Britain in the fall of 1841 took him to Manchester, where Braid was one of the most prominent and respected physicians in that great industrial center.

Upon his graduation from Edinburgh University, Braid had practiced medicine and surgery at three locations in Scotland, the last of which was Dumfries, where he treated a resident of Manchester who had been severely injured in a stagecoach accident. The patient, a prosperous businessman named Petty, was so impressed with the care he received from Braid he urged him to move to Manchester where he would have a far more lucrative practice than in rural Scotland. Braid took the advice and never regretted it. Not that he gained great wealth or attracted notice beyond the community he served. In fact, had it not been for the curiosity that led him to attend one of Lafontaine's stage demonstrations of mesmerism on November 13, 1841, James Braid would have left no imprint on history, except perhaps a footnote in medical annals about his remarkable successes in operating on clubfoot (talipes) and other forms of muscle and tendon constriction.

He was aware, of course, when he went to Lafontaine's presentation, how widespread the public interest in mesmerism had become in Britain. Elliotson's resignation from London University Hospital, not quite two years before, had stirred up a storm of controversy, pro and con, in the British press. People in all ranks of life were arguing over whether there was anything to mesmerism or not. For himself, Braid had early made up his mind it was all humbug—but he had never witnessed any trance inductions, and he was curious enough to want to see just how the "flummery," as he believed it to be, was carried out.

There are varying accounts of how the encounter, and several following ones, actually proceeded. Braid's is brief in the extreme. Lafontaine's account—written nearly twenty years after the event in a highly self-glorifying two-volume autobiography—is sharply at odds with some independent ones, especially that of a Professor Williamson of Owens College in Manchester, who was well acquainted with Braid. Balancing all of these, the following is the probable sequence of what happened.

Lafontaine, who appears to have originally come from Switzerland before taking up residence in France, was a master showman who performed his stage demonstrations of mesmerism on two well-trained subjects, a young man and a young woman. They travelled with him everywhere and it was frequently noted that his rate of successful magnetizings was distinctly lower with volunteers from the audience. He did, nevertheless, possess a considerable and genuine proficiency in trance induction, and had a large following in

France. Many believe that Balzac, in his novel *Ursule Mirouet* bases the phenomenally powerful but anonymous mesmerist, who thwarts the schemes of the inheritance thieves on Lafontaine.

Arriving in Manchester from a poorly attended performance in Liverpool, Lafontaine was eager to outdo himself and gain the publicity that would draw large crowds to his scheduled series of appearances in the industrial city. He had the audience with him right from the start in the first one, on that historic November 13. Probably the only member of the audience who remained unconvinced that evening was James Braid, who detected many of Lafontaine's tricks of showmanship. "And yet . . . and yet," Braid kept musing to himself as he returned home, ". . . it had certainly seemed that when the magnetizer put the young woman to sleep and told her it would be impossible to open her eyes until he released her by spoken command, her eyelids could not be raised by several who at Lafontaine's invitation tried to do so. She could hardly be faking that resistance, but what influence was she really under, and how was it exerted?"

Braid determined to go to a second performance for a closer look. This time he went up on the stage himself and tried to lift the eyelids of the mesmerized girl. Only by exerting strong pressure with his fingers (Braid was a man of robust physique and great physical strength) was he able to do so. He found the pupils of the eyes contracted into small points, evidence of very deep sleep. Next, he pushed a sharp pin under one of her fingernails that should have made her shriek with pain. She remained silent and motionless. Braid could no longer doubt that whatever the nature of the state she had been placed in, it was real. Still the question remained: How was it done?

Watching the process of mesmeric induction as it was carried out by Lafontaine, it appeared to Braid the results were accomplished by his conveying the suggestion to his subjects that they do whatever he commanded them. Though the showman kept up a constant patter about how he was projecting the magnetic fluid, under the influence of which he claimed the subjects became amenable to his will, Braid saw nothing to indicate any such fluid was present or in any way involved. By focusing the attention of his subjects on what he was saying, Lafontaine was placing them in a trancelike state in which they paid attention only to his commands.

Braid concluded that almost any one could train himself to employ the same technique. As a doctor, he immediately realized the usefulness of such a command-enforcing "sleep," which was totally different from natural sleep, in treating a wide variety of ailments, especially those of the nervous system. He started experimenting with some of his patients and friends, and found he was able to put them into trance states identical to those achieved by Lafontaine. Focusing the eyes of his subjects on bright or shiny objects held a short distance in front of them proved the most effective method among a variety he tried. In his own words, Braid's initial induction technique was as follows:

> Take any bright object (I generally use my lancet case) between the thumb and fore and middle fingers of the left hand; hold it from about eight to fifteen inches from the eyes, at such position above the forehead as may be neces-

sary to produce the greatest possible strain upon the eyes and eyelids, and enable the patient to maintain a steady fixed stare at the object. The patient must be made to understand that he is to keep the eyes steadily fixed on the object, and the mind riveted on the idea of that one object. Once the pupils have dilated if the fore and middle fingers of the right hand, extended and a little separated, are carried from the object towards the eyes, most probably the eyelids will close involuntarily, with a vibratory motion.

Having demonstrated the efficiency of his own rapidly developed techniques to some selected audiences, Braid challenged Lafontaine to a competitive appearance on the same stage. The showman accepted, and came back to Manchester for the demonstration, which drew a huge crowd. Both men were obviously feeling the pressure to do well, and neither performed at his best, though Braid appears to have done the better. Lafontaine failed altogether in attempting to replicate Braid's results, and did poorly in employing his own techniques on volunteers, though he was as successful as ever with his pair of responsive subjects. Some have criticized Braid for seeking such publicity at so early a point. However he appears to have felt it was the best way to secure the attention and support of the substantial portion of the medical establishment that had come to believe there was definite therapeutic value in magnetizing, but were still held back by their aversion to the mesmerist doctrine of the all-pervasive fluid and its mystical trappings.

Braid had read, in Alexandre Bertrand's writings, how the Abbé Faria, a generation earlier, had reached the same conclusion about the non-existence of the magnetic fluid, and the primacy of suggestion in the induction of trance. Yet Faria had failed to convince all but a small minority of the many brilliant and competent magnetizers who followed him in France. Braid did not want a similar failure to ensue in Britain. He meant to strike while the iron was hot. In the short run, his success was only partial; in the long run, all modern hypnotherapy would stem from his work.

The lectures and demonstrations Braid continued to give in Manchester soon aroused the interest of medical men in London, who read of them in the new weekly, *The Medical Times,* that had been founded as a more open-minded rival to the increasingly reactionary *Lancet.* Braid soon received invitations to speak in London, and he delivered a series of lectures commencing early in March 1842. (It was at this time Dickens, on his first American tour, was astonished at his quick success in mesmerizing his wife.) Braid's London lectures were well received and he was urged by many who attended them to write a book presenting his findings and conclusions in more detailed form. He commenced the task soon after returning to Manchester in April 1842 to cope with another appearance by Lafontaine seeking to discredit him. He also had to deal with an attack from the pulpit by an Anglican clergyman, Rev. James McNeile, who charged that all mesmeric phenomena were fraudulent acts of the Evil One.

Braid's pamphlet, *Satanic Agency and Mesmerism*, in which he refuted McNeil's accusations, was his first known publication on the subject of mesmerism outside of the Letters columns in *The Medical Times.* Three letters from him appeared in its pages in the course of the year 1842, in which he first introduced the terms "hypnotism" and "hypnosis," from the Greek *hypnos* (sleep), as preferable to the previous ones of mesmerism and magnetizing.[1] Apprehensive, however, that this would be misunderstood as meaning ordinary sleep, he invented a new term "Neurypnology," i.e., the science of nervous sleep, because he believed the sleep was induced by the influence of suggestion on the nervous system. He used the new term for the title of his book which was published in 1843: *Neurypnology or the Rationale of Nervous Sleep: Illustrated by Numerous Cases of Its Successful Application in the Relief and Cure of Disease*. It was a cumbersome term, which today would have an erroneous meaning, implying that hypnosis was the result of a nervous condition. Braid soon came to realize it was an unfortunate choice, and gradually went back to the use of the simpler terms hypnotism and hypnosis. At one stroke they removed the psychological barriers the terms mesmerism and magnetizing had been to the medical establishment's acceptance of this unorthodox therapy. We shall see further on how this led to the great French advances in hypnotism in the last quarter of the nineteenth century.

Braid's book was an instant best-seller by the standards of the time, the first edition of eight hundred copies being snapped up within a matter of weeks. It emphasized the curative potential of hypnosis. The cases Braid described were all from his own experience, some of which he had already reported in his letters to *The Medical Times*. They are truly remarkable, not only in themselves but also because he had taught himself the necessary techniques within the space of a few months. The cases included the rapid remission and total cure of what he diagnosed as lockjaw (tetanus) in a boy of thirteen, drastic improvements in the eyesight of three women who had been slowly losing it despite the use of glasses, restoration of hearing in the totally deaf, complete relief of a neck muscle spasm (torticollis) that had twisted a patient's head around, and regaining of full speech volume by one who for over four years had been unable to speak above a whisper. Braid was almost certainly wrong in his diagnosis of lockjaw in the boy's case, since this was more than thirty years before it was understood to be caused by the toxin of Clostridium tetani, a pathogenic bacillus. What he treated was probably some sort of epileptic seizure, for which hypnosis has often been shown to be effective. Nonetheless, this list of therapeutic achievements is impressive. Even if we assume the underlying causes were psychogenic rather than physical in origin, the cures go beyond what modern hypnotherapy can claim in all but isolated cases.

Braid continued to tell about additional cures in his various published reports over the next seventeen years. Among these further instances of hypnotic healing were those of a young man who suffered from a chronic hysterical condition after being attacked by a dog, and of Braid himself, who cured himself of a severely painful rheumatic congestion in his left arm and shoulder by a simple self-hypnotic procedure. These results seem to be attributable to Braid's ability to implant therapeutic suggestions with conviction. Elliotson, who could not forgive Braid for discarding the magnetic fluid premise, claimed—when he could bring himself to mention Braid at all — the Manchester doctor's successes were due simply to his having an unusual though unadmitted power to project the fluid. Another factor would appear to have been that the average nineteenth century English person had a much greater impressionability of mind, and a much higher imaginative capacity than is possessed by most people today. Generations of movie and TV watching have resulted in an indifference and cynicism the modern hypnotherapist often finds difficult to surmount.

After his initial encounters with Lafontaine, Braid avoided stage exhibitions of hypnotism and soon ceased public demonstrations of it. He did, on occasion, give presentations to small audiences of his medical friends. A particularly exceptional one took place in 1847 when the famous Swedish singer Jenny Lind was paired with a young female subject who was normally incapable of even carrying a tune. The subject very creditably carried out Braid's suggestions to accompany the gifted visitor in a duet.

Although Braid convinced a portion of the British medical profession that the reality of hypnotism had been masked by the erroneous concept of the magnetic fluid, there was still a considerable amount of harshly abusive opposition. Tragically, much of this came from those who should have been his allies — Elliotson in particular, and the literary mesmerists such as Dickens and Martineau. They could not give up the magnetic fluid idea, nor see that it stood in the way of hypnotism becoming a properly regulated part of standard medical practice.

The latter was the objective Braid held constantly in view, and for which he strove. In his book *Neurypnology* he stressed that hypnosis should be solely in the hands of qualified medical doctors, for it was capable of doing much harm when administered by the unskilled, or when used for entertainment.

For about a decade after his conversion to hypnotism Braid adhered to the pseudo-science of phrenology. He attempted to relate various hypnotic phenomena to particular areas of the body and head, desisting only after it became clear he was getting nowhere. He also expended more time and energy than was necessary in publicly insisting on the compatibility of hypnotism with orthodox religion. There had apparently been an inference drawn by some critics that if the effects of hypnotism were simply the result of suggestion and imagination, then the personal Devil who was then still a standing tenet of Christian belief might well be also merely a product of mental conditioning. Such a notion was appalling to Braid, and he went out of his way more than once to denounce it.

Clairvoyance was another point on which Braid took issue with those who adhered to the magnetic fluid doctrine. Contrary to their belief that clairvoyance was a real phenomenon and facilitated by magnetizing, he insisted (in letters to *The Medical Times* and later in pamphlets) that thorough investigation would show all alleged non-physical viewing to result from a heightened perception by the senses and an enhanced imaginativeness—the latter being what today is called the mythopoetic faculty of the subconscious mind. Hypnotic sleep, as he called it, could help to bring about such a state, but he denied it could enable anyone to see distant places or to penetrate either the past or the future. In the twentieth century clairvoyance remains a question lacking final resolution, but one which has no essential connection with hypnotism.

Braid also looked into the phenomenon of suspended animation in prolonged trance, which he called human hibernation. Cases of this were starting to be reported from India, and were being practiced by yogis. He correctly recognized this as a phenomenon of self-hypnosis by persons with a strong mental control of the autonomic nervous system.

Between 1845 and 1850, Braid devoted much of his time and attention to disputing the reality of the "odic force" that the Baron von Reichenbach, an Austrian scientist and experimenter in many fields, claimed to have discovered. Reichenbach asserted that this force (which he named from an ancient Germanic root denoting universal power) was the moving energy of everything in the world, both animate and inanimate. Though it was neither electric nor magnetic, being more subtle than either, the "odic force" was what Mesmer and his followers had misunderstood as magnetism. He contended this was not surprising, for it could be concentrated in iron magnets as well as other metals, and projected from them by the direction of the human will for beneficent purposes. Reichenbach's published writings, which circulated widely in Europe from about 1840 on, aroused vast interest, and both support and rejection. Much of the latter centered on experiments that Reichenbach claimed were demonstrative of the force, but these were not replicable, or only partially so at best, by others who attempted them.

Reichenbach's writings were not available in English until early in 1846, when Braid eagerly read them and proceeded to perform several of the experiments described, as well as some he devised himself for purposes of verification. Braid was soon convinced that all of the results claimed by the Austrian, including the many-colored "auras," could be obtained by purely psychological means, primarily suggestion. The subjects saw what they were told to see. Metals had nothing whatever to do with the postulated force, for which no sustainable proof could be found. All of this was stated by Braid in articles in *The Medical Times* that were also published in pamphlet form. Translated and sent to Reichenbach, they elicited no response from the Baron. This disappointed Braid, as he had hoped to open a dialogue in which the positive factors in the odic force argument could be developed further. The Reichenbach theory continued to attract support, largely from the spiritualist camp, until about the time of Braid's death, and then declined rapidly. By the 1870s it had become a mostly discredited relic.

Braid died suddenly from an apparent heart attack on March 25, 1860, at the age of sixty-five. He left behind him a fairly large body of writings. These do not make easy reading. Braid had always found writing to be a chore and not a pleasurable pursuit. He lacked any gift of lively phrase or vivid simile. All that he wrote conveys a sense of effort and difficulty. Nevertheless, his writings continued to influence the progress of hypnotism long after he had passed from the scene.

However, that influence was not in Britain, but across the Channel in France. The British awakening to mesmerism, magnetizing, and hypnotism, given impetus by Elliotson in 1837 and followed up by Braid, Esdaile, and the literary mesmerists, ran its course within a single generation. By 1870 it was largely forgotten, fading into a new period of eclipse. The death of Dickens in that year, following the deaths of Esdaile, Braid and Elliotson within the preceding decade, marked the end of public interest in the subject. The medical profession, though giving credit to Braid for having bestowed a more acceptable name and a new rationality and respectability to hypnotism, still held back from admitting it into the corpus of standard practice. That would come only after the next great crest in the development of hypnotherapy, which took place over the last two decades of the century, in the work of the great French trio of Liébeault, Bernheim and Charcot. Their work would be based largely on that of Braid, which had started to be transmitted to France while he was still living.

In 1859, a physician of Bordeaux, B. F. Azam, and the noted psychologist M. P. Broca, reported to the French Academy of Sciences their highly successful experiments with Braid's methods. The next year Azam described these experiments in the official French medical journal. In a letter at the end of 1859 Braid thanked Azam for informing him of these proceedings, which finally ended the long resistance of French science and medicine to admitting mesmerism and its later offshoots into the realm of acceptable practice. Though no official statement was ever issued, nor the adverse findings of the four commissions retracted, there was a tacit admission that Braid's discovery and naming of hypnotism made it impossible to deny any longer the reality of what magnetizers had been doing for nearly a century. Henceforth, French doctors would not face official censure if they used it.

However, the human tendency to keep on doing the familiar would delay the great flowering of hypnotherapy in France for another two decades. During that interval, the name of Braid was kept in front of both the public and the medical profession by a popular lecturer, J. P. Durand de Gros, who proposed that hypnotism should be called "Braidism" after the discoverer of its true nature, just as it had at first been called mesmerism after its founder. Durand did not get enough support for the name change, but the discussion helped to spread Braid's name and findings. In 1860, Durand published a textbook of hypnotism entitled *A Course in the Theory and Practice of Braidism or Nervous Hypnotism*, which attracted some interest among physicians and lay magnetizers (as they still called themselves). Not until 1883, however, twenty-three years after his death, did Braid's *Neurypnology* appear in a French translation.

Before we move on from Braid to Esdaile mention should be made that from 1850 on, Braid had to contend with the claims of the American hypnotists known as "electro-biologists" that there was indeed an energy force involved in the hypnotic process, namely the electricity generated biologically in living organisms. They further asserted that Braid was achieving his effects through unknowingly utilizing this electricity, and that they had preceded him in establishing the non-existence of any magnetic fluid. The electro-biologists properly belong in our chapter on mesmerism in America and will be discussed there along with Braid's refutations of their claims.

---

[1] Hypnosis historian Melvin A. Gravitz, Ph.D. discovered that Etienne Félix d' Hénin de Cuvillers, a French student of Mesmer, used the word hypnotism in 1809, almost 40 years before James Braid used the term in his publications.

Dr. James Esdaile
1808 - 1859

CHAPTER 14
James Esdaile Introduces Hypnotic Anesthesia

O f the great trio of British pioneers of hypnotherapy in the early Victorian era, James Esdaile was a very different personality from the two others, Elliotson and Braid. He was the youngest of the three—seventeen years the junior of Elliotson, and fourteen years younger than Braid— and came from a more disadvantaged background than either of them. Though Esdaile's father was a clergyman of the Church of Scotland and able to send his son to be educated as a physician and surgeon at Edinburgh University, his Perthshire parish appears to have been a rather impoverished one. The Esdaile finances could not be stretched to cover the cost of settling young James, on his graduation in 1830, in a practice shared with an established doctor, or as an under-physician in a major hospital. Those were then the two principal ways of getting started in the medical profession, but each required money. The newcomer had to buy his way in, just as in the British Army of that time the only way to get in as an officer was to buy a commission from someone who already possessed one and was planning to retire.

For medical graduates faced with this dilemma, the East India Company offered a solution. Britain's Indian Empire at that time was still the fief of a private trading company that ruled over a domain larger than several European countries put together, and maintained its own large army as well as numerous public services including hospitals and clinics. No such realm had ever existed before, and probably never will again. Its days were numbered; the mutiny of its native troops in 1857 would result in the British Government dissolving the Company and taking over all its holdings. But in 1830, when Esdaile graduated with little in his pocket (Elliotson and Braid were already set up in lucrative practices) the East India Company had numerous openings in its medical services for young doctors willing to face the risks of a tropical climate and its often fearsome and unfamiliar diseases. Doctors were required to sign up for a period of twenty years. Experience had shown the Company that unless bound by such a long-term contract, most of the physicians it recruited would flee back to Britain after a few months, or a few years at best. Having to be constantly looking for replacements was costly, so the Company insisted on holding its doctors in its service for two whole decades.

The drawback to this policy was that unless they were desperate for a position, young medical graduates would hesitate to condemn themselves to twenty years of servitude in such a pestiferous climate. Thus there were always vacancies for those willing to take the chance that they would survive and come back with prestige and some money that would be helpful in further advancement at home. Esdaile was one who saw no other way in which he could put his just-gained medical knowledge to immediate use.

He was twenty-two when in the late summer of 1830 he signed his twenty-year contract with the East India Company and made the long voyage around the Cape of Good Hope to India, where he was installed as the physician in charge at the Native Hospital in Hooghly, down river from Calcutta in a fever-ridden, swampy area. As yet, he had no interest in or knowledge of mesmerism. "I hated the country, the climate, and everything about India, from the moment I set foot in it," he would later write. "My sole ambition was to remain not a moment beyond the expiration of my period of service." Nor did that dislike for India ever change, though from a strictly professional point of view he gradually developed an interest in the remarkable character and variety of the ailments that were brought before him for his attention.

He also started to observe the various healing rituals the native practitioners used to relieve these conditions. In particular, Esdaile noted how a young woman afflicted with epilepsy was apparently healed by a native doctor who put her into a trance-like sleep by a combination of finger stroking, rhythmic breathing and laying-on of hands—all traditional practices of the mesmerist, but known in India for millennia. He began to experiment with these methods.

Esdaile was not the first Westerner to take note of Hindu traditional hypnotism. Among others, a Colonel E. H. Bagnold in the East India Company's military service had, over a span of forty years, observed these practices both among the Hindus and the native peoples of Africa at those places where the Company's ships touched on their way to and from India. In a series of letters published in *The Zoist*, (Elliotson's journal of mesmerism) in 1845 and again in 1850, Bagnold described these methods and their curative results at some length, providing a valuable record of how a primitive form of hypnotism had evolved in cultures as yet untouched by Western concepts of it.

Neither Bagnold nor any one else, however, attempted to adapt these practices to modern medical usage. No one, that is, except Esdaile. He resolved he would seek to induce, by the native methods he had watched, and by what he had read about those of Elliotson, a mesmeric sleep sufficiently deep to permit surgery without pain. (The excruciating pain experienced during surgery in this period was such that agreeing to suffer it was tantamount to signing one's death warrant.) On April 4, 1845, when he had been in India for fifteen years— three-fourths of the time he was contracted to serve—he successfully anesthetized a Hindu patient by mesmeric passes. Within a few months, he had performed seventy-five painless operations, of varying degrees of severity, and reported this to the East India Company's Medical Board. Finding it incredible, they did not even bother to reply.

By the end of the year Esdaile's successes totalled over one hundred, and he went over the heads of the Medical Board to bring the matter to the attention of the Company's Deputy-Governor for Bengal, Sir Herbert Maddock, who appointed a medical commission to look into it. Unlike the French Royal Commissions appointed to investigate animal magnetism, this one actually examined the facts at first hand and reported that the results claimed by Esdaile were real. His procedures, they stated, should be experimented with on a larger scale, and for that purpose Maddock proposed to set up a small special hospital in Calcutta where Esdaile could use mesmerism in the treatment of both white and native patients of all social classes. The results would be periodically reviewed by competent examiners.

There was some delay in getting the project started, but finally the Mesmeric Hospital, as it was called, was opened in November 1846. Despite further striking successes that brought Esdaile's total of painless surgeries to one hundred and thirty-three and demonstrated the effectiveness of mesmerism in the treatment of epilepsy and various forms of paralysis, and despite uniformly favorable reports by the examiners, the Hospital was closed at the end of 1847. It appears some criticism of the use of official funds for carrying on experimentation so greatly at variance with established medical doctrine was behind this suspension.

However, the hospital had been widely supported by the Hindu business and professional classes, and over three hundred prominent personages from their ranks raised sufficient funds to re-open it as a private facility, on September 1, 1848. It was closed again after six months, the Company objecting that under the terms of his contract, Esdaile was not supposed to engage in the private practice of medicine. To satisfy the public demand for his painless surgery and other mesmeric therapy, he was placed in charge of a general hospital on Sarkea's Lane, Calcutta, where he could combine these with regular medical services to the people at large.

The Mesmeric Hospital once again reopened under private management, and Esdaile appointed as his successor an anatomy professor named Webb, who had learned under him how to perform painless operations for cancer and other tumors. However, the foes Esdaile had made in some sections of the Indian medical establishment prevailed in denying the post to Webb, and conferred it on someone with no background at all in mesmerism. Predictably, the Mesmeric Hospital soon failed and was closed for good. When his twenty-year tour of duty

ended early in 1851, Esdaile immediately left India and returned to his native Perth in Scotland. He still detested India
and everything connected with it. He felt its oppressive climate
had destroyed his own health, afflicting him with a form of
emphysema. He was angered by the allegations which were
being made that his mesmeric practice had all been an elaborate
fraud perpetrated on ignorant natives for the purpose of setting
himself up in Calcutta, once released from the Company, to
make vast sums by treating rich and gullible whites. All the
riches of India could not keep him there, he said. As for what he
had done, it had been for the good of all humanity to free it
from the age-old terror of painful surgery. That he had performed painless surgery, even in the most severe operations,
was attested to by the most respectable medical men in India.
He himself had not made a penny out of it, nor had the Company ever increased his salary over that stipulated in his
contract of service.

Esdaile made some effort to inform the medical profession
at large of what he had achieved. He circulated two papers to
all the British medical journals detailing his painless surgeries
under mesmerism. Elliotson's *Zoist* was the only one that
published them, and most did not even acknowledge receiving
them. Those who did alleged that while they did not question
the truth of what Esdaile reported, it had relevance to Indian
natives only and thus did not need to be published in Britain.
One journal objected that Esdaile's account was too technical
and should be restated in more general terms, but when he did
so, the new submission was rejected for lacking technical details
of the surgery.

Esdaile concluded that the British medical profession was
determined to prevent the public from knowing the facts about

the effectiveness of mesmerism for surgical anesthesia. The introduction of chloroform and ether during the 1840s had provided a means of anesthesia that were simpler and easier to use than mesmerism or hypnotism, thus providing a plausible rationale for shutting off all discussion of the latter as an alternative. Esdaile was nonetheless convinced that in selected cases mesmerism was preferable to chemical anesthesia, from which occasional deaths had already occurred due to carelessness in administering it or to unexpected allergic reactions. He felt doctors should be fully aware there was an alternative, and that they should be adequately trained to make use of it. So in March 1852 Esdaile published, at his own expense, a pamphlet on *Mesmerism as an Anesthetic and Curative Agent in the Hospitals of India*, in which he claimed that the medical journals there had been prejudiced against him, despite the measure of official and public sanction he had enjoyed. The journals had repeatedly accused him of either duping credulous natives into thinking they felt no pain, or being duped by them into believing that was the case. They suggested natives actually enjoyed pain, and would go to any lengths to please the surgeon operating on them by telling him what he wanted to hear. There was no unbiased medical press in India, Esdaile charged, nor in Britain either. Not only were his own successes with mesmeric anesthesia not recorded; those achieved by some British and Continental European doctors were ignored also. Only through his pamphlet, and from the pages of *The Zoist*, could the British public learn how anesthesia without chemicals had been successfully employed in hundreds of surgeries.

In all, during his tenure in India, Esdaile performed about three hundred major operations and literally thousands of minor ones, under painless hypnotic anesthesia. Among the major operations were nineteen amputations and one removal of kidney stones, but the great majority was for the removal of the enormous scrotal tumors then common among native men in India as a result of elephantiasis. This is a condition in which there is an enlargement and hardening of tissues, especially of the lower body, caused by the blockage of lymph ducts by parasitic worms. The removal of these immense tumors always resulted in a vast amount of bleeding, which was difficult to control while the patient struggled and writhed in pain under the surgeon's knife. Consequently, the death rate was very high — fifty percent or more — and many of the Company's surgeons had stopped operating on scrotal tumors, regarding them as hopeless cases. Esdaile himself had accepted only eleven cases in the six years before he commenced using mesmerism in 1846. His success rate with these eleven unanes-thetized cases was not reported, but of the one hundred and sixty-one scrotal tumor surgeries he performed with mesmeric anesthesia, one hundred and fifty-three resulted in complete recovery of the patient. The eight who died did so from cholera or other infectious causes unrelated to the tumors. Another summary, that of the Mesmeric Hospital in its first year of operation, 1846-47, lists sixty-two major operations performed under mesmerism with only three fatalities, and six hundred and forty minor operations, all successful and all painless.

Among all of Esdaile's cases, the most famous is the opera-tion he performed on October 14, 1846, for removal of a scrotal tumor nearly seven feet in circumference on a twenty-seven-year-old Hindu. The tumor was truly gigantic, being larger than the man's entire body, and at 103 pounds weighing more than the man did without it. The tumor was tied up in a sheet to which a rope was attached and passed through a pulley in the rafter. This was necessary for Esdaile to be able to cut through its neck with the longest two-edged knife in his kit. The knife had to be pushed in beyond its total length to complete the incision. The removal of the tumor took half an hour to complete, the flow of venous blood from the severed vessels being, in Esdaile's words, "prodigious at first," but was soon controlled with hand pressure and then ligature. During the operation the mesmerized patient remained calm. Esdaile said "I was not sensible of a quiver of the flesh." The patient recovered fully.

Even more dramatic, in Esdaile's own opinion, was an operation he performed on a forty-year-old man for a cancerous nasal tumor that had invaded the sinuses and throat. Under mesmeric anesthesia, the tumor was removed completely and the resulting enormous cavity sewn up without the patient feeling anything. He too made a total recovery. Esdaile's medical memoirs contain these case-notes:

> I put a long knife in at the corner of his mouth, and brought the point out over the cheekbone, dividing the parts between; from this, I pushed it through the skin back to the nose. The pressure of the tumor had caused the absorption of the anterior wall of the antrum, and on pressing my fingers between it and the bones, it burst, and a shocking gush of blood, and brain-like matter, followed. The tumor extended as far as my fingers could reach under the orbit and cheekbone, and passed into the gullet—having destroyed the bones and partition of the nose. No one touched the man, and I turned his head into any position I desired, without resistance, and there it remained till I wished to move it again: when the blood accumulated, I bent his head forward, and it ran from his mouth as if from a leaden spout. The man never moved,

nor showed any signs of life, except an occasional indistinct moan; but when I threw back his head, and passed my fingers into his throat to detach the mass in that direction, the stream of blood was directed into his wind-pipe, and some instinctive effort became necessary for existence; he therefore coughed, and leaned forward, to get rid of the blood; and I suppose that he then awoke. The operation was by this time finished, and he was laid on the floor to have his face sewed up, and while this was doing, he for the first time opened his eyes.

In the records of the Company's official visitors to the Mesmeric Hospital can be found eyewitness accounts of other remarkable painless surgeries by Esdaile, among them, a below-the-knee amputation of a woman's leg, and removal of a man's leg at a point six inches above the knee. Both patients slept calmly though the operations and afterward declared they felt rested and refreshed. Other cases of major surgical procedures Esdaile performed without pain included the setting of a compound leg fracture, involving the sawing off of a piece of bone; successful reduction of severely strangulated hernias; and relief of dangerous urethral stricture.

Esdaile was not a robust man physically. He suffered from some sort of asthmatic or bronchial condition even before he went to India, and thought at first it might be helped by the heat there. Actually, as we have seen, it got worse. He also soon found that, once he started doing it regularly, mesmerizing to induce anesthesia drained his energy. Six weeks of it left him restless, irritable, and unable to sleep. He then began training native assistants to do the induction, and they proved to be even more capable at this than he had been. Only in a few exceptional cases was it necessary thereafter for Esdaile to have to mesmerize a surgical patient into anesthetic trance. Indeed, he seems to have been exceptionally proficient at training others in the procedures of induction. In the fall of 1852, he instructed Dr. Fraser Thompson, surgeon of the Perth Hospital, who was soon able to perform several painless operations. His colleagues then threatened to strike unless the hospital banned all mesmeric practices for any purpose whatever.

After this, Esdaile appears to have ceased any further attempts at getting mesmeric anesthesia admitted to the canon of medical practice. He continued an intermittent correspondence with Braid and Elliotson, but as far as is known did not meet them on any occasion. His health did not improve in the harsh Scottish winters, and sometime after 1855 he moved to Sydenham, near London, where he died on January 10, 1859, in his fifty-first year.

Esdaile had been married three times and been twice a widower, but had no children. Of these marriages and of other aspects of his personal life, very little is known. Outside of his professional activities, he seems to have been a very shy, retiring person, and even within the scope of those, if he met resistance he refrained from pressing the issue further. Nevertheless, on every count he merits ranking among the world's greatest hypnotists. Had it not been for the development of chemical anesthesia at the very time he was bringing hypnotic anesthesia to a level of regular clinical usage, James Esdaile would have been accepted by the medical profession as the pioneer of the painless surgery so long dreamed of. Since hypnosis is the only anesthetic that poses no danger to the patient, medical science has taken a fresh look at hypnotic anesthesia, and today it is being used in selected cases as a valuable adjunct to chemical anesthesia.

Phineas Parkhurst Quimby
1802 - 1866

CHAPTER 15
Mesmerism's Late Arrival in America

G iven that the American nation that came out of the War of the Revolution was a wholly new political and social entity such as had never before existed, it may seem somewhat surprising that at first it was not more receptive to departures from long-established outlooks and practices. Certainly one of the foremost figures of the struggle for American independence, the Marquis de Lafayette, appeared to expect he would be the carrier of Mesmer's message to the new nation, and that it would be enthusiastically accepted by both leaders and people.

Lafayette had joined the Society of Universal Harmony, on April 5, 1784, when it was at the peak of its popularity. This was the very day King Louis XVI appointed the second of the two commissions whose adverse conclusions would bring about Mesmer's downfall. However, the commissions would not report for another five months and by that time Lafayette would be back in America, from where he had returned early in 1782 to watch over the protracted peace negotiations in Paris. Now that the treaty recognizing American independence was concluded, signed, and ratified, and peace formally proclaimed, Lafayette was preparing for his third visit to

America, to be hailed as a principal architect of that triumphant outcome. And he saw himself, at least momentarily, as
also the bearer of news to America of a new and almost
miraculous mode of healing for human ills.

On May 14, a month before he sailed, Lafayette wrote to
George Washington, in rapturous terms:

> A German doctor named Mesmer, having made the
> greatest discovery on animal magnetism, has formed pupils,
> among whom your humble servant is accounted one of the
> most enthusiastic . . . before leaving I shall obtain permission
> to confide Mesmer's secret to you, for you may believe it is a
> great philosophical discovery.

Yet when he landed at New York on August 4 and commenced his cross-country travels, during which he was wined
and dined from one end of the Thirteen States, to the other, he
said no more about Mesmer's marvelous panacea. What
happened to chill Lafayette's enthusiasm for animal magnetism?

Little documentation has survived to provide a firm answer, but it may be guessed Mesmer himself — with his para-
noid concern about being upstaged by his pupils — had
refused to grant the permission, which Lafayette so confidently expected, to become the master's apostle in America. To
Mesmer, letting his doctrines take root in a faraway land,
among people more likely than not to twist them into unre-
cognizable shapes, was something to be avoided, not promoted.

Finally, Benjamin Franklin, who was still in Paris awaiting
the arrival of Thomas Jefferson to replace him as the American

envoy to France, may also have talked to Lafayette. Perhaps Franklin counseled him that the American public, who had taken a long time to see the wisdom of casting off the rule of the British, would think long and hard before accepting the radical overturn of long-standing medical theory and practice that Mesmer sought. It would, in fact, be wisest not to introduce the subject at all in America. If mesmerism was indeed all its founder claimed it to be, it would in good time make itself felt across the ocean, and win acceptance on its own merits. So we can imagine the elder statesman from Philadelphia advising the French "boy wonder" — Lafayette was still only twenty-seven and already a prominent world figure — and something like that probably did happen. Whatever the factors were that caused him to change his mind; Lafayette said nothing about mesmerism on his triumphal half-year tour of America. When he returned to France early in March 1785, mesmerism was already largely discredited. In the Shrove Tuesday ("Carnivale") street masquerades, it had been mercilessly ridiculed. Mesmer himself was preparing to leave France, which he did at the end of June. Lafayette would have realized his own political future would be jeopardized if he were to give mesmerism any further open support. Indeed he may have been influenced by Jefferson (who had now arrived and was a total skeptic of what he saw and heard about animal magnetism) to renounce any remaining private belief in it. In any event, we hear no more of mesmerism among Lafayette's varied interests in the half-century of adventurous life that still lay before him.

Nor do we hear of anything but minimal American notice of mesmerism for more than three decades into the nineteenth century. The reading public must have seen accounts of it being practiced widely in Europe and especially in France, but these aroused no curiosity or emulation. America was still too busy expanding its frontiers westward to be much concerned with the inner frontiers of the mind. There was a brief flicker of interest in 1795, when Dr. Elisha Perkins of Plainfield, Connecticut, found he could relieve pain by stoking affected areas. Perkins attributed the effect (which was wholly due to the patients' confidence, faith, and belief that they would be helped) to electrical currents conveyed through the small metal implements with which he did the stroking with. For a few months he made considerable money by selling sets of the devices, which he called "tractors" — even George Washington was curious enough to buy a set — but by May 1797 his "discovery" had been discredited by the Medical Society of Connecticut, and he made no further effort to promote it. His son Benjamin Perkins was less scrupulous. The young man saw an opportunity to get rich by pushing his father's "find" abroad, guessing that the European press had not covered its discrediting. After first selling the idea, and several sets of "tractors," to the Royal Hospital in Copenhagen, Denmark, Benjamin Perkins went to England where he was astonishingly successful in getting doctors to try the technique. He is said to have made over fifty thousand dollars from selling the "tractors" at thirty dollars each. Finally around 1800 attacks on the devices began to appear in the medical journals, and in the already mentioned treatise of Dr. John Haygarth of Bath on the role of imagination in causing and alleviating physical ailments. It took a decade, though, to fully root Perkins' "tractors" out of English medical practice. The astonishing thing about this episode, on both sides of the Atlantic, is that despite the obvious similarities to Mesmer's magnetizing, no one seemed to realize that the same factor of suggestion was involved in both therapies. Benjamin Perkins, in particular, was very annoyed when anyone suggested he was simply promoting a form of mesmerism. "The tractors work electrically," he insisted, "and Mesmer made no use of electricity."

By the 1840s, after mesmerism—or magnetizing as it had started to be called—had finally been introduced to America by the Frenchman Charles Poyen in his missionary tour of the United States, and after the circulation of an English translation from the French of Deleuze's do-it-yourself handbook, electricity had re-emerged in America as the prime force in the mesmeric technique. The American adherents of this notion called themselves electro-biologists. For a few years they were serious competitors of James Braid, who in England had concluded there was no magnetic fluid involved and all of the observed effects of mesmerism were caused through the influence of suggestion inducing a condition resembling sleep. Had the electro-biologists prevailed with their erroneous conception of an electrical current that the mind could direct and control, the development of hypnotherapy would have been seriously delayed.

Fortunately the danger from the electro-biologists was never as great as it appeared to be. The training and background of the Americans were not up to the standards prevailing in Europe. The electro-biologists who went to England in the 1840s and 1850s were given a hearing, but this convinced few, if any. They could not make as compelling a case for their view as Braid and his supporters were able to do for theirs.

The British medical establishment—outside of those who rejected hypnotism altogether—sided with Braid, and only a handful of mesmerists in France and elsewhere in continental Europe accepted the electrical theory. In a decade or two it had been abandoned everywhere.

To a large degree the defeat of the electro-biologists was symptomatic of a wider failure for American hypnotherapeutic development as a whole. Though the field produced some colorful personalities and some notable results in the way of cures, in nineteenth century America no great pioneers of hypnotism emerged that could rank alongside the British and European masters of the art. There were no far-reaching advances, in either theory or practice, comparable to those in the Old World. It was not until the middle third of the twentieth century that America brought forth one of the world's greatest hypnotists.

However, the rapid but unsubtantial rise of mesmerism in America after its belated arrival, and its stagnation after the mid-century point, makes an engrossing story. Charles Poyen, mentioned above as the prime introducer of mesmerism to America, was an energetic advocate of the art, an effective practitioner of it, and a gifted publicist as well. He was not a deep thinker, but none of the Americans who followed in his footsteps was as interesting a personality.

Poyen was a product of the widespread revival of mesmerism in France in the late 1820s and early 1830s, which resulted from the publication of Deleuze's immensely popular handbook and the naming of the Third Commission of Inquiry. While in the course of training for the medical profession, he became ill in 1832 and was helped by treatment from a female magnetizer. Advised to seek a more thorough cure by moving to a warm climate, he went to the French West Indies where he resided for over a year. He found the owners of the sugar plantations to be fully conversant with the resurgence of mesmerism in the French homeland. They encouraged him to start his own experiments with magnetizing, and suggested the United States would be a fertile field for his advancement in the art.

Coming to New England in 1837, Poyen settled in Lowell, Massachusetts. He taught French and drawing, and gradually expanded the scope of his public demonstrations of magnetizing. He followed the teachings of Puységur more than those of Mesmer, in holding that the exertion of the magnetizer's will was the principal factor in inducing the mesmeric state. At the same time, he insisted on the use of the hands, both in gestures and touching, for transmission of the magnetic power or "fluid" as he still referred to it. He also made occasional use of magnetized water and iron objects as reservoirs of the power, and occasionally talked about it as being similar to an electrical circuit. This was the seed from which the electro-biological doctrine would sprout.

Some prominent persons, including Mayor Elisha Bartlett of Lowell, the carpet manufacturer Alexander Wright, and Francis Wayland, President of Brown University in Providence, Rhode Island, were attracted to Poyen's lectures and demonstrations. They publicly endorsed his claims for the therapeutic usefulness of magnetizing for treating all sorts of ailments. Such support was vital for Poyen in overcoming the widespread resistance he still found to mesmerism, which in the Yankee mind was still equated with the charlatanism that long ago had been exposed by the great Benjamin Franklin. Poyen was surprised at how frequently the objectors cited Franklin, even though they were usually ignorant of the composition and overall findings of the French Royal Commissions of 1784.

Two years after his arrival in New England in 1834, Poyen was presenting his magnetizing lectures on a regular circuit that, in addition to Lowell, Boston and Providence, included Taunton, New Bedford, Salem and Cambridge in Massachusetts, as well as Nashua, New Hampshire, and Bangor and Portland, Maine. In October 1837 he published in Boston a small book under the title *Progress of Animal Magnetism in New England*, which summarized the extensive healings accomplished by him and by the numerous regular physicians who were starting to magnetize on their own. A twenty-two page appendix to the book provided specific instructions on trance induction and impressing one's will on the subject.

New England had thus been won over to the mesmeric doctrine in less than half a decade by what can only be called the fervent evangelizing mission of Poyen, while his converts were making inroads in the medical establishment of New York City, then already the nation's metropolitan center. Poyen's ability to make friends with ease had served his cause well. Entering the last two years of the decade, he was exuberantly optimistic that mesmerism would continue to expand and prosper in the great American nation to which he had introduced it.

However, unexpected disappointments lay in wait for him. Religious congregations, especially of the more fundamentalist bodies such as the Baptists and Methodists, reacted to the sudden popularity of mesmerism by condemning it as contrary to scripture, if not downright satanic. Individual parishioners who had been won over by Poyen's evangelizing were expelled or pressured into recanting. Medical societies were not as a rule quite as harsh in disciplining members who were magnetizing, but such deviants from traditional practice were cautioned to avoid publicity for their unorthodox therapy. Over the course of the year 1838, restraints of this character became more and more common in New England communities that earlier had welcomed Poyen's mesmeric message. Attendance at his lectures fell off sharply.

There is a tragic story from a small New Hampshire town that tells of a popular physician who started magnetizing and was hounded out of the local Baptist congregation and out of the community altogether. His wife, who died of humiliation and grief in 1838, rests under a tombstone that accuses the Baptist church of murdering her. There may have been many other cases, though perhaps none as extreme as this.

In addition, rivals began to appear who made claims that went beyond Poyen's, thus undercutting the ground he had gained. One of Poyen's most fervent and prominent early converts was William Stone, the New York City superintendent of schools, editor of a commercial journal, and former U.S. Minister to the Netherlands. Vastly enthusiastic over the new doctrines he had absorbed from Poyen's presentations, Stone proceeded to conduct mesmeric seances of his own with wholly inadequate controls. Among the phenomena occurring at these seances were instances of exceptional clairvoyance, including an allegedly blind woman's reading of sealed envelopes and locating of hidden objects. Stone was roundly criticized by Charles Durant, another Manhattan disciple of Poyen in a book entitled *Exposition: A New Theory of Animal Magnetism*. Poyen sprang to Stone's defense, calling Durant an ignorant scribbler, but then made his own criticism of Stone for failing to propose any coherent theory to account for the marvelous phenomena he claimed to have produced.

The real grounds of Poyen's attack on Durant were not the latter's taking of Stone to task, but rather the induction procedures recommended in Durant's book. These were largely based on Deleuze's handbook, which Durant appears to have read in French (the English translation by Thomas C. Hartshorn, yet another Poyen disciple, appeared in New York about the same time as Durant's own book), and since Deleuze was a follower of Mesmer rather than Puységur, his techniques were not much to Poyen's liking.

The result of these contrary developments in 1838 was that Poyen came to feel his efforts in America had not been accepted. He concluded he could no longer do any good there, and in 1839 returned to France where he disappeared from historical notice. Perhaps he completed his medical studies and became an obscure physician. Whatever his later fate, his pioneering accomplishment in America had set in motion several chains of events.

Poyen's immediate successor in the role of mesmerist evangelizer of America was an Englishman named Robert Collyer, of whose career little is known. He was a believer in phrenology, as so many in England were in the 1820s and 1830s, and had come to America shortly after Poyen's arrival with the intention of enlightening Americans about the science of the revelatory bumps on their heads. He was shocked by the ignorance he found prevailing among the general public, not only with regard to phrenology but almost every other serious subject as well. Physicians were "dolts and swindlers," preachers "canting hypocrites," politicians and businessmen "corrupt and cheating." Or so it seemed to Collyer, who blamed the common people for not knowing enough to realize they were being imposed upon. Phrenology was, very literally, above their heads—but perhaps, he thought, mesmerism would be easier to grasp as well as being a means of healing some of the sicknesses the doctors could not cure.

Collyer was not very well read on mesmerism, but he studied several books on the art and in 1839 began an intensive course of lectures in Philadelphia, New York and Boston. The crowds who came to hear him were even bigger than those attracted by Poyen. After three months of Collyer's lectures in Boston, the religious and medical opposition to mesmerism had been pushed back on the defensive. People were holding street rallies to denounce doctors and ministers for having withheld the truth—why didn't the Mayor and City Council do something about it? Fearful of mob violence, the Mayor and Council convened and issued a statement which, while falling short of endorsing mesmerism outright, declared it to be helpful, useful, and worthy of further investigation and practice.

Over the next four or five years, mesmerism—or hypnotism as some were beginning to call it—attained in America a popular acceptance and widespread application it has never again seen. In 1843 it was estimated that twenty to thirty lecturers on magnetizing were constantly on their circuits in the Northeastern States, in all seasons of the year; and that there were over two hundred professional magnetizers practicing in Boston and its suburbs. In addition, there were uncounted thousands of amateur magnetizers everywhere, experimenting on their families, relations and friends. Besides the Deleuze handbook in the Hartshorn translation, which had an enormous circulation, swarms of other magnetizing manuals were constantly being made available to the public.

Also widely circulated, though offering no advice on induction techniques, was a slim volume titled *Facts In Mesmerism* that came out in 1842 from the pen of Charles Caldwell, a seventy-year-old member of the medical faculty of Transylvania College in Lexington, Kentucky. Twenty years earlier he had been an early and lone voice on behalf of phrenology; now he hailed mesmerism as a reclaimer of humankind from the grip of religious obscurantism and superstition. Mesmerism, he argued, was the scientific application of the spiritual powers of human beings, rendering obsolete the ritualism and miraculous legends of Christianity, from which only its ethical values needed to be retained.

With their generations-long belief patterns being overthrown by reading books such as Caldwell's (and there were many other similar writings), thousands who would never before have given credence to psychic phenomena became receptive to the new cult of Spiritualism that originated with the famous Fox sisters' rappings and table-tippings in upstate New York in 1848. As the 1850s progressed, so too did the appeal of mediumistic communications with the dead. "Spiritualism," which hitherto had been a not very common term denoting a preoccupation with the higher realms of religious mysticism, was now applied to communicating with the departed through persons who advertised their services and set up offices with regular hours.

Mesmerism, in any guise and under any name, became outmoded. Those who tired of Spiritualism after a surfeit of seances went back to more traditional religious forms rather than to mesmerism. The Civil War that followed, with its enormous burden of personal loss and suffering, accelerated this return to the old and familiar paths of the spirit. It was generally forgotten, especially by the medical profession, that mesmerism had held out a bright promise of relief and cure to the millions who had not benefited from the customary forms of treatment.

However, not all of the achievements during the "American Mesmerist Decade" of the 1840s were lost. (Actually, the period when mesmerism was on the rise was more on the order of two decades, from about 1835 to around 1854 or 1855, and it was not until 1852 that Spiritualism started to be a serious rival.) It left an influential heritage, as we shall see, in the "New Thought" movement of the 1890s, and the new religion of Christian Science whose founder, Mary Baker Eddy, had been treated by a magnetizer inspired by Poyen. It stimulated the creative imagination of such masters of nineteenth century fiction as Nathaniel Hawthorne and Edgar Allan Poe, in works like Hawthorne's *The Blithedale Romance* and Poe's *The Facts in the Case of M. Valdemar*. And most importantly, from the standpoint of modern hypnotherapy, it left a legacy of case histories of effective application in a large variety of ailments. These accounts were rediscovered, providing a substantial body of additional evidence that the therapeutic efficacy of hypnosis had not diminished, a half-century

later and the width of an ocean away from Mesmer.Among
the most effective practitioners of mesmerism for healing in
the 1840s was LaRoy Sunderland. He had been a Methodist
minister. In *The Magnet*, a periodical published by him, he
claimed to have magnetized over fifteen hundred patients,
curing such ailments as rheumatism, stammering, epilepsy,
insomnia, blindness, deafness, and addiction to coffee, alcohol
and tobacco. Along with many other American mesmerists at
that time, he particularly valued the book *Facts In Mesmerism*
by Charles Dickens' friend, Rev. Chauncy Townshend, which
provided a sound psychological basis for what they were
doing, and a solid defense against detractors. Townshend
enumerated four divisions of a living person—the physical
body, the vital "animating" force, the mind, and the soul or
spirit—with the vital force being the one through which
magnetizing worked.

Based on Townshend and on various other English and
European writings on mesmerism that came into their hands,
the American mesmerists had by the end of the 1840s constructed working models of the stages of trance depth into
which they inducted their subjects. These stages were generally six in number, though some models had as few as three,
ranging from light to very deep trance in which it was alleged
clairvoyance and telepathy could occur. Though the most
frequently used six-stage models essentially corresponded to
those distinguished by Carl Kluge in Germany as early as
1811, they seem to have been arrived at independently,
Kluge's work being known to very few of the American
mesmerists.

In sum, American mesmerism had matured rapidly over the fifteen years since its introduction by Poyen in 1834, and in both theory and practice appeared ready to claim its place as a functional part of the standard medical establishment of the country. That it faltered just when its future seemed assured was largely due to two factors in addition to the sudden explosive growth of Spiritualism as a competitor for public attention. The first was a rapid spread of hypnotism—as it was starting to be called in the early 1850s—as a crowd-tickling entertainment at fairs and circuses, which was extremely detrimental to its acceptance as a serious therapy. People who laughed at the antics of hypnotized subjects on the stage were unwilling to let their doctors use the same method on them as a medical treatment. A majority of physicians who would otherwise have been ready to employ hypnotism as a therapy rejected it for fear of losing income from patients who would turn to more conservative doctors. The second factor, the deviation of the electro-biological sidepath, would not of itself have inflicted lasting damage to the growth of nineteenth century hypnotherapy in America. In time its error would have been perceived and the lost ground regained had not the whole developing framework of hypnotherapy been shattered by the excesses of Spiritualism and stage hypnotism. As it was, the failure of the American attempt to promote electro-biology in England, where Braid and his followers refuted it, was a further costly setback to the prestige and credibility of American hypnotherapy.

Electro-biology had in fact sprung from English origins. Among the numerous treatises on magnetizing the Americans were constantly importing from England were several that laid special emphasis on the "electric current" that flowed from the magnetizer's fingertips as he made contact with his subjects. Two in particular who seemed to equate the force at work in mesmerism with electricity were George Sandby, an Anglican parson in Suffolk, and Dr. William Scoresby, who had in his younger years been an Arctic explorer and student of the Earth's magnetic currents.

This idea was picked up in America by J. Stanley Grimes, then in his forties, who in the course of a long and active life of ninety-six years would alter his opinions more than once. At the time he was a college professor of medical jurisprudence, and keenly interested in what was being reported of Braid's successes in trance induction. To Grimes, it appeared that suggestion alone could not produce the observed effects. There had to be a physical cause as well—and what else could it be but the minute electrical currents which, it was already starting to be understood, were constantly being produced in the tissues and organs of the living body? These currents, Grimes proposed, were concentrated by the magnetizer's mental power into a single greatly enhanced one, through which he exerted his will on his subject.

This process he called electro-biology, and soon attracted several converts to his interpretation of it. Some of these, notably Dr. H. G. Darling and Dr. Winslow Lewis, went to England in 1850 on the failed mission to introduce electro-biology there. A French doctor living there, Joseph R. Durand, had no better luck in trying to spread electro-biology in his native country. Grimes later went over to the Braidite camp, and eventually into that of the Spiritualists.

The greatest dissemination of the electro-biological gospel was achieved by John Bovee Dods, who had been a pastor of the Universalist church in Provincetown, Massachusetts. The Universalists were a new denomination, scarcely two generations old, which had risen out of the popular revulsion against the repressive Calvinist dogmas that limited salvation to so few. Imbued already by Universalist doctrine with the expectation of the eventual salvation of all people, Dods discovered in mesmerism what seemed to him a way of speeding this process by relieving sufferers from physical and mental ills. Mainly self-taught in induction techniques, and convinced by the electro-biological explanation of how magnetizing achieved its wonders, Dods took to lecturing around the country on the virtues of the new science and its healing capabilities.

For about three years, from 1850 to 1853, Dods was the unrivaled master of the mesmeric scene in America. Stocky in appearance and fervent in manner, he was a very effective speaker who projected the impression of being far more learned than he really was, and he attracted enormous crowds. For one lecture series in Boston, he drew one thousand people a night for six successive nights, filling every seat in the Marlboro Chapel. At the invitation of Henry Clay, Daniel Webster, Sam Houston, and other noted Senators, he addressed an informal joint session of Congress in the House Chamber of the U. S. Capitol on February 16, 1850. A book-length collection of seventeen lectures sold out three editions before the public's interest declined.

To set himself apart from other electro-biologists, Dods started calling his operative doctrine "electrical psychology."

It was the same, he insisted, as that of his electro-biological rivals, except he knew better how to apply it. The secret was in a small zinc disc in which a five-cent silver coin was imbedded, with a piece of copper wire transfixing them. By having his subjects stare fixedly at it, he could transmit the electrical impulses that made his will dominant over theirs.

Dods' fall was as rapid as his rise. Rivals demonstrated the zinc-silver-copper object had no greater effect in inducing trance than those made of any other materials. His failures in treating serious diseases soon led to a loss of belief in his method altogether. Spiritualism's counter-attraction pulled away even his staunchest adherents. For some years, mesmerism as a therapy rather than as an entertainment—in which role it was continuing to expand—receded to a low level of both public and medical interest.

When public interest revived during the Civil War, it was limited mainly to the New England area and centered around the remarkable personality of Phineas Parkhurst Quimby. Lacking formal education, he had followed Poyen on the latter's final lecture circuit through Maine in 1838, and had quickly learned the technique of induction. Fortunate in finding a good trance subject and assistant named Lucius Burkmar, Quimby became a proficient hypnotist. Gradually he discarded the notions of a magnetic fluid or electrical currents, and relied on suggestion alone. He had been a hypnotherapist, though the term was not yet in use, for over twenty years before the spreading fame of the cures he was achieving started to bring him a large influx of patients from about 1860 on. By the time he died in 1866, he had treated over twelve thousand persons, mostly with beneficial results.

Quimby did not have the literary, organizational, and promotional talents to capitalize on what he had achieved, and to become America's first world-class great hypnotist. In one respect though, he attained immortality. He was the healer and inspirer of Mary Baker Eddy, who was one of his last patients. From his insistence on the supremacy of the mind over all material constraints she derived the basic tenets of Christian Science. That, however, is another story from the one we are telling in this book, and so too is the growth of the turn-of-the-century New Thought movement in America, which also drew on Quimby's teachings.

A handicap all of the American mesmerists in the middle third of the nineteenth century shared was the lack of an academic base. Not until the 1890s would there be a chair of psychology in any American university or college. The American mesmerists were thus in the position of being gifted amateurs, without access to proper research and experiment facilities, or an accepted discipline within which to evaluate the results. The wonder is not that the Americans of that time failed to contribute much to the later development of hypnotism, or that no truly great exponent of it arose from their midst. The wonder is that given their limitations, they accomplished as much as they did.

We now turn to the mainstream of modern hypnotism, as it emerged in France during the last third of the nineteenth century.

VIII.

THE NANCY SCHOOL

THE DAWN OF MODERN HYPNOTISM

Hippolyte Bernheim
1840 - 1919

CHAPTER 16
Liébeault and Bernheim
Found the Nancy School

W e have now reached the point in the evolution of the discipline and practice of hypnotism where it emerged as a distinct and recognized branch of medical treatment. This was during the last third of the nineteenth century in France, when two physicians, Ambroise Liébeault and Hippolyte Bernheim, built the structure of modern hypnotherapy upon the foundations laid by the Abbé Faria and James Braid. Their collaborative effort became known as the Nancy School of Hypnotism, from their location in the city of that name in eastern France. They attracted a wide following in the medical profession across western Europe and in the United States, ensuring that in spite of the periodic swings in and out of favor which had continued to beset medical hypnosis, it would henceforth always have a solid substratum of professional support.

However, at the same time Liébeault and Bernheim were founding the Nancy School of Hypnotism (based on Faria's and Braid's principles of hypnotic induction by suggestion) they were combating an opposite interpretation of hypnotism by one of its most brilliant practitioners, Jean-Martin Charcot, the famous French neurologist and anatomist. Working primarily with psychoneurotic patients in the Salpêtrière hospital in Paris (which gave its name to his version of medical hypnosis) Charcot sought to demonstrate convincingly that the hypnotic state was primarily an artificially induced nervous hysteria. As such it had little, if any, therapeutic function or merit, but could be of great value in determining how neuroses developed and affected human behavior.

The essential difference between the Nancy and the Salpêtrière Schools was that the former had a positive approach—hypnosis was a useful and helpful therapy—while the latter saw hypnosis as a pathological phenomenon, an abnormal exertion of the will of one person over that of another who was impressionable and hysterically reactive. These opposing viewpoints in turn reflected the sharply contrasting personalities of Liébeault and Bernheim on the one hand and Charcot on the other. It is from an examination of their lives and the development of their connections with hypnotism, that their ranking among the truly great practitioners of the discipline can be most fully understood and valued.

Auguste Ambroise Liébeault (he dropped the Auguste in his adult life) was born in 1823, the youngest of twelve children of a peasant family in the province of Lorraine. He was able to get a medical education by working at extra jobs to pay for his tuition. Graduating in 1850 at the age of twenty-seven, he set up as a country doctor in the Lorraine village of Pont-Saint-Vincent. A kindly man who empathized easily with his patients, he met with unusual success in his practice and by

1860 had become a wealthy man by the standards of that time and place.

Hypnotism, or "magnetizing" as it was yet generally referred to, was under the deepest shadow of the mid-century French official disapproval when Liébeault commenced his professional career. As early as 1848, two years before graduating, he had come across what he later recalled simply as "an old book" describing the therapeutic powers of suggestion. It was probably Alexandre Bertrand's 1826 review of the state of animal magnetism in France, which was largely based on the work of the Abbé Faria. After settling in Pont-Saint-Vincent, Liébeault is known to have read Faria's 1819 book, as well as the one which Faria's disciple, General Noizet, published in 1854. Later he obtained French translations of the writings of James Braid.

From these works, Liébeault gained an understanding of the nature of hypnosis and the methodology of induction. Contrary to what Braid taught and what is now generally accepted, he believed hypnotic sleep was the same as natural sleep, differing only in being induced by the exertion of another person's will. This error did not keep him from grasping that therapeutic suggestions could thus be implanted in the mind of the hypnotized person to cure or relieve ailments.

He began to experiment with hypnotic treatment of his patients, and had generally good results with those who allowed him to hypnotize them. Most, however, objected strongly. The Lorraine peasantry was still as a whole uneducated and superstitious, and feared that hypnotism smacked of diabolism and witchcraft. To secure the consent of enough patients to make his experiments meaningful, Liébeault offered a choice: conventional treatment at his regular rates, or hypnotherapy for free. Within four years he had a clientele consisting wholly of hypnotic subjects, but no income. Realizing that to continue this practice was both foolish and ruinous (it had not brought him to any clear formulation of what hypnotism really was or how it should be properly utilized) he retired from active practice in 1864 for a two-year sabbatical. During this time he worked out a consistent system of hypnotic treatment, which he published in 1866 under the cumbersome title of *Sleep and Its Analogous States from the Viewpoint of Moral and Physical Action.*

Doubtless stemming from that pretentious title, legend has it the book sold only one copy in the first five years after it was published, or one copy in each of those five years. Though the book certainly was no best-seller, the legend can be discounted for the book was widely quoted over the last third of the century by both practitioners and writers on hypnotism all across western Europe. Among the professional audience Liébeault was addressing, the book seems to have sold well enough.

Although mistaken in his conviction that hypnotic sleep was the same as natural sleep, Liébeault in his book correctly identified some of the cognitive processes involved in the induction of hypnosis. He was, in fact, the first to do so since the Abbé Faria, whose influence on his thinking was clearly very great.

Successful induction, Liébeault wrote, requires implanting a conviction in the subject that he or she can be put into a hypnotic sleep, and then focusing the subject's attention on a single thought or stimulus. The field of attention had to be narrowed to the point that all critical judgment and initiative were surrendered to the hypnotist. He could then suggest to the subject (whom he believed had become, in deep hypnosis, an automaton) whatever it was that he wanted done.

This is not quite the way that the hypnotic process is understood today, for the mind does retain its individuality even in a profound level of hypnosis; but it was a large advance from all earlier conceptions. Liébeault also correctly related susceptibility to hypnosis to the subject's capacity for vivid imagery—what is now termed, as I pointed out earlier, the mythopoetic faculty of the subconscious mind. The more vivid the images resulting from the hypnotist's suggestions, the greater the subject's openness to induction into deeper levels of hypnosis, or "sleep," in Liébeault's terminology.

He believed all persons were capable of being hypnotized, and of learning to hypnotize themselves. (This is substantially the current view, as every normal person has the potentiality for developing hypnosis and making use of this potential.)

Liébeault's conviction that in deep hypnotic sleep the subject became an automaton, totally under the control of the hypnotist's will, made him fearful that this opened the door to all sorts of criminal abuse the subject had no power to resist. He devoted an entire chapter of his book to strongly worded warnings about this danger, insisting on strict self-control on the part of the hypnotist.

Critics of his mode of practice, which Liébeault resumed after the publication of his book, charged he was slipshod in his diagnoses and often failed to follow the progress of those he had treated. To some extent these accusations are borne out by the accounts of two visitors in the 1880s, when Liébeault's fame and reputation were at their peak. Their impressions of him differ in many respects, however.

The earlier of the two visitors was A. W. van Renterghem from the Netherlands, who would later set up a noted hypnotic clinic of his own, based on Nancy School principles. He found Liébeault receiving patients in an old shed with white-washed walls and stone flooring on the outskirts of Nancy. Liébeault had not re-opened his earlier medical practice in Pont-Saint-Vincent, and was now relying almost entirely on hypnotherapy. For five hours daily, between the hours of 7:00 a.m. and noon, he saw between twenty-five to forty patients, charging only what each felt they were able to pay. The clientele was composed largely of poor working people from the city, and peasants who walked in from miles around. Many said they could not afford to pay anything, and were treated free.

There was no privacy for the patients, and many were talking at the same time, so van Renterghem wondered how Liébeault managed to implant his suggestions amid all the clamor. Liébeault himself was vivacious and talkative, but never for more than a few moments with any individual patient. Employing eye fixation briefly, he would tell the subjects to get sleepy, assuring them they would feel relief from their symptoms.

"I did not see him take a second look at any patient," van Renterghem wrote, "and to me his method seemed a very casual dismissal of sick people suffering from serious ailments like arthritis, ulcers and pulmonary tuberculosis. Indeed I was almost inclined to dismiss Liébeault as a credulous peasant himself. He was a short, wrinkle-faced, dark-complexioned man, the very figure of a peasant who had spent years laboring in the fields under a scorching sun." (Liébeault had indeed probably worked as a farm laborer in his youth, to earn money for his medical education.) "Yet his discussions of hypnotism with me were to the point and he was well grounded in Faria, Bertrand and others who had written on the subject."

Even more importantly, van Renterghem observed, Liébeault's hypnotic treatment did appear to benefit his patients. They would come back, stating they had experienced great relief, or at least enough to warrant a repeat treatment. Some even claimed to have been cured, and they had returned only to thank the miracle-working doctor. Though Liébeault might be careless both in diagnosis and follow-up, the Dutch visitor concluded that his hypnotic therapy had to possess some validity, for if he had deceived them, people would soon stop coming to him for treatment. Instead they continued to come in a steady stream, and very few complained of not being helped. (A modern psychologist would probably agree that at the very least, Liébeault was hypnotically implanting in his patients a conviction they would get better, and as a result their physical condition did actually improve. There is a growing recognition that the placebo effect plays a key role in all forms of therapy as well as hypnosis. As Voltaire once stated, "There is probably more cure in the doctor's words than in many of the drugs he prescribes.")

A rather different picture was drawn by J. M. Bramwell, the leading British hypnotherapist of the late nineteenth century and foremost biographer of James Braid, whose visit to Liébeault in 1889 was some years later than van Renterghem's. In the interval Liébeault had moved into more appropriate premises with spacious waiting rooms for the patients who were now coming at the rate of sixty or more a day. He was very gentle with children, Bramwell noted. "I saw him put instantly to sleep two little girls of about six or seven, who had been brought in together to him. He simply waved his hand in their direction, saying 'Sleep, my little kittens,' adding the suggestions for their getting well. I did not see him pay any further attention to them."

With adults, Liébeault continued to employ a limited degree of eye fixation, but primarily relied on verbal commands for trance induction. The extent to which he had done away with all other forms of induction, or material aids to it, so impressed Bramwell that he credited Liébeault as being even more than Braid the true father of modern hypnotism as strictly a phenomenon of suggestion.

Actually, Liébeault clung to some vestiges of the earlier "magnetic fluid" doctrine. He kept a bottle of magnetized water on hand for treating infants and children too young to be hypnotized verbally. After his retirement from active practice in 1891 — an event marked by a civic celebration honoring him for having brought fame to the city of Nancy — he continued to write articles and also two further books on hypnotherapy. In these he retreated from the position he had hitherto asserted, that hypnotism was an exertion of suggestion on the will of another person; and argued in favor of the existence of an impalpable fluid with magnetic properties, through which the suggestions were conveyed. He retained this belief until his death on February 17, 1904, at the age of eighty-one.

Bramwell would have been more correct in seeing Liébeault as essentially a key transition figure between the magnetizing and hand-passes therapies of hypnotism's first century, and the vast expansion in the understanding and purposeful employment of suggestive therapeutics that would predominate in its second century. Liébeault alone would not have been able to bring the Nancy School of Hypnotism, of which he has to be considered the founder, into international prominence with lasting influence on all subsequent development of the discipline. That the Nancy School did attain these heights was mainly due to Liébeault's friend, collaborator and follower, Hippolyte Bernheim.

Seventeen years younger than his mentor, Bernheim was a native of Alsace, and of mixed French-German parentage, as were most residents of that French border province. Coming from a more well-to-do family than Liébeault he obtained an advanced medical education in the university of the Alsatian capital of Strasbourg. At age twenty-nine he was a teacher in the university and a physician on the staff of the city hospital; then abandoned both positions when he fled from the invading Prussian army in the war of 1870.

Along with thousands of other Alsatian refugees, he sought refuge in the old Lorraine capital of Nancy, which was becoming a center of cultural innovation stemming from this inflow and intermixing of contrasting views and outlooks. A year after the end of the war in 1871, a new university had been founded in Nancy which attracted free-thinking youths from all across France. Soon a new school of decorative arts, pioneered by Emile Galle and Victor Preuve, sprang up and became the catalyst for an unprecedented blossoming of motif and poster art in the France of the twenty-year Belle Époque that ended with the coming of World War I in 1914.

In this creative environment, Bernheim's mind soon reached out to new concepts beyond those of traditional medicine, the teaching and practice of which he had resumed at the new university and its associated hospital. He was appointed professor of internal medicine in 1879, and was already widely known and respected for his innovative research and findings on typhoid fever, and also on diseases of the heart and lungs.

Aware for years of the hypnotic therapy being practiced by Liébeault in his whitewashed old shed on the outskirts of the city, Bernheim was still skeptical about "magnetizing." Though tempted many times to go and see for himself whether it had some validity, he always found some excuse for holding back. Finally in 1882, he heard that one of his own patients, whom he had been treating for a painful sciatica for six months without success, had gone to Liébeault and promptly obtained relief through hypnotic therapy. That convinced Bernheim there had to be something to it. He went to Liébeault's shed clinic and closely watched the procedure of treatment.

Bernheim was so impressed with Liébeault's hypnotic therapy he became the older man's pupil and friend, and started to utilize therapeutic hypnosis himself. He was somewhat more cautious than his mentor in using it, choosing for candidates only those patients he felt would make good hypnotic subjects. His conclusion, after some experimenting, was that people accustomed to accepting commands, such as soldiers and the factory workers of that era, were the most easily hypnotized and the likeliest to benefit from it. (The hypnotic induction used by Liébeault and Bernheim was doctor-directed and authoritarian; so those patients used to giving rather than receiving orders were often difficult to hypnotize. The modern approach to hypnosis is more permissive and patient-centered.)

Bernheim was assertive and authoritarian, though not in appearance. He was short, blue-eyed, soft-spoken, and on first sight was deceptively mild. But he ordered others around; his patients as well as the nurses and orderlies in his hospital wards. It is easy to see how his hypnotic commands would be very effectively carried out by subjects used to obeying peremptory orders, and why those not so accustomed would subconsciously resist.

Even so, the database Bernheim compiled over a ten-year span, consisting of ten thousand hypnotic inductions by Liébeault and himself, largely bore out Liébeault's claim that the vast majority of persons can be successfully hypnotized. Of these ten thousand inductions, eighty-five percent were successful.

In 1884, two years after he first visited Liébeault's clinic, Bernheim published *De la suggestion et de ses applications à la thérapeutique*, in which he strongly supported the position that suggestion was the sole operative force in hypnotism, and that Liébeault's therapeutic use of it was proving its value for curing or relieving many diseases in which the nervous system was primarily involved. Among these, which Bernheim had himself started treating with success, were rheumatoid arthritis, gastro-intestinal ailments and menstrual disorders. He followed up this first publication with an expanded one in 1866, actually a handbook of hypnotic practice, under the title *Suggestion and Its Therapeutic Applications*. The first English translation, by Christian Herter, titled *Suggestive Therapeutics*, was published in 1897 by Putnam's in New York, and was for a while very influential in the establishment of clinical hypnosis in America.

Bernheim's first book was hailed in France and the rest of western Europe as the most practical, useful and scientifically sound text that had yet appeared on hypnotherapy. With its publication the Nancy School may be considered to have arrived on the medical scene, for the book is as much an exposition and defense of Liébeault's methods as it is of Bernheim's. For all practical purposes, the book treated them as a single body of doctrine and application.

It was also a frontal attack on Charcot and his followers at the Salpêtrière, who championed the interpretation of hypnotism as an induced hysterical aberration of the mind. The details of the struggle between the Nancy and Salpêtrière Schools are more properly reserved for our next chapter, which tells how Charcot, despite his errors about hypnosis, has to be ranked among the world's greatest hypnotists. However, we can note Bernheim's definition of suggestion in his 1886 handbook as "the aptitude to transform an idea into an act." All human beings, he stated, possess this aptitude, though in greatly varying degree. Later in his career, Bernheim would stress that therapeutic suggestion did not necessarily require induction into hypnotic sleep to be effective; it could work equally well in the waking state when properly used by a trained therapist. In this he anticipated Freud and the twentieth century psychotherapists, but it was a road that went beyond what Bernheim himself could conceive. He was a medical practitioner not a psychiatrist, and did not have the background for founding a school of psychotherapy.

Bernheim also concurred with Liébeault in regarding hypnotic sleep as identical with natural sleep. Both men were led into this misconception by assuming that, just as in natural sleep the subject's dreams are often influenced by whatever the conscious mind was occupied with just before falling asleep, so in hypnotic sleep the mind retains the impression of the hypnotist and his suggestions. (In a sense that is true, but there is no correlation between hypnosis and sleep. Although the condition resembles normal sleep, scientists have found the brain wave patterns of hypnotized subjects are much closer to the EEG patterns of deep relaxation.)

Liébeault and Bernheim were more correct in recognizing that hypnotic suggestion influences the mind in the same way principles and prejudices built up through a lifetime, and constantly reinforced by repetition, condition what we do or say. But where these are deeply ingrained in our brain cells, and have the strength that comes from familiarity, the hypnotist's suggestions are often something new. They may even be something the subject may never have thought of doing before, and yet they have only the briefest of time — minutes or seconds — in which to exert an imperativeness as great or even greater than that possessed by long-held predilections.

Bernheim further found that the simpler the suggestions, the more readily they took effect. "Words," he wrote, "are the most powerful of vehicles for impressing the subject. The single word *sleep,* when said with sufficient authoritativeness, is enough to put all but the most refractory in the hypnotic state." Healing suggestions needed to be clearly stated and to relate directly to whatever ailment the subject was suffering from.

In a narrow sense the Nancy School was composed of only four men—Liébeault, Bernheim, the forensic medicine expert Henri-Etienne Beaunis and the lawyer Jules Liégeois. The last two were pioneers in the study and recognition of criminal acts committed under the influence of hypnotic suggestion, a topic that is still the subject of inquiry from time to time. They were encouraged in this by Liébeault, who had been concerned about the risk that posthypnotic suggestions of criminal actions would actually be carried out. He saw this as a real danger to society, and believed it should be taken seriously and officials be cognizant of what to look for. Although Liégeois was excessively argumentative and often damaged his position by his vehemence, he laid the foundation of modern legal handling of cases involving actions committed through hypnotic suggestion, as well as acts committed against hypnotized persons incapable of effective resistance. In this endeavor he was greatly assisted by the counsel of Liébeault and Bernheim and the thousands of case histories they made available to him.

In a wider sense, the Nancy School became an international movement that carried the clinical use of hypnotism to new ground in many countries. Offshoots founded on Nancy principles sprang up in both Europe and America, usually founded by medical men who had made the pilgrimage to see Liébeault and Bernheim. Such pilgrimages were becoming as much a ritual of the psychological profession as doing the Grand Tour had once been for young English aristocrats. Here we can mention only a few of the hypnotherapeutic establishments of the late 1880s and the 1890s which had their beginnings in a visit of their founders to Nancy.

Many of the foremost names in turn-of-the-century psychology were numbered among the disciples of Liébeault and Bernheim in Germany, Albert Moll and Albert von Schrenk-Notzing; in Austria, Richard von Krafft-Ebing; in Russia, Vladimir Becherev; in England, Milne Bramwell; in America, Boris Sidis and Morton Prince. They did not agree with their Nancy mentors on every point, and their own practice of therapeutic hypnotism often became subordinate to their pioneering of new avenues of psychotherapy. It was from Nancy, though, that they drew their primary inspiration.

Others went on to take hypnotherapy into novel and exotic settings, reflecting personalities that were colored by the end-of-the-century "decadence" — as it was then called — of the arts. From the standpoint of a hundred years later, the "decadence" seems no more than a garish flamboyance rather than something as destructive of society's standards as Max Nordau in his alarmist book in 1890. However one looks at it, there was obviously a good deal of this flamboyance in the hypnotherapeutic establishment of the Swedish physician Otto Wetterstrand in the 1890s.

Always dressed in the height of fashion, and possessing a blond mustache and a nervous tic of his eyes that he said assisted him in eye fixation of a subject, Wetterstrand received thirty to forty patients every afternoon in his lavishly furnished Stockholm apartment. Claiming to be a devoted follower of Liébeault, he emulated him in the absence of privacy for his patients. They discussed their symptoms with him, and were hypnotized, in the presence of each other.

In addition to his apartment office, Wetterstrand maintained a private hospital for the more seriously ill, staffed by recovered patients whom he trained as nurses. He was a pioneer in keeping patients requiring prolonged therapy in a hypnotic state for as long as eight to twelve days, a duration that later practitioners such as Otto Wolff preferred to maintain only with the aid of drugs, especially trional.

Less flamboyant but still beyond the sedateness of conventional medical practice, was the clinic that A.W. van Renterghem (whom we have already met on his rather skeptical visit to Liébeault's shed clinic) and Frederick van Eeden founded in Amsterdam in 1887, under the name of *Institut Liébeault*. Obviously, van Renterghem had overcome his earlier doubts and was now eager to treat the sick with hypnotherapy on Liébeault's principles. His colleague van Eeden, however, was not a doctor, but an idealistic poet, which did not prevent him from being also a competent hypnotist, whose often daring experiments still await proper follow up by present-day practitioners. For instance, van Eeden sought to prove a child could be taught another language under hypnosis. He gave a ten-year-old girl, who knew no French, lessons in French while hypnotized. Upon waking, she was able to speak and understand some of what she had been taught. In general, modern attempts at subconscious inculcation have not been as effective.

Auguste Forel, a professor of psychiatry in Zurich, Switzerland, and director of a mental hospital, visited Bernheim after Liébeault's retirement, and quickly became highly adept at employing the Nancy techniques of hypnotic therapy. Establishing an outpatient service of hypnotherapy, he had striking success with curing and alleviating several physical diseases. In an interesting variation of usual practice, he hypnotized the staff instead of the patients in his mental hospital, to make them less susceptible to being alarmed, irritated or bored by the inmates.

Another Swiss practitioner, Paul Dubois of Berne, followed Bernheim's precepts so closely he began to claim he was the originator of them. That angered Bernheim, who bitterly charged Dubois with "annexing" the credit that rightly belonged to the Nancy pair of Liébeault the forerunner and Bernheim the fulfillment — which is how Bernheim increasingly saw himself.

The young Sigmund Freud visited the Nancy pair in 1889 and was particularly interested in the success Bernheim was having with breaking down the posthypnotic amnesia that since Mesmer's time had been taken as an unvarying component — i.e., subjects could remember nothing of what they had said or done while in a deep state of hypnosis. Through careful questioning and assisting the subject to concentrate on recollection, Bernheim found he could extract a substantial body of remembered experiences under hypnosis. Freud of course went on to abandon hypnotism as being of no value in his psychotherapy, but Bernheim's memory retrieval experiments undoubtedly influenced his own methods for bringing long-buried memories to the surface.

Bernheim's career reached its height in the year of Freud's visit, when the Paris Universal Exhibition, with its just-completed mighty symbol, the Eiffel Tower, attracted a horde of conventions and congresses to the French capital. Among them were the first International Congress on Hypnotism, held at the Hôtel-Dieu, August 8-12; another on Physiological Psychology, August 6-10; and one of diehard magnetizers, October 21-26. The Congress on Hypnotism was the most widely attended, and drew the largest press coverage; thirty-one European, British and American newspapers sent their reporters to it.

Bernheim was a featured speaker at both the hypnotism and psychology congresses. At the former, he derided people who claimed to be hypnotists when they put two or three susceptible persons into light trance. "Only those who have done authoritative therapeutic hypnosis, under clinic or hospital conditions, and succeeded in inducting eight or nine subjects out of ten, are entitled to call themselves hypnotists," Bernheim asserted.

The intensity of the conflict between the Nancy and Salpêtrière schools was highlighted by Charcot's declining the presidency of both the August Congresses, because of Bernheim's presence. Charcot did not even show up at either gathering, and only two of his then adherents—one being Pierre Janet who later shifted his allegiance to the Nancy position—bothered to attend.

William James from America, then already recognized as the premier psychologist on that side of the Atlantic, was present at both the August Congresses, and chaired one session of the Psychology Conference. Freud attended the Congress on Hypnotism, as did the Dutchmen van Renterghem and van Eeden, who had added the explanatory phrase "clinic of suggestive psychotherapy" to the title of their *Institut*

Liébeault. The extensive newspaper coverage of the presentations and discussions at the Congress of Hypnotism served to raise hypnotherapy in public esteem and acceptance everywhere. Coincidentally, a sensational love-triangle murder and attempted suicide in French Algeria, in which hypnotism was involved, also helped to keep the subject in the forefront of popular attention.

Within a year, new hypnotherapy clinics were springing up all over Europe. Overnight, as it were, Bernheim found his fame being eclipsed by the newcomers, who all had something of their own to offer. When the Second Universal Exhibition and Second World Congress on Hypnotism were held in Paris in 1900, Bernheim was a lonely and overlooked figure. The celebration Nancy held in 1910 for the fortieth anniversary of his arrival in the city evoked from him only a sad and bitter response. His valedictory statement on his retirement in 1913 was equally resentful. To the day of his death in 1921, at the age of eighty-one, he felt he had been denied the recognition that was rightfully due him.

Charcot conducting a clinical lecture at the Salpêtrière.
Jean-Martin Charcot
1825 - 1893

CHAPTER 17
Charcot and the Salpêtrière School

T he career of Jean-Martin Charcot paralleled closely in the last quarter of the nineteenth century that of Mesmer in the preceding century. It can be regarded as a summing-up of the first hundred years of hypnotism and in some respects it was a curious mirror of hypnotism's beginning. Like Mesmer, Charcot was eager for public acceptance and applause, and could not sustain the loss of them. He was an accomplished showman and exhibitionist, and sought a higher culture in his private life. Like his predecessor, he was seriously in error about what hypnotism actually was; yet in the same way that Mesmer had made animal magnetism a household word, Charcot made hypnosis so widely known a phenomenon in his time, there could be no return to the former widespread ignorance of it. Just as Mesmer was an accomplished physician who would have made a name for himself had he never experimented with animal magnetism, Charcot was a brilliant anatomist and neurologist and would have been famous even had he never looked into the effects of hypnosis on hysterical patients.

In their close-fought rivalry, the Nancy School of Liébeault and Bernheim emerged the clear victor over Charcot and his followers, collectively called the Salpêtrière School, after the hospital where he practiced. Yet it was Charcot who received far greater notice in the press, and was mentioned far more often in the conversations of ordinary people. This suggests another parallel with Mesmer: A century earlier there were perhaps hundreds who knew of Mesmer and his work, as compared to the small number who knew about Puységur and his more correct interpretation of the nature of hypnosis.

Charcot was born in 1825. He was of the same generation as Liébeault, born in 1823, and was fifteen years older than Bernheim. He was the son of a Paris carriage-maker whose vehicles were in demand by the wealthy for the high artistry of their design. His family was able to get him the best medical education available in the France of the 1850s. Shy and aloof as a young man, reputedly because of a speech defect which he eventually overcame, he had difficulty in getting a private practice started after his graduation. A heavy mustache gave him a forbidding appearance that turned away potential patients. He finally shaved it off when another doctor insisted that he did so before referring him to a wealthy patient.

Gradually he developed a lucrative practice centering on the care of rich individuals, some of whom he was able to accompany on their vacation trips to Italy and elsewhere, which gained him access to the highest levels of European society. In this, too, Charcot was exactly like Mesmer. His real career did not commence until he was almost thirty-seven years old, with his appointment in 1862 as chief physician in one of the principal sections of the Salpêtrière, at that time the municipally-supported Paris hospital for some four thousand to five thousand elderly and mostly indigent women. Most were permanent residents, for in modern terminology the place was a nursing home on a grand scale.

Charcot had long sought the appointment, for he had served part of his internship within the walls of the Salpêtrière and had soon realized the opportunities it provided for research into a wide variety of the neurological diseases that especially interested him. Now placed at last in a position to fulfill this long-standing ambition, he began immediately to transform the centuries-old refuge for elderly women into an up-to-date research center.

The Salpêtrière derived its name from its having been in the late Middle Ages a site where saltpeter (potassium nitrate), an essential ingredient of gunpowder, was made from human and animal body wastes. It was not a single structure, but an entire complex of forty-five buildings, with adjoining streets, squares and gardens, clustered around a beautiful and historic church. A small city in itself, most of it dated from the early seventeenth century, when it was one of the centers from which St. Vincent de Paul carried out his far-reaching charitable works. Late in that century, King Louis XIV had converted it into a vast hospice for the homeless, the insane, and beggars and prostitutes. Philippe Pinel had there carried out some of his reforms in the treatment of the insane. Hundreds of the Salpêtrière's residents had fallen victims to the September 1792 massacres during the Reign of Terror. Later it had been rehabilitated into the hospital for aged women, but none before Charcot had perceived its suitability as a vast medical and psychological research facility.

Over an eight-year span, 1862 to 1870, when his work there was temporarily interrupted by the Franco-Prussian War and the disorder that followed, Charcot effected his transformation of the Salpêtrière. By exerting great willpower, he persuaded the politicians of the Second Empire to give him whatever he asked for. The Salpêtrière became a virtual temple of the Medical Sciences, with Charcot as their presiding priest. Laboratories, examination and consulting rooms, a museum, an outpatient service that treated men as well as women, and a large auditorium for lectures and demonstrations, were all established.

Charcot assembled a staff of highly competent persons who were devoted to him and furthered his research and treatments at every step. An equally loyal assemblage of students was soon attracted to him, becoming his eager disciples. He himself was inspired—so he said—by the example of Guillaume Duchesne, who in the relative backwater of Boulogne had by long and patient study become the leading authority on neurology. That mantle would now pass to Charcot, whose work on scleroses, ataxia, and anthropathies made him by 1870 the foremost neurologist in the world.

Between 1871 and 1876 he became increasingly interested in epileptic and other convulsive seizures, and in the ability of hysterical persons to imitate them. That led him into an intensive study of hysteria in all forms—there was always a plentiful supply of cases at the Salpêtrière for him to examine—and he carefully described what he believed to be the unvarying successive stages of the full-blown hysterical crisis. Being at this time strongly influenced by Charles Richet, then still in the early stages of a long involvement with the history and effects of hypnotism, Charcot began to investigate whether hysteria could be hypnotically induced.

It did not take him long to be convinced that hysteria, along with practically all forms of mental action, could be readily initiated through hypnotic suggestion. However, he drew the additional and wholly erroneous conclusion that hypnotism was itself a form of hysteria, an aberrant mental function serving no useful purpose. And if hysteria was characterized by a succession of stages, so too — he argued — the hypnotic inducement of hysteria had to progress through a series of steps, each leading into the next.

As he prepared to announce to the world this grand discovery, as he believed it to be, Charcot was on a peak of eminence rarely attained by anyone in any branch of science. He was at this time, in the descriptions of several who knew him closely, an imposing figure physically as well as intellectually. Although short of stature, and on the stout side, he was vigorous and impulsive in his motions. He was always clean-shaven and his black hair was combed back flat. His facial expression was domineering and fiery; it could become ferocious if he was opposed. In general he somewhat resembled Napoleon in appearance, and if the similarity was remarked on by anyone, he never denied it.

There were varying reports about his family life. He had married a wealthy widow with a daughter, and they had a son, Jean, who later achieved fame as an Antarctic explorer. It was alleged the boy was forced by his imperious father to take up a medical career which he was only able to leave after Charcot's death, after which he sought the life of adventure he really craved. Some accounts claim that Charcot was a domestic tyrant altogether, while others state that his wife was very close to him, assisting in his work and with the charitable organizations to which he was a generous contributor.

Whatever he may have been privately, the public Charcot was a charismatic figure, a man of great and ostentatious wealth, sought out by the rich and powerful. He was a private medical consultant to Czars Alexander II and III. He received the Brazilian Emperor, Pedro II, at the palatial residence he maintained on the Boulevard Saint-Germaine. Fluent in English, Italian, and German, he was well versed in the works of Shakespeare, Dante, and Goethe. Every Tuesday night he held a sumptuous reception for Parisian high society, at which literature and the arts were the favorite topics. A capable artist himself, he utilized his vacations to search for and purchase fine specimens of art in all European countries. What he could not buy, he wrote about, with taste and accuracy.

Like Mesmer, he was acquiring the reputation of being a wonder-worker. Stories made the rounds of how he restored long-crippled patients to mobility and health simply by assuring them his examination showed no organic damage. Upon hearing that, they cast aside their braces and crutches and walked out the door. To the extent that these tales had any basis, they rested on his growing competence in hypnotism. There is little doubt that on occasion he did restore psychosomatic cripples to health by instilling the conviction they could walk. Yet he could not see hypnosis as a healing therapy. He was wholly taken up with proving, by actual demonstration, that hypnosis was merely an artificially induced hysteria, in all essential respects the same as naturally occurring hysteria.

"One is spontaneous, the other elicited. There is no other differentiation between them," Charcot declared in the paper he read to the French Academy of Sciences on January 13, 1882. This paper was his formal presentation to the world of his "grand discovery" of the equivalence of hysteria and hypnosis. His carefully reasoned and forcefully presented thesis convinced a large majority of the medical profession to accept his pronouncement. At one stroke it seemed to resolve many puzzling problems of neurotic and hysterical behavior, and to provide a final solution to the nature of hypnosis. Within weeks Charcot was being hailed not only across France but over all Continental Europe as a titan of science, a slayer of the dragons of superstition and gullibility that had so long obstructed a correct understanding of these aberrant mental states. Praise only slightly less adulatory was voiced by many practitioners in Britain and America.

The most important principles of the new doctrine had already been stated by Paul Richet in his book, *Clinical Study of Hystero-Epilepsy, or Grand Hysteria*, which was written in close consultation with Charcot. Appearing a few months before Charcot's "grand discovery" presentation to the Academy of Sciences, it had prepared both the public and medical professionals to be receptive to the principles he expounded.

Hysteria, Charcot stated, always progressed through four stages, though it was possible for a competent physician to stop a hysteric attack in any one of them. Sometimes the patient herself, who was almost always aware of what was happening, could halt the attack at any point. (In conformity with the medical usage of the time, which had uniformly assumed hysteria afflicted only women, Charcot always referred to hysteric patients in the female gender. He was emphatic, however, that hysteria could and did occur in men also, and this was regarded as evidence that he was a radically advanced medical pioneer.)

The first of these four stages Charcot identified as the convulsive one. The patient arched her body into a contortion of contracted muscles, with only the soles of the feet and the back of the head touching whatever surface she was on. This gave way to a general relaxation, sometimes with foaming at the mouth. The second stage, following immediately, Charcot called "clownism." The patient's muscles were again severely contracted, accompanied by jerking arm motions as if she were trying to repulse an unseen attacker. The third stage, which Charcot called the "passionate," consisted of a reliving, both verbally and with body movements, of erotic scenes from the patient's past. This stage was usually brief, rarely more than a few minutes. The fourth and final stage Charcot termed "hallucinatory," and was also very brief. The patient appeared to see all kinds of repulsive animals, such as toads and rats, passing in front of her.

Soon the patient would return to a normal state and be able to describe what had happened, including her hallucinations. This precise sequence of manifestations, which is unknown elsewhere in the medical record, was clearly the product of Charcot's suggestions to the patient. He had convinced himself, from having seen something like it in a limited number of cases, that the manifestation of hysteric symptoms would in every instance follow the same unvarying pattern. He made this prediction self-fulfilling through subtle indirect suggestions to the patient that her attacks of hysteria would always proceed in this way, except when either by her own efforts or his she would be able to halt them at some point. Charcot further conveyed to patients the suggestion that they could anticipate the onset of a hysteric attack, in the same way epileptics sense the approach of a seizure, by noting an onset of pain in what he termed the body's "hysterogenic zones," vaguely around the ovaries. (In men it was around the testicles.) Sometimes this forewarning enabled the patient or physician to cut short the attack or at least mitigate it.

The Salpêtrière technicians devised an ovarian belt which when worn tightly around that part of the body prevented most hysteric attacks. This again was a result of unintended suggestion to that effect. In reality there is no such malady, no such sequence of stages as Charcot claimed, no hysterogenic zone of the body, and hence no objective effect from wearing the ovarian belt. What Charcot had done was this: Among the mentally disturbed inmates of the Salpêtrière there were some with epileptic symptoms and seizures of varying kinds and degrees of intensity, and Charcot had inferred from these a specific hysteric ailment, to which he assigned a specific sequence of symptoms. When in actuality these did not always conform to his theorized stages, he used his authoritative personality and skill at implanting suggestions to instill in the patient the belief that she must behave in line with what he expected and wanted to demonstrate.

The patients caught on quickly. Even when not actually hypnotized, some possessed considerable role-playing talent and could convincingly simulate whatever convulsions or hallucinations Charcot expected from them. We shall see further on how the initial general acceptance of his diagnosis of a specific hysteric ailment, and its virtual equivalence with hypnosis, eroded as the medical and scientific observers of his twice-a-week public demonstrations (with Salpêtrière inmates for subjects) began to detect their essentially stage-performance character.

When Charcot turned his attention to hypnosis, he aserted it had three stages of progression, rather than the four of hysteria. To some extent the three hypnotic stages corresponded to the four hysteric phases, though there were also differences. The first hypnotic stage he identified as the cataleptic one, meaning the subject often underwent contraction of the muscles, similar to that in the first hysteric stage.

The second stage of hypnosis, according to Charcot, was the lethargic one, in which the subject appeared to be in deep sleep, without awareness or volition, and totally insensitive to pain. Instead of seeing this as a useful supplementary means of anesthesia in cases where chemically induced anesthesia is contraindicated (e.g., geriatric patients with pre-existing cardiac problems), Charcot saw it as a form of hysterical reaction to hypnotic induction. He admitted, grudgingly, that at least it was genuine; its occurrence in childbirth cases could not be faked, for no woman could keep from crying out if actually feeling labor pains.

Charcot's third and final hypnotic stage was somnambulism, which could follow either the first or second stages. This too he saw as merely a hysterical syndrome in which the subject acted out bodily motions without awareness of them.

That no such invariable stages were encountered in actual hypnotic practice, either therapeutic or in stage exhibitions, was obvious to hypnotists, both lay and professional, and a chorus of dissent rose from their ranks as Charcot's version became widely publicized. Leading this critical assault on

Charcot, Hippolyte Bernheim in 1884 published his book *On Suggestion in the Hypnotic and Sleep States*, in which—despite his error in equating hypnosis with natural sleep—he showed hypnosis was neither a neurosis nor a hysterical state. On the contrary, it was a normal physiological condition that could be elicited in virtually all individuals not suffering from mental imbalance.

Bernheim developed this line of argument in greater detail in further writings, culminating in an article in 1888 that listed eight irreconcilable points of difference between the Nancy School and the Salpêtrière position. These eight points could be summarized in the single statement that of all people, hysterics were the worst to use for case studies of hypnotism. Their emotional disorders and high incidence of autosuggestion made their responses to hypnotic treatment so formless and bizarre as to render them worthless for analysis.

Modern psychologists and hypnotherapists are rediscovering Bernheim's writings on hypnotic susceptibility and its variations, and finding them still accurate and precise, and readily adaptable into the terminology of today. Charcot's writings on hypnotism remain largely unpublished; psychology, from Bernheim on, has gone so far beyond his mostly erroneous concept of the relationship between hysteria and hypnosis, that they have at most merely curiosity value.

Another outspoken critic of Charcot and his methods with the Salpêtrière hysterics was the noted Belgian physician Joseph Delbouef, who observed them at first hand for several months in 1885-86. Delbouef wrote Charcot was being deceived by patients who enjoyed playing the spectacular roles in his lecture demonstrations of hysteria and hypnosis, and that some of his pupils were assisting these patients in carefully rehearsing their performances. To these and similar accusations from other visitors, Charcot reacted with anger and scorn. He could tolerate no criticism, even from those who were fearful the high reputation his earlier work in neuroses and sclerotic diseases had earned him, would now be undermined by his obsession with hysteria.

His twice-a-week public demonstrations at the Salpêtrière were admittedly in the rank of high drama and bravura, and readily convinced only those who were not careful in discerning the elements of showmanship that went into them. But it is true some of these demonstrations were of lasting worth, such as those in 1884-85 in which he expanded on work that had been started by English investigators into claims of paralytic damage by persons involved in railroad and other accidents. These paralyses, the English researchers asserted, were often the result of self-suggestion, and not of actual injuries. Charcot showed how this was indeed sometimes the case, and how the paralysis could be removed by hypnotic suggestions of healing. Even so, he still regarded these self-induced paralyses as merely hysterical reactions to the trauma of accidents.

Charcot's demonstrations were always in a set pattern. On Tuesday mornings at 9:30, in the presence of his students and the Salpêtrière's medical staff, he would examine new patients. In fact, these patients had previously been examined by his aides, who had reported to him the salient features of each case. Rapidly and with total self-confidence he gave his diagnoses of each, explaining even the most complicated array of symptoms. He had no interest in these patients as individuals. He rarely made any rounds of the wards or followed up on the progress of the patients at these Tuesday demonstrations. They merely served as objects on which Charcot displayed his clinical virtuosity. Often he over-simplified his instant diagnoses to more readily impress his audience. Whether the outcome proved him right or not did not seem to concern him.

On Friday mornings, lectures which were almost solely devoted to the expounding of Charcot's convictions about hysteria and hypnosis were open to attendance by distinguished visitors, French and foreign; as well as journalists and the merely curious. Large illustrations of subjects in the hysteric stages were prominently hung around the spacious lecture-room and on the podium. Promptly at 10:00 o'clock, Charcot would make his appearance, usually accompanied by favored visitors and students, for whom seats had been reserved in the front row.

He would begin in a low, hardly audible voice that gradually rose as he warmed up to his subject. With deft strokes of colored chalk on a blackboard, he outlined the salient particulars of the case he was discussing. Then the patient, most often a woman, would be brought in and put through her paces to demonstrate hypnotically induced hysteria in all of its stages. The great majority of the audience did not suspect that it was more than likely a rehearsed performance and they sat spellbound though the two hours the lectures usually lasted. At the end, all would crowd around Charcot, seeking to shake his hand or in French fashion embrace him, in admiration of his genius. "We were exhilarated, we were swept away in spite of ourselves," was attested by many.

Axel Munthe, the Swedish doctor later famed for his colorful autobiography *The Story of San Michele*, was one of Charcot's pupils who did not greatly value these exhibitions by his
master. He recalled in his life story how the patients chosen as
the center-pieces of the lectures would go through a circus
routine of acts, delightedly smelling ammonia when told it
was rose water, biting into charcoal offered as chocolate,
walking on all fours and barking like dogs, fleeing from a
glove under the impression it was a snake, kissing a top-hat in
the belief it was a baby. Munthe was disgusted by the way
these unfortunate, emotionally disturbed young women were
turned into guinea pigs, repeatedly hypnotized by doctors and
students, their brains skewed by confusing and contradictory
commands, their self-esteem either shattered or destructively
magnified by being put on public exhibit. Most of them had no
future outside of mental-case wards. Munthe's expulsion from
the Salpêtrière, by Charcot's order, came as the result of a
failed attempt to save one young woman from just such a fate
after her parents had appealed to him for help.

Actually, the number of subjects used by Charcot in his
Friday lectures was quite small—probably no more than two
or three dozen—in relation to the total population of the
Salpêtrière. Some became star performers whom he would call
on repeatedly because of the accuracy with which they acted
the roles he had decreed. That they were in fact acting, seems
not to have dawned on him.

The most noted of these Friday-morning stars was named
Blanche Whittman, who faultlessly went through all the three
stages of hypnosis and the four stages of hysteria every time
Charcot called on her. She was called "the Queen of the

Hysterics," and was the model for the woman going into full hysterical crisis in Pierre Brouillet's famous painting of Charcot lecturing to an intent audience. She was not popular among the staff and other patients; they found her bossy, capricious and rude.

Eventually she somehow obtained her release from the Salpêtrière and was admitted to another Paris hospital where she was attended by the psychologist Jules Janet, brother of Pierre Janet, whose contributions to the advancement of hypnotherapy will be discussed in our next chapter. Jules Janet hypnotized Blanche into a lethargic rather than cataleptic initial stage, and before long a second personality began to emerge. Blanche II was much more balanced and self-confident than the first Blanche, behind whom she had hidden, aware all the time of the role-playing that was being carried on but unable to do anything to stop it. Now finally set free by Jules Janet's careful treatment over several months, Blanche II returned to the Salpêtrière not as an exhibitory patient but as an employee in the photography laboratory. Later when a radiology laboratory was opened in the institution, she transferred there but soon fell victim to cancer from being exposed to x-ray radiation, the dangers of which were not then fully understood. Her death came only after years of suffering and multiple amputations. In this second phase of her life, Blanche Wittman retained some of her original characteristics; she was still domineering, capricious, and angry when questioned about having been Charcot's prize hysteric exhibit. Indeed, she would deny ever having been Blanche I or having performed for Charcot.

As the decade of the 1890s began, Charcot was becoming a discredited figure among serious hypnotherapists in both Europe and America. He continued to work frantically to find fresh support for his hypnosis-hysteria syndrome in increaseingly bizarre performances by subjects who were being coached by his pupils and staff, many of whom were doing it to cast ridicule on the master they no longer respected. The press continued to hail him as a Columbus of the hidden mysteries of the mind, and he retained a devoted though diminished following both at the Salpêtrière and in professional circles elsewhere. Among the public his name was still instantly recognized, and novelists unhesitatingly used him as a character—openly or under transparent guises—in the psychological fiction that was becoming popular.

Charcot was not unaware of the increasing doubts and skepticism about his work, and he must have had at least some suspicion that his hysteric patients were being cued by his staff and pupils. He is known to have expressed, in conversations with some intimates, the wish to start afresh his study of hypnotism from its earliest beginnings, and find the source of the errors he was now becoming aware of in his own interpretation and practice. But he could not seem to summon the resolve to halt what he was doing and start all over again. He was having chest pains and was also experiencing a growing dread he did not have enough time left to retrieve his mistakes.

In August of 1893 Charcot decided to take a vacation, in company with two of his most trusted pupils, at Vezelay in eastern France, where St. Bernard of Clairvaux had preached the Second Crusade in the mid-twelfth century. The morning after his arrival, he was found dead in his hotel room, victim of a heart attack at the age of sixty-eight. Three days later, on August 19, he was given a state funeral in Paris, to the accompaniment of lavish accolades in the press and from national officials.

Nevertheless, Charcot's glory faded with astonishing swiftness. Within six years no successor could be found to continue the demonstrations of his theories or to reaffirm their correctness. His most ardent pupils fell away from the doctrines he had propounded. The observances in 1925 of the centennial of his birth laid stress on his achievements in neurology and scarcely mentioned his preoccupation with hysteria and hypnosis from 1880 on. Yet it cannot be said Charcot left no real nor lasting impression on the field of hypnotherapy. His theories and practice strongly impressed two very different men of genius, who would carry something of his imprint into the new century and the use it would make—or fail to make—of hypnotism in the treatment of psychoses. They were Sigmund Freud and Pierre Janet. One finally abandoned hypnotism as a psychotherapy; the other was a bridge to its growth and acceptance.

Pierre Janet
1859 - 1947

CHAPTER 18
Pierre Janet: A Bridge Between Two Centuries

I n the entire roster of the great pioneers of hypnotherapy, there is one name that is usually omitted and often unrecognized even by those who have studied the history of hypnotism. That overlooked name is Pierre Janet, who in his long life of eighty-eight years arguably contributed more than anyone else to establishing hypnosis in the medical canon as a genuine phenomenon and a legitimate therapy in a defined category of ills of both the mind and the body.

Janet's accomplishment was low-keyed and rarely noted by the press or other publicity media. His personality, though by no means self-effacing, was the opposite of the flamboyance of Charcot and that of many of the exponents of the Nancy School and its offshoots. He did not break down any doors of the medical establishment—they had already been broken down many times in the course of the century since Mesmer battered at them. What he did was to consolidate, to assure that a sufficient foundation had been laid from which hypnotherapy could evolve further, whatever the inevitable setbacks it encountered in the future.

Carrying over into almost half of the twentieth century the mannerisms and attitudes of the previous century that had lastingly shaped his approach and outlook, Janet was dismissed by his later critics as a mere relic of a bygone age. Yet even before his death in 1947, some of those critics were becoming aware of his lasting influence and importance as a bridge-builder between the therapies of the nineteenth century and the very different ones of the world that emerged from the two great global conflicts. That valuation of Janet has grown stronger, though hardly as widely disseminated as it ought to be, with the approach of the twenty-first century.

He therefore earns a ranking as one of the world's greatest hypnotists. His life and achievements reflect the high intellectual status of France in the latter half of the nineteenth century, a milieu that made possible the emergence of radical and competing modes of thought and discernment, which have left lasting impressions on all subsequent developments of them throughout the world.

Pierre Janet came from a family that produced several other notable personages. They all shared common characteristics: upper middle class, agnostic, open-minded, non-political. Longevity was another trait that many of them shared. Janet's great-grandfather, Pierre-Etienne Janet, founded a bookshop on the Rue Sait-Jacques in Paris that attracted a large clientele from the Enlightenment circles of the decade preceding the French Revolution—perhaps Mesmer and his followers were among its patrons. The shop survived the Revolution and flourished under Napoleon and the Bourbon Restoration; its founder passed away in his eighty-fourth year, in the year of yet another revolution, that of 1830, that brought the French middle class into power under the Citizen-King, Louis Philippe.

One of the founder's six sons, Pierre-Honoré, also opened a Paris bookshop, specializing in musical works. He died rather young—which was unusual in the family—in 1832, leaving two sons whose offspring would reach distinguished heights in diverse fields of science. The younger of Pierre-Honoré's two sons, Paul Janet (1823-99), became a noted writer on philosophy, the author of three textbooks and several histories that for three generations were standard works in university classes. His son, Paul Junior, was one of the most noted of European electrical engineers of the late nineteenth and early twentieth centuries, and founder of two French schools in advanced electrotechnologies, as well as himself a student of and writer in philosophy, particularly in its relation to science.

The elder and younger Paul Janet both strongly influenced the development and early career of their nephew and cousin, Pierre Janet, in the models they furnished of application to study, theoretics and practice. Paul Janet the elder had already paralleled in his own life many of the experiences that would come to Pierre Janet, and this enabled uncle and nephew to relate to each other in ways that helped the latter to fulfill his potentialities. I will refer to these similarities as they come up in the account of Pierre's life.

Pierre Janet was the oldest of the three children of Pierre-Honoré's older son Jules, a legal editor, and his second wife, born Fanny Hummel. She was the daughter of a building contractor in Strasbourg, the capital of Alsace, where Jules had met her while on a visit in 1858 to his brother Paul, then teaching philosophy in the university there. (It will be recalled that Hippolyte Bernheim also came from Strasbourg, where in that year he was still a student, and later taught at the university.) In the mid-nineteenth century, before its seizure by Germany in 1870-71, Alsace was a fertile breeding-ground of new and provocative ideas, deriving from its mixture of French and German cultural roots. Pierre Janet drew on this inspiriting ambiance through his mother and the many new family connections that came with her.

Born on May 30, 1859, in Paris, where he would spend most of his life, Pierre Janet was a shy, timid and precociously studious little boy. It is said his uncle Paul had been the same at that early stage. At the age of ten, Pierre entered the preparatory school of the College Sainte-Barbe, one of the most prestigious in France, having been attended by many world-famed men including Saint Ignatius of Loyola, and Saint Francis Xavier, and Jean Calvin. His own education there was interrupted first by the traumatic and tragic events of the German siege of Paris and the bloody rising of the Paris Commune, followed by a severe nervous breakdown and intervals of depression, accompanied by a loss of the childhood Roman Catholic faith in which his mother had brought him up. Paul Janet had gone through a similar episode at about the same mid-teen age. Each emerged from it with new, stronger personalities, eager for difficult studies and ambitious for distinction in learned pursuits. Gone were the earlier shyness and timidity.

Graduating from Sainte-Barbe with a baccalaureate degree in 1878 at the age of nineteen, Pierre enrolled for a year of special preparatory training at the Lycee Louis-le-Grand (Paul Janet had done the same) before entering the always hotly contested examinations for admission to the Superior Normal School, as his uncle had done before him. The fortunate few who survived the rigorous screening were admitted to three intensive years of highest quality training for professorships, while also being allowed adequate free time to develop their own independent thinking. Pierre Janet passed the examinations of 1879 along with several who went on to achieve fame in their fields, including the noted sociologist Emile Durkheim.

The director of the Superior Normal School at that time was Ernest Bersot, who almost thirty years earlier had written and published a history of Mesmer and animal magnetism. The book had recently been re-issued in a new and enlarged edition, and Bersot's recommendation of it to Pierre Janet introduced him for the first time to hypnotism. Though it appears to have aroused Janet's interest, he did not immediately pursue the subject. He went on to gain a Bachelor of Science degree and to finish second among eight taking the final exam in philosophy. At the same time he was vastly fascinated by the first International Electrical Exhibition, held in Paris in 1881, to which his cousin Paul Janet the younger took him, and for a while he seems to have considered a career in electrical science.

Then the vast publicity attending Charcot's initial lecture in 1882, linking hypnosis and hysteria, turned Janet's interest back to hypnotism. He determined to become a physician with the ability to examine and judge hypnotism for himself. First, however, he had to become a teacher of philosophy for ten years to fulfill the obligation placed by the French government on the graduates of the Superior Normal School. He would otherwise have to serve three years in the military, which appealed to him even less.

Janet's first appointment as a philosophy teacher was to Châteauroux in central France. Midway through his first year he was summoned away to fill a teaching post that had suddenly become vacant in the port city of Le Havre on the

English Channel. It was a move of prime importance to his future. Châteauroux was a sleepy rural backwater where he might never have come to public notice. Le Havre was the opposite; a growing seaport of over 100,000 in population that had a controversial mayor whose activities were regularly publicized — and criticized — in the city's two uninhibited weekly newspapers.

As bustling seaports have tended to be from remotest antiquity, Le Havre was a wide-open town, with vice and prostitution rampant. The mayor, Jules Siegfried, a Protestant from Alsace who had left the province after the German annexation, was elected on a clean-up-the-city platform, but his efforts were unavailing. The two weekly papers vied in ridiculing him as a soured puritan, and featured stories about the performances in the port's theaters, which would have been banned in any community even slightly more straitlaced.

Probably the least indecorous of the performers on the Le Havre stages were the traveling hypnotists, such as Alfred d'Hondt, known professionally as Donato. They were skilled in eliciting all sorts of farcical behavior from the volunteers they enticed onto the stage. Any who attempted to expose these stage hypnotists ran the risk of being hooted and even physically assaulted by audiences which reveled in the exhibitions they watched. We do not know whether Janet, in his early years in Le Havre, ever attended any of these stage performances of hypnotism. It is known, however, he was aware of them and that they made him all the more determined to remove hypnotism from being put to such exploitative uses if, indeed, it could be applied to better ones. Of that he was not yet convinced, any more than he was of the cor-

rectness of Charcot's theory of the essential identity of hypnosis and hysteria. But before Janet could conduct his own
qualified investigations of hypnotism and arrive at his own
conclusions on its nature and uses, that weary decade of
teaching imposed on him by the state had to be lived through.
He did his best to teach philosophy with enthusiasm, and at
the conclusion of the school year in 1884 he delivered a
noteworthy lecture reminding his audience they should be
appreciative of the rights that had been won, after long and
fierce struggles, for the unrestricted study and teaching of free
philosophical thought. Sharing his house with a mathematician friend, a bachelor like himself, he cultivated a garden in
the spare time he had left from volunteer work at the city
hospital and his reading in psychiatry, which was in preparation for his intended career as a doctor treating psychopathic
disorders.

Janet was also looking for a subject for his doctoral thesis
and chose hallucinatory perceptions, which would have some
connection with his study of hypnotism. Needing an actual
patient around whom to construct a case study, he asked Dr.
Joseph Gibert, a local physician, to recommend one. Gibert
had no suitable one under his care at the time, but said he had
heard of a woman named Léonie who claimed to be capable of
being hypnotized from a distance. He located her and brought
her to Le Havre to be the subject for Janet's first trial of inducing the hypnotic state.

It did not prove difficult at all, he said; in fact, it was surprisingly easy. In a series of experiments lasting from September 24 to October 14, 1885, he readily hypnotized Léonie, both
in person and at a distance, and gave her hypnotic suggestions
that she carried out. Janet wrote up the results, rather over-

enthusiastically, in a paper he sent to his uncle Paul Janet, asking that it be presented to the Society for Psychology and Physiology in Paris. Paul Janet read it to the Society on November 30, 1885, at a meeting that was chaired by none less than Charcot himself. Because of its suggestion of telepathy, the paper created a sensation and its contents were soon widely circulated over western Europe including Britain.

A stream of curious visitors, among them such notables as Charles Richet and the British Psychical Research Society's Frederick Myers, now descended upon Pierre Janet at Le Havre. They were primarily seeking evidence, through further experiments with Léonie, to confirm the reality of telepathy, which they wanted to believe was the factor that enabled her to be hypnotized from a distance. This was a false trail, which as we shall see in a later chapter, had a devastating effect on the British medical profession's acceptance of hypnotherapy. A second series of Léonie experiments was carried out for the benefit of these visitors on April 21-24, 1886. They appeared to confirm she could be hypnotized at considerable distances. Janet however was no longer satisfied. He felt indirect suggestion was somehow involved, and in any case hypnosis and telepathy were two very different things.

Though Janet was able to keep the experiments from being reported in the press, he could not prevent word of them being quickly disseminated through the scientific community. To his dismay, the accounts quickly became distorted. He found himself being quoted at hearsay, with no attempt to check with him as to what he had actually said. Regretting he had written the paper about his first experiments with Léonie, he determined never again to confound hypnotism with parapsychology, and to conduct his future researches solely into the nature of hypnosis and hypnotic phenomena.

Janet was now able to start clinical work with hysterical patients in a small ward that the Le Havre hospital made available to him in the hours he could spare from teaching. Jokingly he referred to the ward as the Salle Saint-Charcot, it being then still the custom in France to name wards for saints. Even though not yet holding a medical degree, he felt by being able to treat patients who had not been conditioned at the Salpêtrière to exhibit symptoms that were expected, he would gain a much better understanding than Charcot and his pupils of the real processes of hysteria and how it related—if it did— to hypnosis. Janet soon concluded there was little connection between the two.

He was discovering any number of other aspects to hypnosis in the subjects he worked with, and in the extensive reading he now undertook in the works of Puységur, Bertrand and others among the pioneers of the art. All that the Nancy and Salpêtrière Schools had been claiming as brilliant new discoveries, had been found long ago by these so soon forgotten pathfinders. Hypnotism, it seemed to Janet, had developed through a continuous process of finding the same things over and over again, and was continuing to evolve through that same process. Janet was so impressed with this point he later collected several of the pioneering writings on hypnotism and in 1919 republished them in his great work of summation, *Psychological Healing* (English translation in two volumes, Macmillan, New York, 1925).

Three principal rules governed Janet's work with the patients he treated with hypnosis: always to have the initial examination in private, never before an audience (as in Charcot's theatrical exhibitions at the Salpêtrière); to keep an exact record of all that the subjects said and did; and to make an exhaustive investigation of their past history and treatments. He found that patients who had been previously hypnotized were sometimes still carrying out suggestions then implanted, and that this interfered with his own therapy for them.

In the summer of 1889 Janet defended his doctoral thesis before the traditional jury of the Sorbonne, and was awarded, a Doctor of Laws degree. Shortly thereafter he was one of the members, along with Liébeault, Bernheim and Forel, of the organizing committee of the first World Congress of Hypnotism, attended by such luminaries as William James and Sigmund Freud. In November of that year he commenced studying medicine, while also having admittance to Charcot's hysterical wards at the Salpêtrière. He still had two years to serve of his ten-year teaching commitment, but had moved from Le Havre to Paris where he taught at the Lycee-Louis-le-Grand and College Rollin. A little less than four years later, in July 1893, he won his medical degree, with Charcot one of the examiners.

Now that Janet was free from having to teach (though he continued to voluntarily hold classes at the College Rollin until 1897), and had become a qualified medical practitioner, he intended to pursue further research into the ramifications of the "subconscious"—a term he later claimed, correctly it would seem, to have originated. His attention was directed to such outward manifestations as amnesia, and how hypnosis might be a therapy for it. For this purpose, Charcot had provided a special laboratory for him at the Salpêtrière. Despite their many and serious differences over the nature of hysteria—differences that were, however, narrowing as

Charcot started to realize he had adopted extreme positions he could not maintain—the two men had a profound respect for each other. Had Charcot lived for a few more years, it is entirely possible that a fruitful collaboration with Janet could have taken shape. But it was not to be. Three weeks after Janet gained his medical degree, Charcot died suddenly. Though his successor as director of the Salpêtrière, Professor Fulgence Raymond, allowed Janet to have the full use of the laboratory provided for him, and Janet did accomplish productive results over a period of seventeen years, Raymond himself was not interested in studying the human psyche and how hypnosis affected it. As a result, Janet worked virtually alone, without the extensive collaboration from all departments of the Salpêtrière that would have been accorded him under Charcot.

Soon after his installation at the Salpêtrière, Janet published a philosophical textbook he had been working on at odd moments for twelve years. It expounds a pragmatic view of life and human responsibilities, somewhat akin to the philosophy of William James, though not derived from it.

In 1894 he married Marguerite Duchesne, a young woman he had met in Le Havre. Through the entire duration of their union, which lasted forty-nine years to her death in 1943, she was his close associate and assistant in his researches and labors. Their three children all attained some distinction.

Over the two decades ending with the outbreak of World War I in 1914, no name was more prominent or more respected in the field of psychology than that of Pierre Janet. He was constantly in demand for lectures in Continental Europe, Britain and the United States, which he visited in 1904 and again in 1906. His articles and treatises, that had begun appearing in the late 1880s, had a wide and influential readership. He was elected Professor of Experimental Psychology in 1902 at the College de France, and then made a member of the Institut de France, the most prestigious educational institution in the country. He could go no higher, but to these heights too he had been preceded by his uncle Paul Janet.

In his person, Pierre Janet was a little below medium height, somewhat stocky in build, with deep black hair and beard that grayed only very slowly with advancing age. His fame and reputation rested rather lightly on his shoulders. Although he was outgoing and always ready to talk at length, even in casual conversation, about his work, he was never over-assertive or dogmatic. He constantly stressed how essential the cooperation and guidance he had received from many had been. These included his uncle, as already noted; his brother Jules, two and a half years his junior, who was a prominent specialist in urology and himself an experimenter with hypnotherapy for psychosomatic disturbances of the urinary function, who had helped him in his early investigations of hypnotism; the small group of obscure magnetizers in the Norman town of Caen he had searched out while in Le Havre; and a host of others, from the lowly to the great. There was, in particular, Alfred Binet, who for several years worked on the theoretical foundation and history of hypnotism in close parallel with Janet, and each credited the other with the advances made. Unfortunately in 1893 a coolness grew between them for reasons still not understood, and Binet's once promising career faded out, and he withdrew into the solitariness in which he died in 1911 at the age of fifty-four. He had, however, left lasting legacies to psychology, he was the first to identify and describe the introvert and extrovert personalities, and the neurosis of fetishism.

It may have been that Janet was offended because the *Psychological Annual* which Binet founded in 1893 and published for some years carried only Binet's own articles and never any of Janet's. However that may have been, it was uncharacteristic of Janet that in this instance he seems to have made no move for reconciliation.

More typical of Janet's dealing with an adversary was his clash with Sigmund Freud in August 1913 at the International Congress of Medicine in London. The two had parted ways long before that over Janet's dismissal of Freud's attribution of an unreal symbolic importance to dreams, and a solely sexual origin for neuroses. Until that encounter, however, they had not stated their differences face to face. Now Janet stood up and in unusually sharp terms attacked Freud for claiming to have discovered the cathartic cure for neuroses, something which Janet claimed to have discovered earlier through hypnotic recall of buried traumas. Freud had cast aside hypnosis as a reliable means of uncovering these hidden psychic wounds, employing instead the interrogative method of psychoanalysis, which Janet scoffed at as being a speculative metaphysics with few if any roots in the real world.

The altercation between him and Freud on this memorable occasion was heated, and Carl Gustav Jung, who was present, had to intervene on Freud's behalf (though he too was parting from Freudian concepts of psychoanalysis) to keep it from getting totally out of hand. Janet soon cooled off and expressed his regrets at having been so intemperate in his remarks. A few months later, when both he and Freud were attending a meeting of the Society of Psychotherapy, at which Freud was attacked in a way that to Janet seemed unjust, he rose spiritedly to his defense. And when, during the war that broke out soon thereafter, French psychologists refused to discuss anything of Freud's because he was a citizen of an enemy country, Austria, Janet opposed such chauvinism. Freud, however, did not respond to these gestures in kind. To him, the break with Janet was final. When in the old age of both men Janet sought to call on him at Vienna in 1937, Freud refused to see him.

Janet did not limit his acquaintances to persons only in his own fields of activity. He was at home with writers and naturalists. It was hardly surprising that, like Charcot, at least one fictional character in a novel was based on him (Dr. Daumier, a sympathetic physician of the Salpêtrière, in Marcel Prevost's 1893 novel, *Autumn of a Woman*). As Janet's income grew, he associated more and more with wealthy and aristo- cratic people, though even then he chose the more cultured types. In 1907 he moved to a spacious apartment on the Rue de Varennes, in the St. Germain suburb of Paris that was the setting of Marcel Proust's novels, which he liked. Here he resided until his death forty years later.

The only people for whom Janet had an aversion were journalists. He was continually in fear of being misquoted and of having more read into his remarks than he intended. He refused all requests for interviews, and only once, in 1928, allowed a reporter to quote part of a conversation he had with another person in the reporter's presence. And it is clearly due to this avoidance of headlines, as well as his placing undue emphasis on what he believed were merely the correct proce- dural steps for integrating hypnotherapy into the medical and psychological canons, that there has been so total an amnesia in his own profession—let alone among the general public—of the achievements of Pierre Janet in hypnosis.

Between 1890 and 1920 the medical profession, by and large, accepted hypnosis as real, and sometimes useful. It did so because Janet was successful in demonstrating both points, so quietly and yet convincingly, no one felt compelled to dispute them. Soon it was easy to forget they had once been resisted so strongly, and equally easy to start forgetting who had largely brought about this change. In the psychiatric field, where hypnotism has scored some of its greatest successes, the dominance of Freud delayed, and even now holds up, a general acceptance. Nevertheless, Janet's work made it easier for hypnosis to be smoothly integrated into the practice of those who on this point do not follow Freud.

Janet was cautious and methodical in all that he did. For every patient or subject, he kept a meticulous case file. Eventually they totaled over five thousand, and would be a priceless resource for therapists today. However, under a strict injunction in his will, all were destroyed after his death. He had feared they would be used in ways that would violate the privacy of those he had treated. Even though most were no longer living, their families or heirs could still be hurt by inappropriate disclosures.

There are, nevertheless, several case histories preserved in his writings that are of great value to practitioners today. In all of them, the real identities and places of residence of the subjects were carefully concealed. All narrate successful treatments of conditions resulting from obsessions and phobias that stemmed from suppressed traumas in the individual's past, and which through hypnotic recall were confronted and expelled. Symptomatic relief for the psychoses was also achieved through hypnotic suggestion. Recall was, however, the principal agency of cure, as it has remained in practically all later modes of psychiatry, which rarely remembers to credit Janet with its first discovery and application.

His numerous, carefully executed experiments with hypnosis also revealed to him the extraordinary capacity of the subconscious to fantasize and to construct elaborate scenarios that the personality feels compelled to act out. This faculty — what Janet's English friend Frederick Myers termed the mythopoetic function—makes possible literary and dramatic creation, but unless controlled can cripple a person emotionally and psychically. To counteract its excessive influence, Janet agreed with another distinguished fellow researcher into the mysteries of the mind, Henri Bergson, that the most effective resource was to direct the subject's attention to the present realities of the world. All this is now pretty much standard psychiatric doctrine; it had not been so before Janet and others like Bergson of his generation defined the concepts and how to apply them. That hypnosis, as employed by Janet, had been instrumental in the basic advances, was often lost sight of in their transmission to later practitioners.

Though Janet continued to be respected and sought out among his colleagues in psychology, and was acclaimed on further lecture tours in the United States, Mexico and South America from 1921 to 1933, his direct influence was waning. His cautious, step-by-step, low-keyed methods did not appeal to the rising psychologists of the new century. What those methods had achieved had passed almost unnoticed into the canon of practice, but there was now little patience to listen further to the man from whom they had come.

All the same, Janet—though sometimes admitting to being disheartened at the way the world was going—continued to be active, writing and researching and treating patients. At seventy-seven he made his last visit to America, to participate in Harvard's 300th anniversary celebration. Though at first fleeing the German invasion in 1940 to go to the unoccupied south of France, he soon decided it was his duty to share the sufferings of the French people under the Nazi heel, and returned to his Paris apartment. During the four years of the enemy occupation, his wife, his brother Jules, his son Michel, his sister Marguerite and son-in-law Dr. Edouard Pichon, as well as his wife's sister, all died from various causes related to the severe living conditions of the time. Only his two daughters were left to him. Yet with the liberation and coming of peace in 1945, Janet—now in his mid-eighties—began taking courses offered by a pupil, Dr. Jean Dellay, on the increasingly prevalent psychotic effects of drugs. He also started writing a book on the psychology of belief, and at the age of eighty-six made a lecture tour of Switzerland.

He was looking forward to new findings when death took him in his sleep on February 24, 1947, at the age of eighty-seven. He was buried in the family grave in the cemetery of Bourg-la-Reine. The epitaph on his tomb bears this simple inscription: PIERRE JANET + 1859-1947.

Sigmund Freud
1836-1939

CHAPTER 19
Freud's Abandonment of Hypnotism

A t this point our gallery of the world's greatest hypnotists should properly have an empty portrait frame, which, because of his superior genius, would have been filled by Sigmund Freud. Had he pursued his early interest in hypnotism, he could indeed have ranked as one of its greatest interpreters—perhaps the greatest of all. As a practicing hypnotist, however, he would probably have fallen short of the highest rating, for he was not adept in hypnotizing his patients, and this was doubtless a factor in his eventual decision to abandon hypnosis as a therapeutic agent. With persistence he might have acquired greater facility in the induction of hypnosis, but it would never have been as easy for him as it was for most of the leading hypnotists.

The other factors that led Freud to discard hypnosis as a principal tool of the psychoanalytic therapy he originated, and which is his claim to immortality, are found in his complex background and personality. He was a product of a rare period in European history that saw the Jewish population of the Austro-Hungarian Empire gain an unprecedented degree of toleration and assimilation into its social fabric. This came about as a result of the 1848 "Year of Rebellions," which, though failing to overthrow the Habsburg Monarchy, shook it to its roots and compelled a drastic re-ordering of the relation of the dominant German minority to the more numerous subject nationalities.

Among these, the Jews (though not a separate nationality in the strict sense) already had an economic and social status above the rest. From 1852 on, virtually all the long-standing discriminatory laws and regulations applying to Jews were dropped. Within the span of a generation, the Austrian part of the Empire — and especially its capital, Vienna, which already possessed a cosmopolitan flavor rivaled only by Paris — saw Jews become prominent in business, finance, the law, and most prominently in medicine and related fields.

It is hardly surprising that many Jews were bewildered by this sudden alteration of what had been in many ways a humiliating position of social subservience to one where they could attain just about any distinction they might want (except in the caste-dominated military profession) by their own merits. Freud's father, Jacob Freud, would appear to have been one of those who did not quite know what to make of this new state of things.

He had been a modestly prosperous traveling dealer in wool cloth, based in the small town of Freiberg, Moravia (now Pribor, Czechoslovakia). Born about 1815, he had buried two wives and married a third by the time he decided in the late 1850s to seek a wider field for his business, first at Leipzig in Saxony where Jewish emancipation was also underway, and then in Vienna. Sigmund Freud, born on May 6, 1856 (four years before the family's departure from Freiberg) was the first child of the third marriage, which would produce six more offspring after him. There were already two sons from the first marriage, of which the oldest was married and had a son.

Jacob Freud's third wife, Sigmund Freud's mother, was Amalia Nathanson, whose father Jacob had come originally from the Ukraine—whether from the Austro-Hungarian or Russian side of the border is not clear, but in any event he appears to have had a profitable stake in the transshipment business in the Black Sea port of Odessa. His daughter probably inherited a share of that, and probably added to it through shrewd investments in the shipping trade, for it would seem that it was her money that ran the Freud household. Her husband became withdrawn, frequenting coffee shops and reading religious books, and doing little or nothing to further his own business interests. A mere shadow beside her domineering and authoritarian personality, he was resented by young Sigmund who felt deprived of a father-figure he could look up to.

It was an ill-balanced family in other aspects too, though not dysfunctional in the modern sense. The vast age difference between Sigmund and his older brothers, and his being only slightly older than his nephew, did not make for harmony. But somehow, under what might be considered the tempestuous but benign tyranny of his mother, the family stayed together and managed to share in some of the good things of Viennese life. There were new books and theater trips and piano lessons and commissioning of family portrait paintings and summer vacations at Moravian resorts, and from somewhere the money came for the advanced education for which Sigmund demonstrated his aptitude and readiness. His mother doted on him, then and throughout his later career, until her death at ninety-five in 1931.

As a youth, Freud was a careful student, having decided early to make medicine his career, but remained uncertain as to which branch of it he would choose to practice. In 1873 he commenced his studies at the University of Vienna medical school, and took his degree in medicine in 1881. Those eight years must have been a strain on the family finances. For the last six of those years he studied under Ernst Brücke, a rigid authoritarian Prussian and unyielding foe of any psychology not founded on strictly materialist bases. From him Freud acquired the hatred for religion — especially all its organized forms — that characterizes his mature work, and perhaps also a strengthening of his already innate bias against the mind possessing any powers underived from sense experience. This would in time block any lasting commitment to hypnosis as a therapy, though for a brief period he was strongly attracted to it.

That attraction had its beginnings in Freud's having met, in the latter part of his studies in Brücke's laboratory, a physician named Josef Breuer who was pursuing a research project of his own. Breuer was then in his late thirties, a Viennese Jew of wide and varied scientific and cultural interests, who made friends easily and usually retained them by being uncritical and approachable. Freud, still unable to find his niche even after receiving his medical degree in March 1881, frequently conversed with Breuer and heard from him about the usefulness of hypnosis in treating difficult cases of psychosis.

One such case that Breuer had just finished with was that of a young woman patient whose real identity was hidden under the pseudonym Anna O. The actual circumstances of this case became clouded over a decade later with embellishments by Breuer that had little or no relation to fact. For all his mental acumen and professional expertise (he had done, among other achievements, a noted study of how the body's sense of balance is controlled by the inner ear labyrinth) Breuer appears to have been given to what Germans call *weaving maerchen*, i.e. the concocting of tales to gratify those we wish to please. As we shall see, Freud at that time was in need of a case history to support his short-lived enthusiasm for hypnotherapy, and Breuer obliged him by embellishing the Anna O story.

When it was first told to Freud in the fall of 1882, it was simply a matter-of-fact account that heightened his growing interest in hypnosis as a mode of treatment. At the time he could not do much to develop that interest, as he had finally decided to enter a three year internship in surgery and psychiatry in the old Vienna General Hospital, then one of the most famous teaching centers in the world. This, Freud hoped, would enable him to go into private practice with some reputation that would attract patients. He would need them for an income to support a family, for by this time he was engaged to marry.

Upon completing the internship, he applied for a six months' travel grant to do research abroad. Having obtained it, he went to Paris with the intention of studying at the Salpêtrière hospital under Jean Martin Charcot, then approaching the zenith of his fame. From October 1885 to April 1886, Freud attended a total of seventeen weeks of Charcot's lectures and demonstrations on hysteria, and came away strongly convinced of the French master's greatness. On his return to Vienna, Freud opened an office for practicing treatment of nervous diseases and a little later married his fiancee, Martha Bernays.

Initially, in his practice, Freud sought to apply Charcot's principles; that hysterical symptoms could be relieved or cured by hypnotic suggestion, and conversely that they could be hypnotically initiated or stimulated. Very soon, though, Freud began to develop a further principle that Charcot had left vague and poorly defined. This was that hysterical symptoms were primarily the product of stubbornly-held ideas. The "ideogenic concept," as it came to be called, soon dominanted Freud's treatment of hysteria cases, and at this stage he was finding hypnosis to be effective in diagnosing such "fixed" ideas and purging them from the patient's mind through a process called "catharsis" — a purifying or figurative cleansing of the emotions.

By this time he had made the acquaintance of Wilhelm Fliess, a Berlin specialist in ear and nose diseases, and a powerful thinker on the functioning of the human psyche, who would in a few years displace Breuer as Freud's principal confidante and influence on his theories. As Fliess had not yet taken a strongly anti-hypnosis position and was still somewhat neutral toward it, Freud did not hesitate to write him on December 2, 1887, about "all sorts of small but peculiar successes" he was having with hypnotherapy of hysteric patients.

Catharsis was a much-discussed topic during the decade of the 1880s, owing to the publication of a book by Jacob Bernays, an uncle of Freud's wife, which sought to relate Aristotle's classic description of mental and spiritual purging to modern conditions. It played a key role, as we shall see, in the Anna O episode and its later misinterpretation and elaboration by Breuer and Freud. The latter was still—despite his "small successes"—feeling his way around, so to speak, in the hypnotic discipline and its application to catharsis.

Having come to doubt that Charcot's obsessional identification of hysteria and hypnosis was correct, Freud decided to investigate for himself how the Nancy School was utilizing hypnotherapy. In 1889, after having translated and published one of Bernheim's handbooks, he made an extended visit to Nancy and discussed at length with both Bernheim and Liébeault their mode of treatment. Watching the simplicity and speed of the Nancy procedures—usually two or three sessions sufficed to identify the fixed idea that was causing the patient's symptoms, and to get rid of it by hypnotic suggestion—Freud now started to have a fresh doubt as to whether there was any need for the more involved cathartic process. Then he swung around again to at least a modified acceptance of the latter. This was after reading some of Janet's writings, especially *Psychological Automatism*, in which case histories were cited of the recovery through hypnotic recall of an original traumatic event, the hidden psychotic influence of which was then removed by hypnotic suggestion.

Freud may have met Janet at the 1889 World Congress on Hypnotism at Paris, which he attended during his stay in France that year. Although there is no direct proof of such a meeting, Janet's influence on Freud is clearly evident through the first half of the 1890s. Where Breuer had been leading him in the direction of a step-by-step recall of a whole sequence of suppressed traumas in a patient's past, on Freud's return from Paris he followed Janet in concentrating on the recall and elimination of a single episode, of which any later ones were probably mere offshoots.

Yet Freud could not commit himself to any one approach. He was torn between his lingering admiration for Charcot as the greatest living neurologist, his attraction to the simplicity of the Nancy School's suggestive therapeutics, and the greater satisfaction he found in the more thorough methods of Breuer. And behind all these were the first stirrings of wholly new ideas of psychology, implanted by Fliess in his expanding correspondence with Freud, and destined to transform psychotherapy to an unprecedented degree.

The vacillations in Freud's own course at that time are clearly discernible in his various public statements between 1889 and 1895. On April 27, 1892, he told the Viennese Medical Club that Bernheim's mode and utilization of hypnosis and hypnotherapy were superior to all others, and advised all physicians to go to Nancy and learn it at first hand. In a lecture to the same club a year later he supported, with only a slight modification from Janet, Charcot's ascribing of hysterical paralyses to unconscious self-hypnosis. And in the interval between those two conflicting statements, he had delivered a paper to the club in which he described the new theory he was working on with Breuer, that involved a detailed search for past traumas and their one-by-one cathartic removal.

Freud was in fact working with Breuer on a book that would have a half-dozen case histories, including Breuer's pioneering experience with Anna O, of hysterics cured by hypnotic recall and catharsis of hidden traumas. Early in 1893, Freud was so impatient to get the book published, even though only two of the case histories (Anna O and Freud's patient Emmy von N) had been written, that he issued these two as a separate item under the title of *A Preliminary Communication on Studies on Hysteria*. It was well received by the Vienna medical profession and favorably reviewed in their journals. Perhaps that is why Freud was so anxious for publication; he felt a need for peer approval to confirm that he was on the right track.

However, a dozen years had passed since Breuer's treatment of Anna O, and in the retelling of it many times over that span, he had built it up into an elaborate fantasy that later researchers found difficult to square with the facts. Breuer seems to have wanted to go out of his way to oblige Freud with a dramatic case history in support of their mutual thesis of recall and catharsis; maybe he had sensed a fraying of their friendship and wanted to satisfy Freud's demand for something so out of the ordinary as to compel acceptance by its very strangeness.

Anna O was in reality Bertha Pappenheim, a highly educated and cultivated young lady from one of the most distinguished of Vienna's old Jewish families. In 1880, at the age of twenty, she became ill with what were clearly psychosomatic ailments from the stress involved in nursing her terminally ill father. Following his death in April 1881, she gradually recovered and went on to a notable career as philanthropist and social worker, and devotee of the arts. She died in 1936 at seventy-six, and was honored on a West German postage stamp in 1953.

While it can hardly be questioned that through Breuer's employment of hypnosis Bertha Pappenheim was able to identify and dismiss the traumas resulting from her father's unexpected illness, it is also clear that the account of that treatment, as printed in the *Preliminary Communication* of 1893 and in the book *Studies on Hysteria* published two years later, is largely fictitious. It covers a far longer span of time than the actual duration of her care under Breuer, and abounds in exactness of coincidence that cannot be found in any other authentic hypnotherapy case history. In addition, Bertha Pappenheim was clearly a first-rate actress, and to a large extent brought about her own cure, acting out what had made her ill and manipulating Breuer's reactions to her doubtless secret amusement and enjoyment.

To what extent Freud may have suspected that the Anna O story had been greatly exaggerated is unascertainable. He needed the story for his book, for the other case histories in it fell far short in narrative interest. Collectively, however, along with Anna O, they make the case that—in Freud's words— "what hysterics suffer from is reminiscences," and that most of those are hidden and have to be recalled with the tool of hypnosis, which will also get rid of them. Further, that this traumatic hidden memory has a life of its own; it continues to wreak harm until it is exposed and dealt with.

At that point, in 1895, Freud stood on the threshold of a psychoanalysis mediated through and by hypnosis. By now, however, he was undergoing a severe psychic crisis of his own. From it would come in a few years both his recovery and his masterwork, *The Interpretation of Dreams*, which marked his emergence as the originator and disseminator of the premier psychiatric doctrine and therapy of this century. In that achievement, hypnotism no longer had a share. Freud had fallen out with Breuer and Fliess, and now saw hypnosis as an outworn superstition. This led to Freud's claim that his doctrine of psychoanalysis was not only distinct from all others that had preceded it, but that it superseded and replaced them all. Though all previous history of psychotherapy stood in refutation of this assertion, it was widely accepted, and hypnotism has had to progress through the past ninety years on a path separate from though parallel to the one Freud pioneered. It may be that they are now at last converging.

When the Nazis invaded Austria in 1938, they burned Freud's books and banned his theories. Freud fled to England, where he died of cancer of the jaw and palate in London on September 23, 1939.

Svengali
The film was based on "Trilby," the 1894 novel by George du Maurier

CHAPTER 20
British Hypnotism's Rocky Road

While hypnotherapy was making its great strides in France through the Nancy School, and was kept in the public eye with the Charcot-Nancy controversy, across the English Channel the quarter-century from 1865 to nearly 1890 was one of quiet progress. Though there were no outstanding figures following in the footsteps of Braid, Esdaile, and Elliotson, as pioneers and innovators, a silent growth of acceptance by the medical profession continued through this period, especially during its earlier phase. However, after about 1888 there was a change, leading to a pronounced aversion on the part of medical men to even mentioning hypnotism. While many still used it, they cautioned patients not to talk about it, and articles on hypnotism disappeared from British medical journals.

The principal reason for casting hypnotism under a cloud of silent disapproval was the rapid growth in public awareness of the Society for Psychical Research, founded in 1882 by Frederic H. W. Myers, a flamboyant personality who sought by a wide variety of sensationalistic experiments to prove the survival of human personality after death. Hypnotism was a prominent feature in some of these experiments, and was not always used with proper caution and restraint. It is not surprising that reputable physicians did not want to be associated with the dubious practices of Myers and his colleagues, though the psychic researchers won a large following at all levels of British society.

Prominently associated with Myers in founding the Psychical Research group was a very different personality, Edmund Gurney, born in 1847 to a prominent and distinguished family. A remarkably handsome man, he was also endowed with a wide-ranging intellect and an enormous capacity for work. Esteemed among all of his broad circle of friends and acquaintances as a man of uncompromising integrity and probity, he seemed fitted for success in whatever he undertook. His greatest ambition was to be a musical performer, but he lacked the skill for this and felt unfulfilled and unsatisfied despite the critical acclaim for his book on musical theory, *The Power of Sound,* which appeared in 1880. Realizing by then that he could not compose music any more than he could play it — he could only write about it, far better than most, but that was not enough for him — he tried law and medicine, but found he was too sensitive to the feelings of others to succeed in either.

In addition to his other psychological handicaps, Gurney was a manic-depressive, alternating between moods of boundless enthusiasm and crushing despair. He needed above all else some cause into whose service he could pour all of his vast energy, and his zeal for which would sustain him in his dark hours. In Myers' crusade to find the holy grail of survival after death, he found that cause. From 1881 on he dedicated himself unreservedly to it, working impossibly long hours as the Society's secretary, editor of its journal and proceedings, and author-compiler of the two-volume, 1300-page work on *Phantasms of the Living* that the Society published in 1886. He did all this without pay, being a person of independent means.

His principal interest gradually became the quest for evidence of thought-transference (i.e., telepathy) over long distances through hypnotic trance. With two young men, one of whom had some skill in hypnotizing; he carried out in the resort town of Brighton a series of experiments that appeared to confirm the reality of this. Since he had no hypnotic ability himself, Gurney had to rely on the honesty of these collaborators. When in June 1888 he discovered that they had been deceiving him, it was too much for him to bear. He had already become highly skeptical of many of the Society's asserted proofs of survival after death. In a lonely hotel room he committed suicide by inhaling chloroform, in a way that enabled his family and friends to publicly label his death an accident. There was never any doubt, though, among those who had known him, and in medical circles generally, that it was suicide.

This marked a very dark moment for the practice of hypnotherapy in Britain. Hypnotism, rather than Gurney's mistaken attempt to use it for telepathy, took the blame both among doctors and the public for having brought about the ruin of so brilliant a man. For about a year, there was real danger that the British medical profession would act to ban the practice of hypnotherapy altogether. That this was averted, and the medical employment of hypnosis in Britain proceeded to wider use in the twentieth century, was mainly due to the existence of a core group of practitioners who had developed their skills in hypnotherapy during the silent quarter-century, and were prepared to fight for its continuance.

The waging of that struggle drew heavily on the energies and talents of this core group, preventing them from achieving a rank among the great hypnotists of the world. This is not to disparage them in any way, but simply to state the fact. By opposing an adverse tide of opinion among their peers, in the press, and in the public mind they saved what they believed was useful and helpful, but at the cost of some of their own prospects of advancement.

At the head of this core group must be placed J. Milne Bramwell, who did not begin using hypnosis in his own private medical practice until 1889, when the anti-hypnotism uproar in the wake of the Gurney suicide was at its peak. He quickly became convinced of the therapeutic value of hypnosis, and being a wholly open-minded person, agreed to serve on a committee that the Society for Psychical Research set up in 1893 to resolve once and for all whether any connection existed between hypnosis and telepathy. In two papers that he wrote for the Society's Proceedings in 1896, Bramwell presented the total lack of evidence, even with very good hypnotic subjects, for telepathic results, leaving aside entirely the question of whether telepathy was itself a real phenomenon. With that, he severed all further connection with the matter, his participation on the committee and the thoroughness of his two reports having served to notably lessen the agitation against hypnotism.

Bramwell had meantime been familiarizing himself with the teachings of the Nancy School, which he visited in person. He also researched the careers of his great British predecessors, especially James Braid, whose pioneering work he presented anew to the medical practitioners of his own time. Finally in 1903 he published his classic book, *Hypnotism: Its History, Practice and Theory.* For over two decades it was the standard work on the subject in English, and did much to counteract the negativity of the London surgeon Ernest Hart's 1896 book *Hypnotism, Mesmerism and the New Witchcraft,* which sought to dismiss hypnotherapy as "rarely useful, generally useless and often injurious." That was effectively refuted by the numerous detailed accounts that Bramwell provided of cures and alleviations achieved through hypnotherapy in his own practice.

Next to Bramwell, Charles Lloyd Tuckey was the most influential British defender of the clinical use of hypnotism in the aftermath of the Gurney incident. His courageous founding on October 8, 1889, of the Hypnotic Society of Britain did more than anything else to reverse the demand that had been growing for banning hypnotherapy. A disciple of Liébeault and the Nancy School, Tuckey was ahead of his time in avoiding induction techniques that unduly suppressed the client's own personality. He foreshadowed the client-centered approach that would become common among hypnotherapists of the latter half of the twentieth century.

R. W. Felkin, whose primary field of expertise at the University of Edinburgh was tropical medicine, utilized hypnotherapy in his practice, employing Nancy School techniques. His book *Hypnotism, or Psycho-Therapeutics,* published in 1890, was an early rebuff to the anti-hypnosis agitation. Felkin investigated the hypnotism-at-a-distance phenomenon, which Bramwell had also done, and agreed with him that hypnosis had no connection with telepathy. People could be hypnotized over the telephone, or even by letter, but in all such cases there was a clearly identifiable material mode of transmitting the suggestion.

This conclusion was further reinforced by the work of George C. Kingsbury. Kingsbury stated in his book *The Practice of Hypnotic Suggestion: A Handbook for the Medical Profession*, published in London in 1891, that his own experiments, and those of others he cited, added up to the simple fact that any object could be used to convey a suggestive signal over a distance limited only by how far it could be seen or heard. Kingsbury was also a disciple of the Nancy School and had visited Liébeault. In his book he objected to the growing use among some practitioners of chemicals such as chloroform, morphine, and nitrite of amyl as agents of hypnotic induction. Such, he felt, did not induce true hypnotic trance, but only a narcotized sleep. He also urged hypnotherapists to stop relying (as some were still doing) on magnets as aids to induction.

Ralph Harry Vincent's *The Elements of Hypnotism* was the most widely read and used of the medical-level books on hypnotherapy that appeared in England during the 1890s. First published in 1893, it went through a second edition four years later. What made it particularly useful was its comprehensive review of all the recent advances on the European Continent. In this respect it had no rival until Bramwell's book superseded it in 1903. In his own practice, Vincent followed mainly the Nancy School techniques, and like most hypnotherapists of that period was convinced that morning inductions yielded the most beneficial results.

In addition to their struggle to overcome the negative impression of hypnotism resulting from the Gurney episode, all of these noted British proponents and practitioners of hypnotherapy in this final decade of the nineteenth century had also to contend with the even worse impression created in 1894 by the publication of George Du Maurier's sensational novel, *Trilby*. This story is about a wistful Irish waif named Trilby who is a model in Paris' Latin Quarter, then considered the depths of decadence and wickedness. She is hypnotized by an artful villain named Svengali into being a concert singer of a talent far beyond what she naturally possesses. The novel enthralled the public on both sides of the Atlantic. Its setting, in the world of Parisian art students, one of whom the author himself had been nearly half a century earlier, was sufficiently realistic to make most readers believe it was based on fact. After all, hadn't there always been a widespread suspicion that hypnotism enabled wicked men to place beautiful women in their power? For tens of thousands of readers *Trilby* confirmed this suspicion, especially since the lovely Irish heroine's hypnotist was a scoundrel who, as her concert manager, made a fortune by exploiting her. When finally she snaps out of her trance, recognizes her old art student friends in the audience, and immediately loses her singing ability, the villainous Svengali drops dead from a heart attack. Trilby herself dies some time afterward, for Victorian mores required that she be punished, despite all her charms and good qualities, for having posed nude in her modeling days, and because she cohabited — though involuntarily — with her rascally hypnotist.

It took more than a little courage on the part of the British practitioners of hypnotherapy mentioned above, as well as the many of lesser note to continue with it during the two years or so that the *Trilby* craze whipped the British public into a hysteria of demand for the outlawing of it. However, the majority of the medical profession had, by 1894, moved beyond the anti-hypnotism agitation that followed the Gurney suicide, and they firmly resisted all attempts at making hypnotism illegal. The one exception was a Dr. Norman Kerr, who waged a one-man crusade seeking prohibition of all public displays of hypnotism, including medical teaching seminars, and the restriction of its use by physicians to last-resort cases in which nothing else had availed to relieve pain. Hypnotism, he declared, led to deterioration of the brain function, physical decadence, and moral perversion. Kerr did not succeed with his campaign in Britain, though some coun-tries — notably Belgium, Argentina, and the Austro-Hungarian Empire — enacted laws during the 1890s limiting hypnotism to medically licensed practitioners. These stemmed from per-ceived excesses in stage exhibitions of hypnotism, and not from the *Trilby* hysteria, which affected mainly Britain and to a lesser extent the United States.

Du Maurier, the creator of *Trilby*, had been for thirty years the prominent illustrator of the humorous weekly *Punch* and also of other periodicals and books. He did not take up novel-writing until his late fifties. *Trilby*, published when he was sixty, was his second book. Like the first, *Peter Ibbetson,* it had numerous illustrations by the author which made his heroine very real to readers, so much so that her fate affected them as much as if she had been an actual person.

In *Peter Ibbetson*, Du Maurier had made use of a sort of self-hypnosis on the part of his two main characters to enable them to live a life of fantasy which they could not do in the real world. For *Trilby*, he drew on his memory of having witnessed, back in his art student days, a fellow student and noted exponent of the free-living Bohemian lifestyle, Felix Moscheles—son of the famous pianist of the same name—hypnotizing a pretty Belgian shopgirl. The fictional Trilby was modeled on her, and on her real-life descent from an engaging sweetness and innocence to a career of promiscuity.

The outcry against hypnotism in Britain generated by *Trilby* might have lasted longer had not Du Maurier died on October 8, 1896, two years after the book's publication. He had often expressed amazement at the way his story was taken so seriously by the public; to him it had been merely a pleasant fantasy and a re-living of long-ago memories. The numerous press obituaries for him emphasized this, and apparently had an immediate effect in subduing the public clamor. Nevertheless, the names of Trilby and Svengali had permanently entered the English language as synonyms for abuse of hypnotism, and to this day they color some people's perception of the art.

Hypnotherapy in Britain had survived a very rough passage, and with the advent of the new century (fittingly marked by the publication of Bramwell's classic summation of the previous one, in 1903) it was ready and eager to advance to new high ground. Several practitioners of the new generation contributed to this forward progress.

Henry C. Miller of Edinburgh revived and modified earlier group-induction techniques, going back to Mesmer's time, for hypnotizing several patients at the same time and enabling the therapist to devote more time to each. J. F. Woods called attention to silent stroking as more effective than spoken commands in hypnotizing many patients. A. Betts Taplin of Liverpool, President of the British Psycho-Medical Society, pioneered the concept of induction by progressive relaxation, with primary emphasis on making the patient feel as much at ease and comfortable as possible. He even made sure that the wallpaper in his consulting room was of a soothing color. Edward Wingfield, also a president of the society, was one of the first to insist that the patient fully understood the procedure before commencing induction. He was also more than half a century ahead of his time in introducing the now familiar concept of divided consciousness, or neodissociation, which holds that the actions of which we are aware are governed by a split-off part of our consciousness, the severing being effected by induction. This split-off part, being mostly or wholly beneath the conscious level, has so little power of discrimination that it readily accepts the suggestions of the hypnotist.

Other figures of note from this period, ending with the commencement of World War I in 1914, could be mentioned, and one who cannot be overlooked is Alice M. Hutchison who in 1912 became the first known female medical practitioner of hypnotherapy, and in 1919 published her *Hypnotism and Self-Education*, anticipating by decades many of today's psychotherapeutic principles.

Almost certainly, had Western civilization been able to avert its plunge into the First World War, one or more of those we have cited above would have gone on to rank with the world's greatest hypnotists. As it was, the terrible swath of slaughter that the war cut through an entire generation of young British men left the nation in a dispirited and despondent mood from which it did not recover for years. Professionals went through the motions of their disciplines without any feeling of achievement or progress. Spiritualism revived as millions sought contact with those they had lost—a development to the detriment of psychotherapy and medical hypnotism.

Elsewhere, however, hypnotism emerged from the trauma of the Great War, as Britain called it, and went on to new horizons of understanding and attainment. In particular this was true in the United States, which had suffered less severely from the war. It was also true in France, where, although the psychic shock was even greater than in Britain, there survived a strong foundation of professional support of hypnotism that bore significant fruit in the post-war years. We shall look at these important American and French developments in our next chapter.

X.

THE TWENTIETH CENTURY

Emile Coué
1857-1926

CHAPTER 21

"Every Day In Every Way"
Charms the Roaring Twenties

The rapid post-World War I decline of interest in hypnotism and hypnotherapy had in a way been foreshadowed by the general abandonment of hypnotherapeutic practice among the American medical establishment from the 1890s on. There seems to be no single overriding reason for this. Among the likely causes, which impacted each other in ways that reinforced their overall influence, was the increasing belief that science was establishing material causes for all effects, and was in the process of finding material remedies for all illnesses. The introduction of the germ theory of disease in the 1880s by such prestigious figures of science as Louis Pasteur, Joseph Lister and Robert Koch, led physicians to the conclusion that mentally-operative therapies were no longer necessary and had probably been mostly fraudulent anyway.

This attitude was not confined to American doctors in the turn-of-the-century period; it was starting to spread in Britain and Continental Europe as well, feeding on a strong undercurrent of the materialistic "positivist" philosophy of Auguste

Comte that had gained credence in intellectual circles from the 1830s on. Nevertheless, it took the shattering impact of World War I to reduce British and European professional medical acceptance of hypnotherapy to a level as low as that in America twenty years earlier.

Another factor in the rapid decline in America was that there were very few outstanding practitioners of hypnotherapy compared to those in Britain and Europe. Only very few American hypnotists were on a level with their distinguished counterparts across the ocean—for instance, Boris Sidis, a friend and student of William James, who in 1914 opened a psychotherapy institute at Portsmouth, New Hampshire, and John D. Quackenbos who practiced in Manhattan from 1894 to at least 1907. They can be credited with certain advances in the understanding of hypnosis. Sidis, and to a lesser extent F. H. Gerrish, pioneered in the exploration of the hypnoidal (now called hypnagogic) state between waking and sleeping, while Quackenbos sought to reclaim youths who had gone morally and criminally astray by sympathetic and reassuring hypnotic suggestions—an endeavor in which he was remarkably successful. Yet the sum of their achievements falls far short of those of the same period in Britain and Europe.

The practice of hypnotism in America was falling back into the hands of self-taught amateurs. That is not to undervalue their contributions, one of which was the eminently practical handbook of instruction in hypnotism and suggestion published in 1903 by the stage hypnotist Herbert Flint and his wife in Chicago. This made little impression, however, on members of the medical profession, who looked to the academic community for example and direction; and the academics were largely turning their backs on hypnotherapy.

William James, though never a practicing hypnotherapist himself, made a valuable contribution to the scientific advancement of clinical hypnotism by his open-minded approach to it in his numerous philosophical writings on the structure of the human mind. In 1892, however, he gave up his chair of philosophy at Harvard, and thereafter spent much of his time writing and lecturing in Europe; he did not care for the laboratory work that was necessary for further advances in mental functions. His replacement, Hugo Muensterberg, a materialistic, domineering German from the University of Freiburg, laid down as an unshakable axiom that nothing took place without an uninterrupted link of physical circumstances. According to him, the phenomenon of hypnosis did not exist in fact, and never would.

Muensterberg's pernicious influence, lasting through three decades until his retirement in 1921, devastated the advancement of therapeutic hypnosis in America. The public's notion of hypnotism once again became one of farcical stage antics. Even though hypnosis played a role in some serious psychological investigations — such as that of Morton Prince into the phenomenon of multiple personalities in the famous case of "Sally Beauchamp" — it was only as an unorthodox method of limited use and validity.

Morton Prince, to be sure, was no follower of Muensterberg. He accepted the reality of trance phenomena, seeing them as upwellings from the depths of human consciousness. He was a competent hypnotist and wanted to hypnotize Mrs. Pearl Curran (the channel for "Patience Worth," the disembodied novelist) to see if hypnosis would bring to light the suppressed creative personality. However, Mrs. Curran refused to be hypnotized, and Prince did not press the point, any more than he ever sought to use hypnosis therapeutically. He was too careful of his reputation and standing with the medical establishment to take the risk.

Joseph Jastrow was another potent devaluer of hypnotism in American medical practice during this period. In his post as Professor of Psychology at the University of Wisconsin, he echoed Muensterberg in denouncing hypnosis as a fraud, involving deliberate or unwitting collusion, hallucination, or defective observation. It is hardly surprising that by the time William McDougall came from Britain to take Muensterberg's place at Harvard in 1921, only a handful of physicians in America were still using hypnosis in their practices.

McDougall's open-mindedness and willingness to admit that there might be something of value in hypnotism as a therapy for certain conditions, started to change this situation for the better. Newspapers and magazines began to claim that medical uses of hypnotism merited further experimentation. Many doctors quietly took to trying it in a limited way. Had this process of step-by-step reintroduction of hypnotherapy gone on through the 1920s, free of any further dramatic input, it is possible that the 1930s would have seen hypnotism widely accepted and used by American doctors. That however was not to be, for the 1920s became an era in which every sort of novelty, good or bad, was accepted uncritically, only to be discarded as soon as something else new and sensational came along. It was not without reason that the era was later recalled as the "Roaring Twenties," a time when anything was likely to win attention and just as likely to lose it.

That was the fate that befell what could have been an international revival of hypnotherapy from the sound and solid foundations that had been laid by the Nancy School a generation or two earlier. In fact, the revival which had its beginnings in that very place, the French city of Nancy, was known at first as the New Nancy School. Soon, however, it acquired the name of Couéism, from its chief proponent, the French pharmacist Emile Coué. He was a pharmacist from 1882 to 1910 and thereafter a student of hypnotism and suggestion who established a free clinic in Nancy. He became famous for his autosuggestion formula, "Every day in every way, I am getting better and better." With an unreasoning faith in the efficacy of his self-suggestion mantra, Coué claimed that by this means he could teach people self-healing even to the extent of effecting organic changes.

From this the descent into ridicule was short and swift. Predictably, after a brief heyday when it was trumpeted to the skies as the newfound magic cure for every human ill, Couéism was rejected and scorned even more rapidly that it had been accepted and hailed. Yet in its essence what Emile Coué propounded was based on the way that the human psyche and imagination actually function, and the modern application of self-hypnosis is really a revived form of his doctrine. Tragically, it took half a century for it to be assimilated into medical practice.

While Coué cannot be ranked with the world's greatest hypnotists—though he was a very successful practicing hypnotherapist—the story of his rapid rise to world fame, and his equally swift descent into historical oblivion, is nonetheless an essential part of the development of modern hypnotherapy. It needs to be known and appreciated far more widely than it has been.

Emile Coué was born February 26, 1857, in Troyes, a city in east-central France, about one hundred miles southwest of

Nancy. His railroad worker father was able to send him to study at the Paris School of Pharmacy, and to provide a modest capital with which he opened his own drug store in Troyes in 1882. Becoming interested in what he was hearing about Liébeault's and Bernheim's successes in drug-free treatment of patients, and having himself seen the curative effect of a placebo he gave to a customer who kept demanding a drug he was not authorized to sell, Coué went to Nancy during the winter of 1885-86 and stayed for several weeks, closely observing what was being done.

He made further visits to Nancy School adherents in western Europe and even in the United States, where he is said to have been impressed by a now forgotten treatise from the pen of a Chicago hypnotist, W. B. Fahnestock, who argued that most people could put themselves into trance and did not need another to do it. When Coué started his own hypnotherapy clinic in Nancy, he contended that there was no suggestion other than self-suggestion and that all hypnosis was really self-hypnosis. He claimed to have treated between fifteen thousand and forty thousand patients annually, mostly without charging a fee. As his method increasingly diverged from that of the original Nancy School toward one of pure self-hypnosis, it came to be identified as that of the New Nancy School.

It attracted little attention outside of France until 1921 – the year of Muensterberg's replacement by McDougall at Harvard – when a Dr. Monnier-Williams from London, who had heard of Coué's practice, came to examine it for himself. He was sufficiently impressed to open a similar clinic in London. The French press now began to give widespread notice to Coué, who proceeded to set up a Psychological Society of

Lorraine, with himself and his wife as founders and directors. For a mere five francs, anyone could become a member; ten francs would secure membership of the inner council. Soon, branch institutes were springing up all over France. A book that had appeared the previous year, titled *Suggestion and Autosuggestion,* by Dr. Charles Baudouin of the University of Geneva in Switzerland, with a dedication to Coué, became an overnight best-seller. In a matter of weeks, the British and American press started to extol the virtues of this marvelous new way of finding happiness. People began demanding to find out more about it; and the demand was soon met with a plentiful supply.

In London, a Miss Richardson opened the Coué Institute for the Practice of Conscious Auto-Suggestion; in Paris, Mlle. Anne Villeneuve, who had studied under Coué, opened a similar institute. Coué himself, now in his mid-sixties, came to New York early in 1922 to coordinate plans for a National Coué Institute to be located in that city. An eager disciple, Archibald Stark Van Orden of Ramsay, New Jersey, founded the Coué League of America, with himself as Secretary. Two books by Coué appeared in American bookshops in rapid succession—a translation from the French, *Self-Mastery Through Conscious Auto-Suggestion,* followed by *My Method, Including American Impressions,* which he wrote in English after returning to France. Professor Baudouin had already prepared an expanded and revised edition of his earlier book, which was published in the United States by Dodd Mead, and became the bible of the Coué movement here.

All this was typical Roaring Twenties hyperbole. For two or three years Coué's name and face were as well known to newspaper readers as those of Al Capone or the Prince of

Wales. Everybody was repeating the simplistic mantra, "Every day in every way, I am getting better and better," that Coué and Baudouin declared was the central keystone of their system. Very few, however, grasped what was really meant by the mantra and how it could effectively alter their mental and physical condition for the better. Because of this lack of understanding, disappointment was, before long, almost universal. New sensations — Teapot Dome, radio, Lindbergh's Paris flight, and many others — soon crowded Couéism off the stage. Millions of people reached the conclusion that it had been just another fad in an age of fads. And that is how Coué and his doctrine are remembered today, if they are remembered at all. Yet what Coué taught was very much in the mainstream of hypnotherapy as it had been developed through almost a century and a quarter by Mesmer and his successors. All that was really innovative in Coué's approach was his recognition that the patient's imagination was more important than will power in the therapeutic use of suggestion.

Coué proposed that by training one's imagination to produce a confident mental expectation of beneficial results, the body would mobilize its mechanisms of self-repair and defense against intrusion and injury. That such expectancy and conviction could be instilled through hypnotic suggestion, in a trance state, had been demonstrated in innumerable cases. But the trance state was not necessary. Coué insisted that the mere recitation of a proper formula, repeated consistently and correctly over time would do the job just as well, in fact even better.

The key point in Coué's assertion is the "correct persistence" in the recitation of the autosuggestion formula. Coué pointed out that training the imagination is not an easy thing. Merely repeating any mantra or formula will not get the imagination under control, or enable it to direct the autonomic nervous system, which carries out most of the bodily functions (digestion, breathing, heartbeat, and so on) without our ever thinking about them. Coué devised a four-step method— which included trance induction and hypnotic suggestions— for enabling his patients to commence the rigorous process of training their imaginations. Patients were instructed to suggest to themselves that three times a day they would feel like eating, that they would do so without any digestive distress, that they would have an easy daily evacuation of intestinal wastes, that their bodies would properly assimilate what had been eaten to facilitate and strengthen every natural function, that they would enjoy nightly refreshing sleep, and be able to fulfill whatever demands of work or effort—within reasonable limitations—that might be placed upon them. These, and several other autosuggestions, were to be imagined as actually happening, not because of an act of will, but simply as the result of picturing them to one's self as real. Eventually this process would become effortless and natural, and it would not be necessary to repeat the visualization technique.

A strict translation of the original French mantric formula was, "Every day, from every point of view, I am doing better and better." To facilitate its use by English speakers, Coué shortened it to, "Every day in every way I'm getting better and better." Repeated twice daily, the formula reinforced the basic suggestions. Without first having instilled positive expectancy, recitation of the formula was to no avail.

Because of the simplicity of the autosuggestion concept, the public was soon convinced that Coué was a charlatan. By the time he died on July 2, 1926, in Nancy, at the age of sixty-nine, he was discredited by doctors, hypnotists, and the public alike.

For the better part of a half-century Coué remained discredited, and even now has not been fully recognized as having anticipated the benefits of self-hypnosis. Coué understood what had been known for centuries, that mantras could dissolve the sense of physical separation from the inner self. The repetition of such formulas enables the conscious personality to call on the vast powers of the subconscious. Although Coué did not realize it, the wording actually matters little; the great English poet Tennyson, for instance, used to put himself into an "inspirational trance" by repeating his own name.

According to Coué, the method is effective only if the repetition has become habitual and confidently expectant, and this requires thorough training of the imagination. Coué said that this training should be largely intuitive and unforced. He differed on this point from Baudouin, who called on the intellect and will to tame the imagination and make it the trusted order-bearer of the conscious mind to the subconscious. But that, Coué argued, would constantly create conflicts between what the intellect thought was best and what the subconscious instinctively knew to be best. This disagreement between Coué and Baudouin was another factor that hastened the demise of public obsession with Coue's autosuggestion doctrine. If he and his chief disciple couldn't agree on a key point, many were quick to draw the conclusion that there had to be something wrong with the whole idea.

The medical profession had never warmed up to Coué and was happy to see him and his teachings disappear from the headlines. A few doctors did, however, think that perhaps

Coué had been on the right track. So many patients seemed to have nothing organically wrong with them, yet were always complaining of various symptoms. A. J. Cronin, a London practitioner later noted for his medical novels, decided to try telling some of them that they were suffering from "asthenia," a term he abridged from Freud's "neurasthenia." The patients were delighted to discover in him a doctor who, unlike all the others, accepted that they were actually sick. And they readily submitted to the placebo injections he gave them, and for which he charged high fees. The almost uniformly successful results gained him a reputation that soon had other doctors employing similar methods.

Yet neither Cronin nor those who took their cue from him saw in this placebo therapy any connection with suggestion or hypnosis. The medical profession was solidly in agreement with Pierre Janet's somber assessment in 1925 that "Hypnotism is dead — until its next revival." Hardly any expected that revival to occur within any foreseeable future. Instead, science and medicine fled for refuge to the behaviorist sanctuary proffered by John Broadus Watson at Columbia University, which started in 1912 and attained a peak in the depression psychology that was almost universal in 1932. It would remain in the establishment forefront through World War II and the immediate post-war years, attaining a new prominence and avid acceptance in the 1960s, with B. F. Skinner as its principal advocate. Behaviorism, which asserted that only observed behavior had any scientific validity, drove any investigation of states of consciousness into the limbo of unacceptability. There was no way, Watson and later Skinner claimed, to observe mental processes accurately. Thus science could learn nothing from them, or about them.

The behavior of organisms, on the other hand, could be observed and recorded with rigorous precision, and reduced to mathematical formulas. Under this reductionism dogma subjective processes such as sensation, perception, emotion, and creativity, unlinked to any definitely locatable stimulus or impulse, were declared out of bounds. Like all other dogmas, this was an attempt to legitimize a particular set of practices. It shut the door, through almost half the century, to any widespread examination or further development into the effect of suggestion and imagination that had been growing from the time of Mesmer through the Coué episode in the 1920s.

Nevertheless, developments were taking place that would lift hypnotherapy to still greater heights of theory and practice from the mid-century on. Across the Atlantic, behaviorism found less academic acceptance than in the United States, thanks to the opposition of such figures as Professor C. D. Broad at Cambridge University, who, in 1923, derided Watson's premises as so silly and preposterous that "only very learned minds could conceive and believe in them," a shining example of the British genius for understated sarcasm. On the European continent, in addition to Pierre Janet, who continued his lonely labors in behalf of hypnotism and its use in therapy, there were still some who remembered what Georg Groddeck, a now forgotten pioneer from whom Freud borrowed his concept of the Id, had said in 1917: bacteria by themselves did not cause illness, which only occurred when our inner defenses of immunity broke down, for reasons usually related to what the mind thinks or believes.

In addition, both in the United States and Europe medical fads continued to sprout and flourish, to the enrichment of the doctors and product-makers who practiced and promoted them. Removal of the appendix and of "septic sacs" in the intestines, radical extractions of sound teeth to uncover such sacs in the gums and jawbones, yeast diets for skin conditions, and a host of others arose and had their day in the limelight. That they did actually benefit many is undeniable — but it was because of the power of suggestion, which instilled belief in the effectiveness of the treatment. When each episode of belief had run its course, the therapy in vogue lost its efficacy and yielded to the next one. Very few in the 1920s and 1930s viewed that as an illustration of the potency of imaging and suggestion.

In America, the revival of hypnotism in medical practice stemmed from the publication in 1926 of William McDougall's *Outline of Abnormal Psychology*, with its explanation of hypnotic control as a temporary yielding by the mind's authority to suggestions in which it has acquired confidence. The work in the 1920s and early 1930s of Clark Hull at the University of Wisconsin and Yale University was equally influential. Along with these was the emergence into active hypnotherapy of Milton Erickson, who was to become the greatest hypnotist of the century. We now turn to these developments.

Clark Hull -- Milton Erickson's academic mentor
1884 - 1952

CHAPTER 22
The Arrival of Milton H. Erickson

The 1920s were a time of indecision about, and opposition to, the validity and usefulness of hypnotism as a therapy. On the one hand, there was an intense public interest—shared to some extent by medical professionals—in finding out more about how the human mind works and what could be done through it to overcome disorders of the body. On the other hand there was a general skepticism and impatience on the public's part that denied innovative approaches an adequate trial, and among the professionals a hesitancy and distrust of anything that did not fit into their textbook preconceptions.

In addition to the already cited book by McDougall in 1926, which derived in part from the seminal work of the British psychologist Halse Rivers in diagnosing shell-shock and other psychic traumas of front-line soldiers in World War I, there were many books—by popular writers such as Camille Flammarion—that kept hypnotism and the subconscious mind in the public eye. Yet there were very few doctors offering hypnotherapy, and few places where medical students or practicing physicians could seek professional training in hypnotism. Nor would this state of affairs alter materially for an entire generation.

Nevertheless, the advent of a new and scientifically sound hypnotherapy was foreshadowed in the early 1920s, while the Couéism fad was at its height. At the University of Wisconsin Clark L. Hull, who held the chair of psychology, began holding seminars on hypnotism with both graduate and undergraduate students. Hypnotism had interested him throughout his long academic career—he was then in his late fifties—and though he strongly doubted that hypnosis had much medical value, he was eager to determine whether it could be pinned down in its various modes into textbook categories.

Among the students to whom Hull gave investigative assignments was one who was destined to be the world's greatest hypnotist of the twentieth-century, and to rank with the most eminent of the past. He was Milton H. Erickson, whose life history had some remarkable points of similarity to Hull's. The latter had originally been educated as a mining engineer, but after being partially disabled by an attack of polio, he turned to a career in psychology because it was less demanding physically.

Erickson was born December 5, 1901 in a Nevada mining camp. His father had been a farmer, and shortly after Erickson was born he gave up mining to return to Wisconsin to resume farming. Erickson's ambition as a youth was to become a farmer too—a modern, up-to-date one. At seventeen he had already published an article in a national magazine on why young people did not want to stay on farms and what could be done to persuade them to do so. Then, just after finishing his third year of high school in 1919, he was stricken with polio which left him almost totally paralyzed. Through a combination of mental imagery and stubborn determination, Erickson recovered sufficiently to go to the university and train to become a medical doctor, the career he chose as an alternative to farming for which he no longer had the physical strength.

Erickson realized that his recovery from a state of helplessness had been largely due to his having developed the ability to self-induce a trance state (i.e., self-hypnosis) in which he imaged step-by-step each stage of regaining his body's mobility. He was thus readily drawn to Hull's classes on hypnotism, and the shared elements in their lives made them at first highly responsive to each other. In the summer of 1923, with Hull's encouragement, Erickson carried out a number of experiments that sought to investigate the nature of hypnosis, the processes of induction, and the relative roles of the hypnotist and the subject, including which was the more important in trance development. His findings give rise to lively debates in Hull's seminars that fall, and it was soon clear to him that there was little, if any, common ground between him and his mentor. This recognition moved Erickson to commence a new special investigative project of his own that winter, which led him to conclude that the controlling factor in hypnosis was the subject's individuality and how it interplayed with the suggestions of the hypnotist. This was in agreement with his own experience of introspective self-hypnosis.

Although Erickson summarized his findings in two papers, he did not publish them at the time, for they went against Hull's conviction of the absolute priority of the hypnotist in the induction and facilitation of hypnosis. To Hull, the subconscious mind of the subject was a blank tablet on which the hypnotist could imprint whatever commands he wished. Erickson strongly felt this to be an erroneous concept, but since he was at the beginning of his professional career, he felt he could not afford publicly to oppose or offend Hull, who was becoming an authority to whom all deferred in the field of hypnotism. Thus Erickson remained silent, though he gradually dissociated himself from Hull's further researches, which were soon transferred to Yale, where he was appointed to the Sterling Chair of Psychology. In that position he was, from the late 1920s to mid-century, the foremost figure—albeit a lonely one—in American hypnotherapy. His book *Hypnosis and Suggestibility: An Experimental Approach*, published in 1933, set a standard of scientific control and statistical verification of hypnotic phenomena that even now is a model for the profession. Yet he largely abandoned his own work in hypnotism after the publication of the book, leaving it to others to put its central philosophy into practice. That, unfortunately, was still a rigid insistence that the subject did not contribute in any way to the hypnotic process or its outcome. It was a position that would block any further broad advances in hypnotherapy for a third of the century.

From 1933 on, Hull devoted his energies and abilities to an attempt to quantify the primary laws of psychology, as he conceived them to be, into a neo-behaviorist scheme of things, on the model of Newtonian physics. From these primary laws, he argued, all individual behavior, however complex, could be derived under a set of secondary laws, together with social and group behavior in all their variations. He devised several mathematical equations to express these laws, which he published in 1943, in his book *Principles of Behavior*. For a decade beyond his death in 1952, this work was a Bible of psychological theory and practice, seemingly assuring Hull a niche among the immortals of science. Then in the 1960s, almost overnight, his fame and influence faded as the impractical and untenable nature of much of his premise became increasingly evident.

Today, Clark Hull is remembered by few, even among professionals, and most of those few blame him for having held back the development of modern hypnotherapy with his failed numerical straitjacketing of the human psyche.

Milton Erickson, however, held a more generous view of his academic mentor in hypnotism, recalling how Hull had encouraged and directed his youthful interest in the discipline. He also valued the statistical solidity and scientific respectability that Hull's landmark *Hypnosis and Suggestibility: An Experimental Approach* gave to American hypnotherapy when it was sadly lacking in both. In addition, Hull's university seminars on hypnotism had been important since they took place in a time of rapidly declining interest on the part of professional medicine.

Erickson's balanced assessment of Hull's contribution to hypnotherapy is probably in line with what is likely to be the eventual judgment of medical historians. Though Erickson and a host of practitioners after him went far beyond Hull, the fact remains that without the scientific credibility he provided, it might have been another fifty years or more before hypnotism was again used in therapy. And the maturing of Erickson's own genius and attainment of pre-eminence in hypnotherapy would have had to surmount even greater obstacles than the many he overcame in his climb to fame and recognition.

Many of these obstacles were connected with his physical health. He had a near-fatal attack of polio at seventeen, and going back even further, there were physical deficiencies that hindered his early education. He was tone-deaf and red-green color-blind; he had a severe dyslexia which vanished in an instant flash of visual illumination when trying to follow his frustrated teacher's explanation that the characters M and 3 were not the same. This occurred when he was in either first or second grade. From that moment he had no further problem with learning to read except that until he was in his second year at high school he was unable to find words in their alphabetical sequence in the dictionary and had to keep turning the pages until he found the word he was looking for. Then, just as suddenly as the reading disability had disappeared, this one also vanished in a flash of insight.

Recalling these sudden illuminations some sixty years later, Erickson concluded that they were the result of his having self-induced, without realizing it, a trance state in which the intense concentration on his reading limitations brought about their elimination. Whether or not that was so, there can be no question about the role of concentration, imagery and self-hypnosis in Erickson's recovery from polio. From a state of total paralysis, and a partial loss of his speech faculty, he regained within eleven months the ability to walk, though still needing crutches, and was again able to speak clearly. His recovery enabled him to graduate from high school in 1920, and work at a sit-down job in a cannery all summer to earn money for college. He entered medical school at the University of Wisconsin that fall.

Long afterward, Erickson told his second wife that there was some physical therapy involved in his recovery. A local practical nurse treated him with hot packs and massage, and by moving the paralyzed limbs, while also motivating him to move them on his own. This was essentially the same method later employed by Sister Kenny in Australia, which aroused the fierce opposition of the medical profession. Nevertheless, Erickson believed it was the depth of concentration and clarity of imaging that was the principal factor in his overcoming the extreme degree of incapacitating paralysis he had suffered.

His hearing, which had been only average, became exceptionally sharp and sensitive as his body sought to compensate for its loss of mobility; and he availed himself of this heightened auditory faculty to start to identify every sound in the house and all that he could hear from outdoors. Soon he could accurately determine who was making what sound, and what activity and mood it denoted. Next, he used his eyesight, which also appears to have acquired a heightened acuteness, to scan the windows closely, while he sat in bed and also in the rocking chair into which it shortly became possible to lift him. This intense focusing on the windows, and concentration on the idea of reaching them and looking out, induced an autohypnotic state in which he was actually starting to rock the chair and very gradually slide it toward the window.

He concentrated on recalling the movements of his hands, feet, fingers and toes in grasping tools and utensils, in walking and climbing trees, and visualized performing the same actions again. Before long he was indeed renewing those motions. From watching closely his baby sister's learning to walk and to balance herself, he visualized himself doing the same all over again—and was soon doing it.

He was, however, still having to use crutches through his freshman year at the university, and had a general feeling of physical weakness. Determining to toughen himself through a stretch of outdoor living, he set out in June 1921 on what he assured his parents would be a two-week canoe trek down the Wisconsin River and back. He was actually gone ten weeks, going from the Wisconsin into the Mississippi, and down that river to beyond St. Louis, then back up against the current in both streams; a total of twelve hundred miles. On his return he was in much stronger physical condition, with powerful shoulder muscles developed through strenuous paddling, and again able to ride a bicycle. He now discarded the crutches, though he continued to carry a cane and occasionally used it for balancing. In addition he had met a great variety of people and learned much about conducting himself in many different situations.

Yet there was a physical price to be paid for these gains. Erickson's right shoulder muscles never regained the strength of those in his left shoulder; and to keep the left shoulder from becoming markedly higher and giving him a disfigured appearance, he stood long hours in front of a mirror, twisting himself until the two shoulders were approximately level. That, however, resulted in a severely twisted spine that had already been damaged by the polio. This would cause severe problems in later life. For the time being, however, Erickson had achieved a nearly normal physical appearance and capability of movement.

After his investigations into hypnotism under Hull in his senior year, he went on to postgraduate medical school at Wisconsin and qualified in 1928, at the age of twenty-six, for his medical and master of arts degrees. His first internship in general medicine was at the Colorado General Hospital, and in psychiatry at the nearby Colorado Psychopathic Hospital where he worked under Dr. Franklin Ebaugh, one of the more noted psychiatrists of the 1920s.

After a year at these Colorado institutions, Erickson was appointed assistant physician at the Rhode Island State Hospital for Mental Diseases, where he did some intensive studies in the relationship of mental deficiencies to family and environmental factors. His findings resulted in seven papers being published in professional journals, which started to bring him into notice and led to a better paying tenure at the State Hospital in Worcester, Massachusetts, where in four years (1930-34) he progressed from junior physician to Chief Research Psychiatrist. It was at Worcester that he first started to use hypnotism extensively as a therapeutic tool. The hospital staff was opposed to this, fearing that hypnotism was potentially dangerous to sanity, and he had to overcome this hostility through carefully controlled experiments in which he demonstrated its safety. His resulting paper, published in 1932 in the *Journal of Abnormal and Social Psychology*, was a significant first step toward the wider professional utilization of hypnotism in medical practice.

While Erickson was thus advancing in his career, his personal life was unhappy. In his first year of postgraduate medical study, at twenty-three, he had married, and by the early 1930s was raising a family of three children. This was a heavy burden on him with his still relatively low earnings. In hindsight, he realized that early marriage had been a serious mistake on his part. The focusing on himself that had been necessary for him to overcome his paralysis had resulted in his failing to develop adequate social and personal relationships with others. He retained a naiveté and immaturity of judgment in the areas of loving and caring that ill fitted him for marriage. After his divorce in 1934, in which he obtained custody of the children, he determined to seek a better understanding of all the things he had been deficient in, and to apply this painfully gained knowledge in his professional practice. In the 1940s and 1950s he was the first to work with families to bring about healing of shattered relationships.

Erickson received an appointment in 1934 as Director of Psychiatric Research at the Wayne County General Hospital in Eloise, Michigan, a Detroit suburb. Five years later this position was expanded to cover Psychiatric Training as well. He remained a total of fourteen years at the Wayne County institution. It was at Eloise that Erickson started to attain true maturity both as a person and as a healer.

A prime factor in this further growth was his meeting Elizabeth Moore, whom he married in 1936. She became his fellow researcher and inspirer, a mother to the three children he already had, and of five more she would bear. Without her steadying and strengthening presence, Erickson could not have become the dominant leader of the hypnotherapy revival in the 1960s and 1970s.

At the time of his second marriage he was thirty-four and physically still vigorous and active, though the limp on his right side that he never fully overcame was becoming more pronounced and he now had to use a cane all the time. However, he could walk surprisingly long distances, and he still had powerful shoulder muscles.

His physical deterioration started in 1947, at forty-five, when he was knocked off his bicycle by a dog and suffered extensive skin abrasions. Given a tetanus antitoxin injection, he developed a severe reaction from which he had great difficulty recovering. In particular he seemed no longer able to tolerate the chill and dampness of the Michigan winter. A friend and former Detroit psychiatrist, Dr. John Larson, who was Superintendent of the Arizona State Hospital at Phoenix, invited Erickson to come and join his staff. With his family, Erickson moved to Phoenix in the early summer of 1948, and in the warm dry climate his health improved markedly. He also found an outlet for his energies in helping Dr. Larson institute numerous progressive changes at the hospital, which had been run in an outmoded and obsolete manner.

In the spring of 1949, political opposition forced Larson's resignation, and Erickson also decided to leave the hospital staff and go into private practice. He was ill again twice within a few months, apparently from allergic reactions to the desert environment with its sand and dust. To reduce exposure to them, he set up his office in the home he had bought in Phoenix, so he did not have to travel to and from another location.

His condition then seems to have become stabilized, until 1953 when he suffered what was diagnosed at the time as a second attack of polio, but is now believed to have been an episode of post-polio syndrome, traceable to the original attack twenty-four years earlier. There were further episodes of this through the remaining twenty-seven years of Erickson's life; and while these were not as severe as the first one in 1953, each caused a further muscle impairment until in the end, as will be seen further on, he was reduced to virtually total invalidism.

It was while first coming under this weight of steadily worsening physical debility that Erickson heightened his initial prominence in the hypnotherapeutic field. He had already, while at his post in Michigan, attracted the notice of Dr. Margaret Mead, who consulted him in 1939 regarding the spontaneous trances of the native dancers she had filmed in Bali. They collaborated during World War II on still classified government projects assessing the Japanese character and the effectiveness of Nazi propaganda. At this time he also became the associate editor of the *Journal of Diseases of the Nervous System*, and was interviewed several times by newspapers and radio stations, as well as national publications such as *Life* and *This Week*. In addition he frequently spoke to civic and youth groups, and at graduations, taking advantage of all these opportunities to promote a wider public understanding of hypnotism.

The response was still slow and meager, but the seed was being sown that would bear abundant harvest later on. In the decade of the 1950s Erickson became a nationally known figure, featured in the news media and consulted by famous athletes, the U.S. military, and the airline industry for improved performance by both individuals and groups. Even though the emphasis was still mainly on the psychology involved, and his masterly application of it through his psychiatric techniques, the fact that hypnotism was the most important of them was finally getting across to the public and to some portion of the medical profession. A giant step forward to greater acceptance of hypnotherapy was the founding, in 1957, largely by Erickson's initiative, of the American Society of Clinical Hypnosis, with him as its first president and first editor of its Journal. He was the president for two years, and editor for ten years.

All this came about despite his physical disabilities that grew worse every year, as also did the demands on his time and strength. Be the late 1950s invitations to speak and demonstrate his inimitable techniques to professional groups across the country and abroad were coming at such a rate that Erickson was away from home for at least a week every month. And still his greatest attainments, in the sense of developing a coherent philosophy of what he sought for his patients and how he achieved it, lay ahead of him. They would make the 1960s and 1970s a period when Erickson towered over the fields of psychiatry and hypnotherapy, laying new foundations and opening new approaches that will occupy his successors far into the twenty-first century. We will now take up the panorama of those two epochal decades.

Milton H. Erickson
1901 - 1980

CHAPTER 23
Erickson the Master Wounded Healer

A t the Seventh Congress of the International Society of Hypnotists held in 1976, Milton Erickson was the first recipient of its newly created Benjamin Franklin Gold Medal award for the highest level of achievement in the theory and practice of hypnotism. He was cited as an outstanding innovator, distinguished clinician, and the leading creator of the modern view of hypnosis as a discipline and therapy. This was followed in July, 1977 by the publication of a special issue of the American Journal of Clinical Hypnosis (of which he had been the founder and first editor two decades earlier) in honor of his seventy-fifth birthday. It included a tribute by Margaret Mead, who was the first figure of national prominence in psychology to recognize Erickson's genius.

Now, halfway through the eighth decade of his life, Milton Erickson was known and looked up to everywhere in the Western world as the premier figure in the field of hypnotherapy. Though he had given up active practice and was totally confined to his wheelchair, he was still avidly sought out by those in the rising generation of psychotherapists who hoped to be his disciples and to carry to new heights his legacy of creative and innovative healing through hypnosis.

Some of these new aspirants to Erickson's heritage, notably Ernest Rossi and Jeffrey Zeig, have risen to prominence since his death on March 25, 1980, at the age of seventy-eight. Yet there is still no general agreement among professionals as to exactly what constitutes an Ericksonian approach to therapy. There are many who say they are doing—or trying to do— what Erickson did, but no one is following him exactly on the path he took.

Indeed, it is hardly possible that they could, for Milton Erickson was a law unto himself, a master innovator who early in his career had understood that he would have to go beyond textbooks and theories. They were the indispensable foundation, but what he built on them was based on his own best insights and judgment. He had come to trust them through years of experience, from which he learned that he had to approach each case on its own merits. No two patients were alike. What worked with one may not work with another. At the same time, there were certain general principles, mainly of common sense, that could usually be relied upon to produce results. Effective treatment involved determining the best mix and application of these principles to each individual case.

Erickson did not always succeed. Though he never revealed any scorecard of successes and failures, he freely admitted that he had encountered many patients he could not help. Some were simply not hypnotizable and offered no other access to their twisted inner complexes. Some who could be hypnotized lacked the inner wish to be helped. An important part of any therapist's practice, he taught his pupils, was learning how to detect that a patient could not be helped. His techniques for doing that were, however, very much his own, and not easily adaptable—if at all—for use by others who were not at ease with his often very unconventional approaches. Whether for diagnosis or treatment, those approaches spanned a very wide range, broader in scope than those of any of Erickson's predecessors. He himself never sought to systematize them—he avoided systems of any sort—but their often dazzling variety can be roughly grouped under the headings below.

To a great extent Erickson employed indirect suggestion, confusion, puzzlement, and metaphor. "I try," he would say, "to get the patient to learn about himself, in an unstructured way." Erickson's suggestions and leading questions—at which he was as expert as any trial lawyer—concentrated the patient's attention to the point where he or she would enter the hypnotic state without the customary induction ritual. He utilized traditional induction procedures too, very capably, when the occasion called for them, but they were not his primary tools.

To say that Erickson often employed metaphor is to oversimplify his vast assortment of techniques of analogy and anecdote. He was a charismatic story-teller, whether he was addressing an audience or a patient. Few could resist becoming wholly wrapped up in his tales, which often seemed to have no relation at all to the patient's situation or problem. They had a very distinct purpose however, which was to open up the patient's mind on both conscious and subconscious levels to what was wrong with him or her, and the need to take definite steps to change the anomalous behavior.

When the situation called for it, Erickson could be extremely authoritative, issuing preemptive commands instead of softly spoken suggestions. He knew when to employ shock techniques to compel patients to make choices instead of evading them. Sometimes he enabled those with bad habits to overcome them through even greater indulgence, until they grasped just how harmful and self-destructive those habits were.

Erickson was particularly effective in situations where he could make use of his talent for creating high drama, in which the patient played the leading role. He did not write the script, but he provided the setting and the strategy, leaving it up to the patient to devise — aided by his suggestions — the tactics to play out the drama to a successful conclusion. To critics who charged him with being manipulative, he countered that all psychotherapy was manipulative in one way or another. What mattered was the objective and the values involved.

With Erickson, the values were always those of traditional morality, softened only to the extent that common sense and sensitivity to suffering demanded. He was not religious in any church-going sense, though he had experienced mystical states at various times in his life. He believed very strongly that there was a right way for people to behave, with consideration and respect, toward themselves and others. If a religious conviction or affiliation helped anyone to cultivate proper behavior, that was well and good, but he never relied on or employed religious motivations in seeking to effect beneficial change in a patient.

One criticism of Erickson was that when inculcating a sense of values into patients, he tended to lecture them in the fashion of a moralizing Dutch uncle. Some resisted this and claimed it was demeaning, but the majority appear to have accepted it and it seems to have achieved its purpose. Perhaps his speech rhythm, which was about seventy-five words a minute (half that of most people) and resembled the intonation of a priest or lector reading a text aloud, acted as an induction mode, facilitating a trance-like absorption in and acceptance of what he was saying.

So strong was the impression that Erickson's voice made on his hearers that it made his posthypnotic suggestions more emphatic and effective. "My voice will go with you," he would say, and the memory of it would reinforce the suggestions within the patient's subconscious. However, it was not his custom to make hypnotic suggestions overt; usually they were concealed inside the anecdotal story or other narrative device he used to concentrate the patient's attention.

As a psychiatrist, Erickson was concerned with retrieving and identifying a patient's core emotions from early life, and he made very effective use of hypnosis for this purpose. He realized, perhaps more clearly than most practitioners, that the validity of such retrievals depended on how much they were influenced by the patient's eagerness to please and satisfy the therapist. In many cases the memories brought up were not of real events, but what the patient thought the therapist wanted and expected. With this in mind Erickson worded his questions to patients in hypnosis in ways that tended to elicit truthful answers. He was careful not to prejudge the responses, but he had usually formed a pretty accurate idea of what the patient might be concealing from what had come out in pre-induction questioning.

Therapists who attended his seminars and workshops often despaired of ever being able to match his flexibility and eclecticism in their own practice. They realized that these were qualities in which he excelled uniquely, and that this was the key to his preeminence. Patients quickly realized that they were being treated by a learned person who was at the head of his profession, and this made them feel special also.

On a philosophic level, Erickson did not subscribe to Freud's belief in the incompatibility of human biological urges and civilization. This, to him, seemed to fly in the face of the common sense perception that the vast majority of people were able to live normally with those urges inside the constraints that civilization imposes. The goal of psychotherapy, as he saw it, was to free those persons shackled by attitudes of rigidity and timidity that prevented them from functioning usefully within civilized society. For this purpose, hypnosis — which he once defined as any state of absorption in which the attention could be concentrated on a single thought or idea — was by far the most effective means. It unlocked the vast hidden powers of the unconscious, a term Erickson preferred to the subconscious.

Whatever the name, he looked on that postulated region of the psyche (the unconscious) as a source of power and strength, a reservoir of resources to be drawn on by the conscious surface personality for its better and more healthful functioning. This was diametrically opposite to Freud's view, which regarded the subconscious with suspicion, as a hiding-place of malignant memories and impulses. Erickson, though he had no illusions about people's propensity to deviousness and trickery, had a more generous conception of human nature than did Freud. This optimism helped him to take an active interest in each patient and to convey a belief that relief or cure was possible and attainable.

At the same time, he did not believe there were limitless powers of healing in the human unconscious. There was a boundary to everything, and the human body — marvelously constructed as it was, with capabilities of resilience and recovery of which conventional medicine had no conception — still had its ultimate design limits beyond which it could not be sustained. The amplest evidence of this was his own steadily deteriorating physical condition. He helped and frequently healed others; himself he could help less and less as time went on, and nothing he did would much longer sustain his increasingly crippled body.

Erickson was in fact the epitome of the archetypal "wounded healer," who appears in the mythology and folklore of peoples around the globe. The archetype is present even in the Christian figure of the divine Jesus, who on the cross is mocked by the crowd shouting, "He saved others, himself he cannot save." Facing up to the reality that his physical deterioration was irreversible, Erickson nevertheless called on his own inner resources to allow him to continue helping others as long as possible. In spite of pain that became nearly constant, and virtually total loss of mobility, he lived into his seventy-ninth year and to the very end was still active in many ways. This was a medical miracle that owed very little to conventional medical therapy, though he made use of it to the extent that he felt it was of value.

Erickson's physical breakdown intensified steadily from about 1967 on, even while he was attaining the peak of his fame and recognition. The once powerful shoulder muscles weakened to the point that he needed both hands to lift spoons, knives, and forks when eating. Walking, even with a cane, became too exhausting by 1969, when he had to give up traveling. A year later he moved into another home in Phoenix which had been remodeled for wheelchair living. Even so, he continued to do research, write papers, do organizational work and editing, and see patients. By 1974 he had to give that up, as with further loss of cheek and tongue muscle control he could no longer wear dentures or enunciate as clearly as before. He also had to give up much of his reading, as he could no longer maintain eye-focus for an extended length of time.

Yet he did not become totally inactive professionally. He was increasingly in demand for teaching sessions at his home. At first, in the mid-1970s, he was able to do these both mornings and afternoons, five days a week, then in the afternoons only, and finally only on four days a week. So many were the requests to attend these sessions that, when he died on a Tuesday evening in late March 1980, his teaching schedule was filled through the end of the year, and there were applications that would have extended it through the following year.

Through collaboration with his favorite disciples Ernest Rossi and Jeffrey Zeig, Erickson was able to continue contributing to the professional literature on hypnotherapy. The demand for papers by him — satisfied to some extent by reprinting earlier ones from as far back as forty years that had attracted little notice on their first appearance — had grown enormously since the publication in 1973 of Jay Haley's *Uncommon Therapy: the Psychiatric Techniques of Milton H. Erickson, M.D.* It was this book that first made a large sector of the medical and psychiatric professions, which had not previously paid much notice to the acclaim Erickson had been steadily gaining from his peers, more fully aware of the breakthrough character of his methods. As Mesmer and the Nancy School had done in their centuries, Erickson in his century lifted hypnotism to previously unattained levels as a therapy, laying the foundation for still further gains in the century ahead. And as had been the case with Mesmer and the Nancy School, Erickson's achievements have not been immediately followed by new ones of equal stature. No corpus of hypnotherapeutic theory or practice has appeared that can be identified as strictly Ericksonian, because his unique approach was simply beyond imitation. He set examples and laid down principles that can be built upon, amplified, and further developed, but no matter what the degree or direction of these advances, they   inevitably depart from both the spirit and the letter of his approach. To the extent, however, that therapists adhere to his openness and diversity of approach, they can claim to be practicing a form of Ericksonian therapy.

Five years after Erickson's death, D. Corydon Hammond of the University of Utah School of Medicine, in a symposium at the Tenth Congress of the International Society of Hypnotists, held in Toronto, Canada, delivered an analysis of the varying attempts at following in Erickson's footsteps. Hammond's paper is a valid statement of the Ericksonian legacy and of how it is being handled.

Some of the misinterpretations that Hammond described are surprising in light of how clearly Erickson elucidated his techniques in a vast body of writings. For instance, Erickson's entry into self-hypnosis in the diagnostic process, which was on occasion helpful to him in grasping the nature of the patient's problem, has been misunderstood as being his standard method. The harmful result has been training sessions in which aspiring therapists are encouraged to go into hypnosis and trust their unconscious to come up with the esoteric metaphors and paradoxes that Erickson often employed—and to expect such superficial methodology to produce results as positive and lasting as those that he obtained.

That is merely an evasion of the hard work and careful planning that Erickson devoted to each individual case. He had no intention of founding any sort of cult, or of propounding dogmas of either theory or practice. He did believe, because he had seen it proved over and over again, that the results you get are in direct proportion to the effort you put into solving the problem.

Some of this misapprehension stemmed from the teaching seminars he conducted in his last years. Because of his increasingly severe physical limitations, they were not formal classes in any sense. He would reminisce informally about a great many cases in his experience and describe in more or less general terms how he treated them. Such narrations often gave the impression of his having achieved literally magical results through very simple means. But he left out the arduous trial and error through which he had arrived at the correct diagnoses and the appropriate techniques of treatment in each case. He made it sound easy because he was no longer up to telling how hard it was. His results were miraculous only to those who did not appreciate their really common sense nature.

Again, many who claim to be Ericksonian in their practice are actually employing only one, or at best a few, of his many approaches. Often it is asserted that the true Ericksonian method is to implant hypnotic suggestion indirectly. Actually he used direct suggestion about as frequently as indirect, but because indirect suggestion had rarely been used and was unknown to many practitioners, he naturally emphasized it in his case histories. Why talk at equal length about what was known already?

Ernest Rossi summed up Erickson's genius as an extreme flexibility in applying whatever was appropriate to the given situation—of knowing when to use what. "It is natural," Rossi said, "when we encounter a genius who does something new (such as indirect suggestion) to jump on that one facet as being the total of what makes a genius. That totally misses the eclecticism that is often a hallmark of geniuses, and certainly was emphatically so with Erickson."

Kay Thompson, another therapist familiar with Erickson's work at first hand has said, "We simply don't believe in ourselves enough . . . we don't believe we have the power to make the direct approach work for us, as he made it work for him. We chicken out and resort to the indirect approach—and don't do so well with that either—because we lack the belief and skills needed for the direct one. Erickson was successful with both methods because he had fully mastered each."

Again, the later followers of Erickson have made metaphor and story-telling a prime factor in their modes of treatment, even though therapists such as Robert Pearson, who worked with Erickson, have said that at most metaphor accounted for no more than a fifth of his hypnotic work. The misconception here was that Erickson did not trust patients to obey him or follow his directions, so he conveyed suggestions in the form of metaphorical stories that distracted the patient and diffused resistance to what he was instilling. Rather, according to Pearson, Erickson wanted to give his patients time for integrating what they had already been told. Stories were a way of giving that time without boring them. Nor were they mere idle tales, spun on the spur of the moment. Erickson invariably made a direct connection between them and the patient's problem, and was careful in making essential points to that end.

Erickson said that he often spent more time in reviewing the details of each session with a patient than in the sessions themselves. He wrote down everything that was said, and what he planned to say at the next session. It was this exhaustive preparation and reviewing that made his words and actions appear effortless and spontaneous. Many who claim to be his followers, Kay Thompson has charged, think they can do the same simply by entering self-hypnosis and trusting their unconscious to come up with the right words. "They've put nothing into their unconscious, so nothing useful comes out of it," Thompson said. "They don't want to do the painstaking, exhausting work Erickson did." Nor, it would seem, do they want to give their patients the hours of intensive training in developing the hypnotic state that Erickson always provided before he undertook the implantation of therapeutic suggestions. Even with a patient who had previously been hypnotized, he insisted on a minimum of twenty minutes in the hypnotic state before the patient was given appropriate posthypnotic suggestions.

Erickson put the interests of his patients ahead of his own. He gave them sixty minutes out of every hour, rather than the fifty which has become more common in the psychotherapy profession, and even with the onset of inflation in the early 1970s his fees never exceeded $40.00 an hour up to the time he gave up private practice. He did not amass monetary wealth, but he left to his family and to his colleagues a legacy of high and strict principles, dedicated application, and a conviction that service to others had a value above all else.

As hypnotism stands on the threshold of the twenty-first century, its advancement needs to be in accordance with the standards that Milton Erickson set and followed throughout his long professional career. In the final chapter I shall examine the current trends in the profession and suggest where the next great hypnotists of the world may come from.

Ernest R. Hilgard, Hypnosis Pioneer
1904 - 2001

CHAPTER 24
Future Trends: Hypnotism Comes of Age

With Milton Erickson the present roster of the world's greatest hypnotists comes to a close, for no other individual practitioner has attained a comparable level of accomplishment. To say that, however, is probably to undervalue the vast theoretical and practical advances that have been made over the past seventy years in the understanding and application of hypnosis as a valid therapeutic tool. These advances have been made by an array of professionals working along three principal lines of investigation, of which Erickson's was the most individual and idiosyncratic.

Most of these advances were achieved in America, and they have laid the solid foundations on which hypnotism will move firmly ahead to even greater attainment. And from this twentieth century base will spring the great hypnotists of the twenty-first century.

The first of the three lines of advance grew out of the teaching and clinical work of William McDougall and Morton Prince at Harvard in the 1920s. McDougall left Harvard for a professorship at Duke University in 1927; however, in his seven years at Harvard he stimulated the curiosity and interest of several students who went on to do important work in hypnotism and to influence others to follow in their footsteps.

Among McDougall's students who pioneered in hypnosis research, the most prominent were William S. Taylor, Paul C. Young, Frank A. Pattie, George W. Estabrooks, and Henry A. Murray, who succeeded in 1929 to the headship of the Harvard Psychological Clinic that Morton Prince founded in 1927. (Paul C. Young performed the first hypnotic experiments leading to an American doctorate in psychology.) In 1931 Murray and a graduate of the clinic, Donald W. Mackinnon, co-authored a book on the status of hypnosis research at that time. Another graduate, Robert W. White, Murray's successor as head of the clinic, was the teacher of Martin T. Orne, who after World War II would become one of the most important figures in the field of hypnotism.

None of these men of the generation between Prince and Orne were known outside of their own professional circles, and the hostility toward hypnotism was so great in the medical establishment at the time that they had to avoid any publicity about their interest in it. Yet their contribution to the later emergence of hypnosis into medical acceptance was considerable. They kept alive a spark of research out of which new insights and techniques would emerge.

The second line of development was that which centered around the work of Clark L. Hull, a psychologist at the University of Wisconsin and then at Yale from 1923 to 1931. We have already mentioned the influence of Hull on Erickson's early interest in hypnosis, and the publication in 1933 of *Hypnosis and Suggestibility*, which for an entire generation was the authoritative text on the subject. This work was the first modern (20th century) scientific book on hypnotism. At the time that it appeared in print, Hull had stopped all his research in hypnosis, and in 1931 closed the hypnosis research laboratory he had opened at Yale two years earlier. Why he rejected hypnotism is not fully known. He was, as we have noted, strongly attracted to the behavioristic doctrine of Skinner, and to developing his own theory of learning. There are also stories of severe disagreements with the Yale Department of Psychiatry, which is said to have disapproved of Hull's hypnotic procedures as being overly intrusive into his research subjects' personalities and lives. Whatever the truth was, Hull's abandonment of the field was devastating to his twenty pupils in hypnosis. Eleven went on to other studies; nine found academic or clinical positions in psychology, but only two of these, Arthur Jenness and Griffith Williams, ever did any hypnotherapeutic work in their professional careers. Even that had a later beneficial result, for along with the influence of the Harvard line, it made available during World War I a number of young psychologists with experience of hypnotherapy who were ready to use it in the treatment of the symptoms of battle neuroses caused by the psychic trauma of war. These victims were hypnotized and regressed in time to the period of the traumatic experience, and encouraged to relive the event and to get rid of the emotions relating to the experience. (J. A. Hadfield coined the term "hypnoanalysis" for this procedure.)

This employment of hypnosis as an abbreviated psychotherapy for battle traumas, which resulted from a shortage of mainline psychiatrists for the thousands of cases that flooded into the armed services hospitals, led to its being more favorably regarded by the post-war medical establishment. The clinical use of hypnosis in World War II and the Korean War also created a new wave of enthusiasm for hypnotherapy. The cumulative evidence was incontrovertible that hypnotherapy had proved superior to pain-killing drugs in alleviating or removing the pain of burns and severe wounds, and that it was of definite value in restoring healthy minds and psyches to men who had been inwardly scarred by the horrors of combat.

In 1955 the British Medical Association passed a formal resolution approving hypnosis as a valid therapeutic technique for treating neuroses and for relieving pain in surgery and childbirth. In 1958 the American Medical Association and the American Dental Association made comparable resolutions recognizing hypnosis as an accepted form of treatment in medicine and dentistry, and they encouraged training in hypnosis for students in those fields. Also in 1958, the American Psychological Association recognized hypnosis as a respectable psychotherapeutic tool, and certifying boards were set up for both the experimental and clinical usage of hypnosis in 1960. With this new legitimacy an increasing number of health professionals began to make use of hypnosis.

By that time, the third line of development, the idiosyncratic approach of Erickson, had merged with the other two. Erickson had already experimented with and applied many of the hypnotherapy techniques that the wartime psychologists employed, and had formed a circle of collaboration with a few other psychiatrists who did not accept Freud's rejection of hypnosis. They all found themselves in good company with the expanding post-war establishment of associations to further the development of the scientific and therapeutic aspects of hypnosis, and to promote the setting up of research facilities.

Milton V. Kline, a psychologist, and Jerome M. Schneck, a psychiatrist, both of the new generation of clinical hypnotists that emerged after World War II, founded in 1949 the Society for Clinical and Experimental Hypnosis. Three years later, the Society began publishing its Journal, with Kline as the first editor. This gave an impetus to the formation in 1958 of an International Society with the same title by Bernard Raginsky, a Canadian psychiatrist. It merged its Journal with Kline's for a worldwide readership. That same year also saw the founding by Erickson of the American Society of Clinical Hypnosis, whose Journal he would edit through its first ten volumes, to April 1968. For a while there was some rivalry between Kline's and Erickson's societies, but this gradually faded out, with most clinical hypnotists taking membership in both, and attending joint meetings in which the international society sometimes participated. Together these societies spurred universities and funding sources such as the National Institute of Mental Health and the Office of Naval Research, as well as private sources like the Ford Foundation, to set up and endow laboratories for hypnosis research.

One of the most influential among the first of these research centers was that established by Martin T. Orne, whom we noted above as a student of Robert White at Harvard, where he took his Ph.D. degree in 1958, having earlier obtained a medical degree from Tufts College. Orne's laboratory, set up in 1960 as the Studies in Hypnosis Project at the Massachusetts Mental Health Center under Harvard's auspices, was transferred in 1964 to the University of Pennsylvania under the name of the Unit for Experimental Psychiatry. Orne was now a professor of psychiatry and in full charge of the program, along with his wife, Emily Carota Orne, who had been associated with the laboratory from the beginning. In 1962, Orne also took over as editor of the International Society for Clinical and Experimental Hypnosis Journal which was founded by Raginsky.

The most outstanding among Orne's many contributions to both the theory and practice of hypnotherapy, has been the clear distinction he drew between the essence of hypnotism — that is, the phenomenon of suggestibility by itself — and the artifacts, or the physical effects produced by hypnosis in the bodily organism. Even among the most careful investigators of hypnotic phenomena there had always been some uncertainty about the relationship between the act of suggestion and its results. After Orne, there could no longer be any such intermingling of cause and effect, and this resulted in greater clarity in the definition and application of hypnosis.

Another important hypnosis research laboratory was established in 1957 by Ernest R. Hilgard at Stanford University. Hilgard, a student of Hull (though not in his hypnosis class) at Yale, where he graduated with a Ph.D. in 1930, became a professor of psychology at Stanford in 1933, and continued to maintain the interest in clinical hypnosis he had acquired from Hull. He was thus, although collaterally rather than directly, from the first or Hull line of hypnotherapy development in the era between the two great wars.

Hilgard's hypnosis research facility at Stanford was set up with the active collaboration of André M. Weitzenhoffer, who a year earlier had gained his Ph.D. from the University of Michigan with a dissertation on hypnosis. Three years prior to that, he had published *Hypnotism: An Objective Study in Suggestibility*, the best review and update of the field since Hull's book two decades earlier. While planning the research center with Hilgard, Weitzenhoffer published a second book, *General Techniques of Hypnotism*, a comprehensive text on induction methodology. Weitzenhoffer and Hilgard were joined on the center's senior staff by the latter's wife, Josephine R. Hilgard, holding degrees from Yale and Stanford, whose wide experience in both child guidance and adult psychoanalysis made her a most valuable adjunct. Interviews conducted by her and her associates with a wide range of hypnotizable persons became the basis of the Stanford Hypnotic Susceptibility Scales, which are now the accepted standard in the profession. Over an eight-year span, from 1959 to 1967, these scales were carefully adjusted and refined to produce significant rates of correlation between measured hypnotizability and the degree of pain relief attained. They provide clinical hypnotists with a tool that enables them to judge with a high level of accuracy how readily a patient can be hypnotized and how helpful the treatment is likely to be.

There is hardly an aspect of hypnosis that was not advanced in one way or another by the work at Stanford in the 1960s and 1970s. Erickson was involved in some of these research projects, which also influenced Charles Tart's investigations of the physiological and subjective patterns of the alternate states of consciousness revealed by the widespread experimentation in the 1960s with mind-altering drugs. Tart expanded his studies into the consciousness-altering practices of Eastern religions. He found unique response patterns associated with waking states, dreaming states, and other alternate states of consciousness, such as drug-induced states, and was eventually able to distinguish three distinct states of consciousness: wakefulness, ordinary sleep, and "paradoxical" sleep, the third state being the one into which hypnotic induction provides an entry that can be controlled and adjusted. There are, of course, numerous intermediate stages between these three primary states of consciousness, but all of the intermediate phases will in almost all cases shift rather rapidly into one or another of the primary states.

A third laboratory that made significant contributions to a more thorough understanding of hypnosis was founded in 1959 by Theodore X. Barber, who had completed four years of post-doctoral study at Harvard, part of it under Orne. Greatly skeptical at first about the validity and usefulness of hypnosis as a therapeutic tool, Barber went on to define and delimit the boundaries of stage hypnosis on the one hand and professional clinical hypnosis on the other. He drew the distinction between the two more clearly and sharply than it had ever been drawn before, and this emboldened many researchers to seek new and more far-reaching applications of hypnotism. Barber himself, and many who were trained by him, have been in the forefront of these pioneering studies that are opening up vast new horizons for the hypnotists of the twenty-first century.

These horizons are unfolding from the entirely new formulation of the mind-body problem, away from the static dualistic state in which it has largely existed since it was first defined as an axiom by Rene Descartes in the seventeenth century. A vast corpus of research, much of it originally done by psychologists who were not hypnotists but who provided clinical hypnotists with whole armories of innovative uses for hypnosis, has established as attested scientific fact the interrelationship of the mind and the body as a single biochemical unit. Neither exists nor acts independently of the other. The mind influences and controls the functions of the body to an extent that is only beginning to be understood in all of its remarkable ramifications, and the body in turn affects the state of the mind through its own conditions of health and illness.

A generation, or perhaps two, of concentrated psychobiological research and experimentation on the frontiers of the expanding mind-body concepts that the second half of the twentieth century has brought forth may be needed before all their implications and potentialities are adequately grasped. Only then is it likely that new great hypnotists, with healing capabilities far beyond those possessed by any in the past or at present, will arise to astound the world as Mesmer and the Nancy School did in their times.

To review even briefly these new approaches and paths of hypnotherapuetic inquiry is beyond the scope and purpose of this book. We can, however, point out some of the most prominent aspects of the mind-body relations that are currently being explored through hypnosis, and what they promise for clinical application. The references at the foot of this chapter will also help to guide the interested reader to detailed sources of material.

Scientific research is increasing our understanding of the process by which the mind mediates physiological processes. Basically, the brain conveys ("transduces," is the technical term) information and instructions to the nerves, muscles, circulatory and disease-fighting systems of the body through the hypothalamus, a small organ in the lower part of the brain which acts as a filter and modulation box for receiving and transmitting sensory, verbal and mentally imaged impressions. That it was through this center, and the networks it connects with in every part of the body, that hypnotic commands are transmitted and acted upon, was suspected by Hippolyte Bernheim a century ago. Hans Selye, beginning in the 1930s, identified the component parts of what came to be called the hypothalamic-limbic system. (The limbic system is the area of the brain that helps to maintain homeostasis, a stable environment within the body.) More recently, Stephen Black in England has defined its pathways and routings, enabling therapists to better understand how the system operates, how it can break down under stress and assault, and how it can be reached and directed through hypnosis.

In simplest terms, there are three main routes through which the hypothalamic-limbic system functions. The first is the autonomic nervous system, which controls bodily functions automatically, without conscious intervention. (Respiration, circulation, and metabolism are all within the purview of the autonomic system.) The stability of the autonomic nervous system is critical to good health. Many psychosomatic diseases involve a disturbance in the balance of the sympathetic and parasympathetic branches of the autonomic nervous system. When the body and mind suffer from chronic over-stimulation of the fight or flight response, the physiological resources of the body are depleted by energy-using sympathetic activity without corresponding energy-restoring parasympathetic activity. In this state of chronic stress and fatigue, the weakest aspect of an individual's physiology breaks down and a disease state ensues. The ability of hypnosis to establish autonomic equilibrium and relieve stress, suggests its value for the prevention and alleviation of psychosomatic illnesses.

The second of the main hypothalamic-limbic system routes is the endocrine system, channeled through the adrenal and pituitary glands, which secrete the hormones that regulate the rate at which the body carries out its work. This also is now known to be open to modulation by hypnotic suggestions.

The third route is the immune system, the body's front line defense against disease, centered in the thymus gland, the lymph nodes, and the spleen, where the blood cells and antibodies are formed that mobilize against invaders of the body. Enhancement of the immune system has been shown to be possible through hypnotic suggestion, and may someday prove as effective as vaccines and antibiotics in warding off infections. Neuroscientists working with psychologists and immunologists have developed a healing discipline called "psychoneuroimmunology" — the inner healing effect of mind on immunity.

On all three routes, the hypothalamus activates hormonal messengers called neuropeptides. In the late 1960s scientists began to isolate neuropeptides; at first only five were found, but now more than fifty have been identified and additional ones are currently being discovered. The neuropeptides that have come into public awareness are the endorphins, which act like natural opiates or pain-killers, but many of the others appear to function as boosters of the immune system.

Ernest Rossi was the first American researcher to study the neuropeptides and the key role they play in hypnosis and information transduction within the brain and the network of nerves that convey the brain's commands to every part of the body. In *The Psychobiology of Mind-Body Healing*, co-authored with David Cheek, Rossi explains how the neuropeptides circulate within the brain itself as neurotransmitters providing an intricate two-way communication system linking the mind, the immune system, and all other systems of the body. The implications that hypnosis can enhance the immune system and influence such complex physiological processes are profound.

In 1899 Wesley Cook, professor of physiology at the University of Chicago, published an influential and definitive book titled *Practical Lessons In Hypnotism*, which covered all that was known about hypnotism at that time. Cook stated that:

> Hypnotism is the most practical science of the age. It enters into our everyday life, and confers advantages that cannot be acquired through any other medium. Its practice is no longer a mere pastime for amusement, as professional men of the highest standing now recognize its value and seek to profit by its benefits; and scientists regard it as a natural phenomenon, for ages kept dormant, but apparently destined to perform an active part in the welfare and development of future generations. . . .
>
> Prejudice, bigotry, avariciousness and narrow-minded sophistry have until lately succeeded in smothering the science of hypnotism. Men who were bold enough to make known the marvelous nature of the hypnotic power they

were able to manifest, were denounced as wizards, charlatans, impostors and mountebanks. But now the tables are
tuned. Those who were formerly denounced are now regarded as scientific investigators; and the doctrines they
taught are being eagerly learned by the most noted scientists. What was held up for ridicule is now regarded as a
dignified science. What was attributed to evil machinations
is now regarded as one of the greatest of blessings to the
human race.

Cook's stirring words were prophetic — hypnotism has tri-
umphed. The future will undoubtedly see an increased
acceptance of hypnosis, and with its present impetus of
development it is destined to startle the world by its marvelous revelations. We believe that hypnotism will come to its
fullest flowering with the integration of classical methods of
the past and modern psychoneuroimmunology techniques via
the pathways of mind-gene-molecule communication. To
acquire this ability is the goal of research now being pursued
in many facilities around the globe. When that goal is attained,
hypnosis will have fulfilled the hope that the world's greatest
hypnotists, from Mesmer to Erickson, have always held for
it — that it would be the most effective and least intrusive of
healing agents.

EPILOGUE
What Might Have Been

T here was a moment, brief and evanescent, when hypnotism in its initial guise of animal magnetism might have gained in the English-speaking world the prestige that a little later it obtained in France from its acceptance by Balzac, then the foremost literary figure in that nation, at a time when writers had a greater standing in society than did medical men and scientists.

The literary personage who could conceivably have filled this role in England was the poet and essayist Samuel Taylor Coleridge. The moment of history in which it might have happened was around 1800, a few years after the end of the French Revolution, Mesmer's departure into obscurity, and the short-lived fad for animal magnetism in London, resulting from Mainaduc's and Loutherbourg's public exhibitions described in Chapter 11.

Coleridge was still in his late teens, attending classes at the charity school of Christ's Hospital, during the four years — 1788 through 1791 — that the popular infatuation with animal magnetism ran its course in London; and there is no evidence that he was caught up in the craze. Six or seven years later, however, when he had settled down at Nether Stowey in

Somerset, as the near neighbor of William Wordsworth, to the serious work of writing some of the greatest lyric poetry in the English language, Coleridge became interested in the properties of magnetism in both inanimate and living substances.

This interest appears to have been triggered in a passage in a minor work of the Anglican devotional writer William Law (1689-1761). In this passage, written about 1737, or more than thirty years before Mesmer introduced the concept of animal magnetism, Law wrote that everything in existence was magnetized, in fact there was nothing else in existence but magnetism and the innumerable impediments to its greater or lesser functioning. This applied also to the relationships of humans to each other, and to their relationships toward God and of God toward them.

Coleridge understood that to mean that just as certain material substances like iron and magnetite stones could be strongly attracted toward each other, and influence their motions as in the compass needle, so humans could be strongly attracted and exert a controlling influence on each other for good or evil. Was not this the principle that accounted for what he had heard about the magnetizings by Mesmer and his followers? They had learned to apply certain simple and basic techniques for bringing under their volition and direction, an impalpable universal fluid that conveyed this attractional force.

It further appeared—so Coleridge gathered from all he could find out about this animate form of magnetizing—that its motive force was mainly directed outward through the eyes. In the first version of *The Rime of the Ancient Mariner*, completed in 1798, Coleridge attributed this quality to the

Mariner who fixates with his "glittering eye" the Wedding Guest protesting . . .

> *That which comes out of thine eye, makes*
> *My body and soul to be still . . .*

Coleridge also expanded this concept to include the application of the terms "single touch" and "double touch," originally employed a half century earlier by the Swiss mathematician Leonhard Euler with respect to inanimate magnets. By touching only one end of a lodestone (a piece of magnetite) to a susceptible metal such as iron, no more than a limited degree of magnetic attraction can be conveyed to the latter; but with a "double touch," i.e. touching both ends of the lodestone to the metal, a much greater effect is achieved.

Similarly, Coleridge now reasoned, superficial human relationships involved only a "single touching," and yielded little for their participants. Those relationships, however, marked by harmony and rapport—a "double touching"—were productive of lasting good for both parties; for they were magnetically attracted to each other. Yet even this, on the basis of what had assertedly been achieved through Mesmer's animal magnetism, was far short of what Coleridge believed could be done by consciously exerting the capability of attraction.

Coleridge grew excited over what seemed the unfolding prospects for overcoming physical and moral ills by magnetically (i.e., hypnotically) influencing behavioral and biophysical processes.

Though his youthful plan to found a utopian community in Pennsylvania had never materialized, Coleridge still

nurtured ambitions of being a mover for vast social reforma-
tions. But where was he to go for authentic information on this
wonderful new mode of healing?

Mesmer had dropped from sight and was perhaps dead;
France was an enemy country under an expanding military
dictatorship; the introducers of animal magnetism to Britain
had been showmen and charlatans in part or in whole, and in
any case were no longer around. In Germany, though, it was
possible that some serious practitioners of magnetizing might
be found. Coleridge had heard that the great Blumenbach had
expressed himself favorable to magnetizing as a therapy.

Johann Friedrich Blumenbach was then in his late forties,
the head of the faculty of medicine at the University of Goettingen. He was looked up to by men of science on both sides of
the Atlantic, as the founder and expositor of the new sciences
of physiology and anthropology. His pioneering studies of
skulls from every part of the globe had led him to divide all
humankind into five main divisions — Caucasian, Mongolian,
Malay-Polynesian, African, and Native Americans. So great
was his prestige that if indeed he were to lend it to the magnetizing art, its future as a force for human betterment was
assured.

To Germany, then, Coleridge hastened as soon as he could,
in the fall of 1798. He was enthusiastic over the prospects he
visualized, of returning to England as the herald and prophet
of a new dispensation of healing. It was not an unrealistic
aspiration; it could have come true, had he found animal
magnetism to be as solidly established in German scientific
circles as he wishfully imagined it to be.

He was soon disillusioned. "There's nothing to it, or at least not much," Blumenbach told him when they met in Goettingen. "I merely commented that it was an interesting experiment with human imagination. I do not see it—nor does any medical person of any standing in Germany—as any sort of medical or behavioral therapy." It would be almost a decade and a half, before the Prussian Academy of Sciences would shift from that position and seek out Mesmer in his retirement.

From the moment Blumenbach dashed his magnetizing vision, Coleridge's own career gradually crumbled. He returned to England at loose ends, unable to concentrate on anything for any useful length of time. He jumped from project to project; he began poetic epics that he could not complete. His marriage fell apart, his friendships broke up, his health was shattered, he became addicted to opium. Only as a lecturer on Shakespeare and other literary topics, was he any longer able to function at all.

In 1816, a physical wreck at forty-four, Coleridge was taken as a live-in patient by a doctor in a London suburb, and there passed the remaining eighteen years of his life. His mind still retained much of its original brilliance, though he could not bring it to focus on anything for long. And when he heard of the publication of Wolfart's book, containing the transcripts of the German doctor's conversations with Mesmer in 1812, along with a translation of Mesmer's own 1799 book critical of Puységur, Coleridge insisted on obtaining a copy. He could read German with ease.

That copy still survives, with Coleridge's marginal notes stating how he was finding that animal magnetism did after all confirm his "long, long ago theory of a mode of *double touch* . . ." Reflecting on the fact that "sincere, sensitive, warm-hearted men" appeared to have been the most successful practitioners of the magnetizing art, rather than those of sober judgment, Coleridge further commented in his marginal notes that this stemmed from the former being those with double touch capability, while the latter related to others with only a limited single touch.

Other notes reveal that he has heard of Blumenbach now reversing his earlier adverse judgment, ". . . but that great man was now old and worn out by his mighty labors of intellect, and could not now be the verifier of animal magnetism as a transforming force for humanity, that he might have been when still in his full vigor of repute and achievement." In writing that Coleridge seems to be saying, "And that is my own fate also."

Prematurely old, broken in health and spirit though not in mind, Coleridge could only muse on what might have been had Blumenbach been open to the prospects of animal magnetism in 1798, and sent him back to England as a herald who had already gained an audience with his powerful poetry and would be listened to. Death would remove Coleridge from the scene in July 1834, even as John Elliotson was introducing animal magnetism into British medical practice. Probably he was never aware that it might have been done three decades earlier, had Coleridge's genius not been as tied to ill fortune as it was.

NOTES AND REFERENCES

A note about the references:

The extant literature on hypnotism and its practitioners is volumi-
nous. To burden a book intended for general readership with a
ponderous apparatus of numbered footnotes referencing hundreds if
not thousands of scholarly and professional works would defeat its
very purpose. It is important, however, that sufficient documentation is provided to satisfy those who wish to go to the scientific
literature for supporting references and suggested reading.

As a compromise, in the informal bibliography that follows, references are categorized by topic under chapter headings. Additional
sources are listed for those who wish to pursue further research.

There are three major current sources for the history of hypnotism,
to which every writer on the subject has to be heavily indebted.
They are:

Edmonston, William E., Jr. *The Induction of Hypnosis*. John Wiley &
Sons, New York, 1986.

Ellenberger, Henri F. *The Discovery of the Unconscious: The History and
Evolution of Dynamic Psychiatry*. Basic Books, Inc., New York, 1970.

Laurence, Jean-Roche & Perry, Campbell. *Hypnosis, Will and Memory:
A Psycho-Legal History*. The Guilford Press, New York, 1988.

These will be referenced by author names only, as follows: Edmonston; Ellenberger; Laurence & Perry. All other references will cite author, title, date and location (if known) of publication.

Chapter 1
Temples of Sleep

The best general survey of hypnotic practices in ancient cultures is in Edmonston, chapter 1, "The Ancients," pp. 1-25. This includes comprehensive extracts and paraphrases from the Ebers and Leiden Papyruses, as well as a full listing of relevant Biblical passages. There are also (pp. 17-21) several illustrative citations about ancient healing practices involving suggestion, from the three basic articles by W. W. Lloyd in the British journal the *Zoist* (vol. 3, nos. 10-11 and vol. 5, no. 19; 1845-1847.)

A more detailed account of the Hellenic and Roman *asklepeia* or curative sleep temples can be found in Mary Hamilton, *Incubation or the Cure of Diseases in Pagan Temples and Christian Churches*, London, 1906. E. J. and L. Edelstein in *Asclepius: A Collection and Interpretation of the Testimonies*, Johns Hopkins Press, Baltimore, 1948, provide an anthology of ancient descriptions of the healing temples and the hypnotic rituals employed to perform their cures.

Ellenberger, chapter 1, pp. 3-15, has several excerpts from foreign-language works, descriptive of shamanic practices resembling hypnosis; as well as (p. 33) a summary account of the *asklepeia*.

The Jewish hypnotic fixation practices utilized by the thirteenth-century kabbalist Abulafia are detailed in Edmonston, chapter 2, p. 33; and at more length in M. K. Bowers and S. Glasner, "Auto-Hypnotic Aspects of the Jewish Cabalistic Concept of Kavanah," *International Journal of Clinical and Experimental Hypnosis*, no. 6, pp. 50-70, 1958.

Edmonston's chapter 2 gives a summary narration of the lives of Paracelsus (pp. 35-39), Fludd (pp. 41-42) and Greatrakes (pp. 45-49); the latter in considerable detail, from original sources. A more hostile, though still useful, account of Greatrakes can be found in Charles Mackay, *Extraordinary Popular Delusions and the Madness of*

Crowds, London, 1842, and New York, 1932, pp. 312-316. Edmonston and Mackay both employ the alternative spelling, Greatraks.

For William Maxwell, see Laurence & Perry, pp. 16-17. They also treat the St. Medard convulsionaries at length, pp. 36-42, deriving principally from the first volume of Louis Figuier's four-volume work, *Histoire du Merveilleux dans les temps Modernes,* Paris, 1860, still extant only in French.

Chapter 2
Mesmer Revives an Ancient Art

There are numerous biographies of Mesmer, but few are either authoritative or balanced in treatment. Stefan Zweig in *Mental Healers* (Viking Press, New York, 1932) devotes a third of the book to a word portrait of Mesmer—Mary Baker Eddy and Sigmund Freud are the other two subjects. Zweig's account of Mesmer is essentially fair though flawed by several errors of fact. These are corrected in Ellenberger who has drawn on the researches of several German and Austrian writers such as Justinus Kerner (1856), Rudolf Tischner (1928), F. Schuerer-Waldheim (1930), Karl Bittel (1939), Joseph Rudolf Wohleb (1939), and Bernhardt Milt (1953). Their investigations have established the facts of Mesmer's birth, parentage, education, early career, and marriage, beyond further serious question.

Mesmer's life, through the events narrated in our chapter 2, is conveniently summed up by Ellenberger on pp. 57-60. A similarly concise and factual summation of Fr. Gassner's life is given by Ellenberger on pp. 53-57.

Edmonston treats Gassner and Mesmer very briefly, on pp. 49-51; citing however the important detail of Mesmer plagiarizing his doctoral thesis from Richard Mead's 1704 treatise. The basic source for this is from F. A. Pattie's "Mesmer's Medical Dissertation and Its Debt to Mead," in the *Journal of the History of Medicine and Allied Sciences,* no. 11, 1956, pp. 275-287.

Some additional details on the life of Fr. Gassner, and the career of Mesmer through his appearance before the Munich Commission of Inquiry, can be found in Laurence & Perry, pp. 3-9. They give (p.

4) an extract from Mesmer's letter to the Altona Scientific Journal, in which he asserts that he has successfully magnetized a great variety of substances to produce curative results. A footnote on p. 23 describes the glass harmonica. See Zweig, op. cit., pp. 10-11, for Mesmer's acquaintance with Mozart and other cultural personages in Vienna.

Mesmer's own writings have been collected and published in French by R. Amadou, (Ed.), *F. A. Mesmer: le Magnétisme Animal,* Paris, 1971.

Chapter 3
The Paradis Case Leads to Mesmer's Exile

The growing coolness toward Mesmer in Vienna, and the Paradis episode, are described with some lack of accuracy in Zweig's *Mental Healers,* pp. 35-43. Ellenberger treats the Paradis case very briefly, pp. 60-61. Laurence & Perry go into more detail, especially regarding the Jesuit intervention against Mesmer, pp. 9-12 and note on p. 22. For Mesmer's departure from Vienna and letters of recommendation given him, see Laurence & Perry, p. 49. For his letter to the Prussian Academy of Science and its negative reaction, see Zweig, p. 46 and Edmonston, p. 52.

The Strange Case of Mademoiselle P, by Brian O'Doherty (Pantheon Books, New York, 1992) is an excellent fictional account of the Paradis case, which adheres very closely to the facts. Its concluding chapter is an accurate portrayal of the closing phase of Mesmer's life. The author's recasting of Mesmer's long-afterward recollection of his treatment of Paradis is based on the English translation by Capt. V. R. Myers (in Gilbert Frankau's *Mesmerism,* MacMillan, London, 1948) of Mesmer's 1779 treatise narrating his accomplishments.

Chapter 4
Mesmer in the Paris of the Enlightenment

Robert Darnton's *Mesmerism and the End of the Enlightenment in France,* (Harvard University Press, Cambridge, Massachusetts, 1968) provides in Chapter 1, pp. 3-50, a comprehensive discussion of the social and cultural milieu of Paris at the time of Mesmer's arrival and residence in the French capital. See also Ellenberger, p. 61, for the contrasts between Paris and Vienna.

The most detailed account of Mesmer's first months in Paris, to his closing of the clinic at Créteil, is given by Laurence & Perry, pp. 49-56. They also describe with great clarity the complex adversarial relationships between the French scientific and medical bodies at that time. President Le Roux's name is misspelled "Leroy" in Laurence & Perry, following Mesmer's own usage.

Touching by kings of scrofula sufferers is cited by Laurence & Perry, p. 45, and Edmonston, p. 31.

Chapter 5
The Transitory Triumph of Animal Magnetism

Mesmer's *baquets* and their exotic surroundings are described in Edmonston, pp. 53-54, citing principally A. Binet and C. Féré, *Animal Magnetism*, D. Appleton & Co., New York, 1888 (pp. 10-11). The events of Mesmer's stay in Paris, from the setting up of his city clinic at the Place Vendôme to the founding of the Society of Universal Harmony, are concisely narrated in Laurence & Perry, pp. 56-72; and — rather accurately — by Frank Podmore in *From Mesmer to Christian Science*, 1909 (1964 reprint, University Books, Hyde Park, New York), pp. 41-60.

The ultimate source, from which all later ones derive either directly or indirectly, is the 14-volume collection titled *Recueil Générale des Magnétisme Animal*, in the Bibliotheque Nationale in Paris. Compiled in 1787 on the eve of the French Revolution, it includes virtually every published document as well as several unpublished ones, on the subject of animal magnetism, written during the nine years beginning with Mesmer's arrival in Paris. His own writings in this collection can be found in the work by R. Amadou, cited above under Chapter 2. The *Recueil Générale* has also been drawn on heavily by D. Barrucand in the early chapters of his *Histoire de l' Hypnose en France*, Paris 1967.

Robert Darnton, op. cit., is the most thorough as well as the most readily available source for the history of the Society of Universal

Harmony, and for the careers of Bergasse and Kornmann. Darnton also has made copious use of the original sources in the *Recueil Générale*. Some interesting details on Mesmer's rejection of the French Royal Court's offer, and the rapid growth of the Society of Universal Harmony, can be found on Darnton's pp. 50-52. For a summary of the Society's rules and organization, see pp. 75-77. Lafayette's interest in mesmerism and discouragement by his friends in America are noted on pp. 88-99. Darnton does not arrange his material in a narrative sequence, making it difficult to locate and relate specific items to events in the careers of Mesmer and d'Eslon in Paris. Nevertheless, the wealth of Darnton's extracts from (and referencing to) obscure sources, amply repay anyone interested in Mesmer and the beginnings of modern hypnotism for the toil of plodding through his tightly-written text.

Chapter 6
The Fall of Mesmer — But Not of Mesmerism

The *Recueil Générale* and the already cited French-language works of Amadou and Figuier, especially the second and third of the latter's four volumes, are the original sources for the events connected with Mesmer's rapid fall from the dizzying heights he had attained in Paris at the beginning of 1784. The general reader without access to these primary resources can find a fairly comprehensive overview in Laurence & Perry, pp. 73-99. Specifically, Claude Bertholet, pp. 73-74; Father Hervier, pp. 74-75; Court de Gébelin, p. 76; Thouret's book, *Recherches et Doutes sur le Magnétisme Animal*, pp. 77-78; *The Modern Doctors* (stage play by Jean-Baptiste Radet), pp. 80-81; Mlle Paradis' appearance in Paris, p. 82; the Commissions of Inquiry and their findings, pp. 83-93, with de Jussieu's dissent on p. 92; the responses of Mesmer and d'Eslon, pp. 93-95. For most, though not all of these, Laurence & Perry give page references to Figuier.

For Mesmer's failures with Prince Heinrich and Princess de Lamballe, see Laurence & Perry, p. 104; and p. 105 for Caullet de Veaumorel's book on animal magnetism and Mesmer's response.

For the crank genius Jean-Louis Carra, see Darnton, op. cit., pp. 98-99 and 107-110. See Darnton also for d'Espréménil's denunciation of *The Modern Doctors*, p. 65; also for the rapid spread of self-appointed mesmerists throughout France, and J. H. D. Petetin's discoveries at Lyon, pp. 66-68. A more detailed account of Petetin is given in Laurence & Perry, pp. 121-123.

The reports of the two Commissions of Inquiry, and the secret one not published, are preserved in the *Recueil Générale*.

Chapter 7
Puységur Discovers Artificial Somnambulism

The original sources for the lives and opinions of the Puységur brothers are the four autobiographical and doctrinal works by the Marquis de Puységur, which were published in Paris in 1784, 1785, 1807, and 1812. The first two are preserved in the *Recueil Générale*, along with two smaller volumes by his brother, the Comte de Chastenet. All are extensively quoted in the third volume of Figuier, 1860, which in turn is the principal basis for Laurence & Perry's account, pp. 107-120, of the Marquis de Puységur's concept of "artificial somnambulism" and the criticisms of it by Mesmer and others. The magnetizing of Victor Race is cited, in the Marquis' words, on p. 108. Mesmer's critique is summarized on pp. 113-114. The Marquis' escape from Napoleon's execution order is noted on p. 127, which cited an 1825 memoir by P. Foissac in defense of magnetizing.

Ellenberger on pp. 70-74 provides details of the lives of all three Puységur brothers, including the imprisonment of the Marquis under the Reign of Terror and his death after attending the coronation of Charles X. For these details, and the uprooting of the Buzancy oak in 1940, Ellenberger cites the data provided to him by the Vicomte du Boisdulier, a direct descendant of the Marquis. He has also drawn on the family genealogy by Robert de Puységur (Paris, 1873).

Edmondston quotes, pp. 55-58, some of the Marquis de Puységur's magnetizing techniques.

For Mesmer's life after his departure from Paris in 1785, and the circumstances of his retirement and death in Switzerland, see Laurence & Perry, p. 106; Ellenberger, pp. 68-70; Edmonston, pp. 51-52; and Zweig, pp. 86-95; also the substantially factual concluding chapter of Brain O'Doherty's above-cited novel, *The Strange Case of Mademoiselle P*.

Chapter 8
The Abbé Faria Does Away With Magnetic Fluid

The most adequate general account of the Abbé Faria's life and opinions is in Laurence & Perry, pp. 135-141. It is based largely on the biography of Faria by D. G. Dalgado, *Mémoire sur la vie de l'Abbé de Faria*, Paris, 1906; and on the third volume of Figuier's 1860 work, *Le Magnétisme Animal*. The anecdote about Faria and the canary is from p. 302, vol. 2 of the four-volume (1843) posthumous compilation of F. A. R. Châteaubriand's miscellaneous writings, under the title *Mémoires d'Outre-tombe*. Noizet's account of his first impressions of Faria is from the first page of his *Mémoires sur le Somnambulisme et le Magnétisme Animal*, Paris, 1854.

Brief summations of Faria's career and influence are given by Edmonston, pp. 63-64, and Ellenberger, pp. 75-76. The latter also scans the work of Deleuze, Noizet and Bertrand on the same page.

Deleuze is treated in considerable detail in Laurence & Perry, pp. 130-135, and in Edmonston, pp. 64-74, which give copious extracts from his 1825 handbook of induction methods. Laurence & Perry also summarize the career and writings of Bertrand, pp. 142-144; and on pp. 147-148 describe the setting up of the French Third Commission of Inquiry into Animal Magnetism. Bertrand and Noizet are briefly noted in Edmonston, pp. 75-76.

The flamboyant career of the Baron du Potet, and his "Magic Mirror" technique for induction are described in Edmonston, pp. 80-82.

Chapter 9
The German Sidepaths

The primary sources are in German-language works, mainly of the 19th century, which with a few not readily available exceptions have not been translated into English. Parts of Kerner's 1829 two-volume work on the *Seeress of Prevorst* have from time to time appeared in occultist periodicals in English. A fairly objective biography of Anna Catherine Emmerich, by the Very Rev. Carl E. Schomeger, appeared in German in 1867; there have been at least three English translations, the most recent from TAN Books, Rockford, Illinois, in 1976.

Ellenberger, pp. 77-81, has summarized and quoted from the sources, and provides a bibliography of them.

Edmonston on pp. 90-93 reviews Reichenbach's "Odic Force" theory and its supposition of the magnetizing influences of metals.

Chapter 10
The Mid-Century Eclipse In France

The primary sources are Figuier's third volume and several 19th century French-language works, some of which are listed below; and the seventeen annual volumes (1845-61) of the Journal de Magnétisme, likewise in French only. For readers of English, the following are the most readily available secondary sources.

Dr. Cloquet's painless surgery and the report of the Third Commission of Inquiry are discussed in Laurence & Perry, pp. 149-50; the Fourth Commission of Inquiry and the hostile book by Burdin and Dubois on pp. 154-55; the cases of Ricard and the Mongruels on pp. 156-58. Teste's manual and techniques are summarized and cited from in Edmonston, pp. 77-79. Mesmerist influences on Romantic Era literature in France and elsewhere are examined in Ellenberger, pp. 160-163. The introductions to Balzac's novels in the Penguin softbound reprints, especially those to *Ursule Mirouet* and *Cousin Pons*, provide considerable information on the importance of mesmerism in French society and culture in the 1820-1850 period.

The novels themselves, particularly *Louis Lambert*, shed much light on how animal magnetism was understood and practiced.

The memoirs of Baron du Potet, revealing both for his own experiences and the general course of magnetizing in mid-19th century France, appeared in several editions in Paris; that of 1842 was published in H. A. Lee's English translation of *Magnetism and Magic* by Allen & Unwin, London, in 1927. Another work by du Potet, more in the nature of a manual, titled *Traité Complet du Magnétisme Animal*, appeared in at least four editions, the last in 1882. None of these are available in English.

The most comprehensive source on the Ricard and Mongruel cases, and several similar ones, is L.-J. J. Charpignon's *Rapports du Magnétisme avec la Jurisprudence et la Médecine Légale*, Paris 1860. There is also the polemic by L. P. Mongruel, *Le Magnétisme Militant*, sharply critical of the French medical establishment, Paris, 1851.

Chapter 11
John Elliotson Introduces Magnetism to Britain

For the exhibitions of magnetizing by de Mainauduc and Loutherbourg, see Laurence & Perry, pp. 164-165. A more comprehensive account, including Dr. Haygarth's conclusions of the role of the imagination in causing and relieving disease, can be found in Charles Mackay's *Extraordinary Popular Delusions*, op. cit., pp. 334-338.

The account of the poet Shelley's brief involvement with magnetizing is based on Richard Holmes, *Shelley: The Pursuit*, E. P. Dutton & Co., New York 1975, pp. 625-636.

Edmonston, pp. 87-90, concisely sums up Chenevix's seminal demonstrations and writings; Elliotson's career including his founding of the *Zoist*; and the techniques of W. J. Tubbs, on pp. 87-90. Laurence & Perry give only a solitary page (167) to Elliotson, and Ellenberger passes him by altogether, perhaps because no satisfactory full biography of him is in existence. The only readily available sources for Elliotson are the accounts in John H. H. Williams' *Doctors Differ*, pp. 13-60, London 1946, and the lengthy interweavings of Elliotson's life and work with the mesmeric interests of Charles

Dickens in Fred Kaplan's *Dickens and Mesmerism,* Princeton University Press, Princeton, New Jersey, 1975; especially pp. 13-54. Williams and Kaplan both draw essentially on the files of the *Lancet* and on passages in the fifth (1840) edition of Elliotson's *Human Physiology,* pp. 680-681 et passim. J. Milne Bramwell's section on Elliotson, pp. 4-10 in his *Hypnotism: Its History, Practice and Theory,* London, 1903, Julian Press reprint, 1956, derives mainly from the same original sources, and to a lesser extent from James F. Clarke's *Autobiographical Recollections of the Medical Profession,* London, 1874. Clarke's pp. 159-164 describe du Potet's presence in London and influence on Elliotson. There is also a useful account of Elliotson's hospital demonstrations of magnetizing in the first issue (July 1911, pp. 272-284) of the University College Hospital Magazine.

Neither Williams nor Bramwell cite the specific numbers of the *Lancet* and the *Zoist* that they have drawn on. Kaplan does so — extensively and copiously — and those interested in tracing the original accounts in the files of those publications are referred to Kaplan's footnotes, found mainly on his pp. 27-56. Kaplan also draws heavily on the letters of Charles Dickens, preserved in the Nonesuch (London 1938) and Pilgrim (Oxford, 1965 and 1970) edited collections, for the magnetizing demonstrations witnessed by Dickens.

Kaplan has in addition edited a compilation of Elliotson's writings on magnetism, principally from the *Zoist,* titled *John Elliotson on Mesmerism: Collected Works,* Da Capo Press, New York, 1982. Elliotson's monograph *Numerous Cases of Surgical Operations Without Pain in the Mesmeric State,* Philadelphia, 1843, has been reprinted (pp. 3-56) in the tenth volume of D. N. Robertson's compilation of *Significant Contributions to the History of Psychology,* University Publications of America, Washington, D.C., 1977.

Chapter 12
Charles Dickens Heads the Creative Mesmerists

Kaplan is the principal generally available source for Dickens' mesmeric abilities and his employment of them. The narrative portion of Kaplan's account of Dickens, pp. 55-105, which includes the Mme. de la Rue episode, is based on the above cited Nonesuch and Pilgrim collections of Dickens' letters. Specific references to these letters are given extensively in Kaplan's footnotes. Citations are also given from additional letters of Dickens in the Berg Collection in the New York Public Library, the Pierpont Morgan Library, and the Huntington Library in San Marino, California; and those in the Welcome Institute for the History of Medicine in London. The involvement of the actor William Macready in Dickens' mesmeric pursuits is documented in the two-volume edition of Macready's diaries, edited by William Toynbee, London 1912.

For Harriet Martineau's experiences with mesmerism, see her autobiography, edited by Maria Chapman, London, 1878; her *Letters on Mesmerism*, London, 1845; and F. Fenwick Miller, *Harriet Martineau, Kennikat Press*, Port Washington, New York, 1972.

For Chauncy Hare Townshend's influence among the literary mesmerists, see Edmonston, pp. 98-100.

Chapter 13
James Braid Coins a Name That Sticks

The primary sources for Braid's life are J. Milne Bramwell's already cited 1903 work on the history of hypnotism, and his earlier 1896 book (pp. 21-26) *James Braid, His Work and Writings*. A shortened version (pp. 127-166) appeared in vol. 10, part 30, of the Proceedings of the British Society for Psychical Research.

The most important of Braid's writings can be found—mainly abstracted and extracted—in *Braid on Hypnotism*, edited by A. E. Waite, Julian Press, New York, 1960. His 1855 monograph, *The Physiology of Fascination*, is reprinted in full, pp. 365-389, in *Foundations of Hypnosis from Mesmer to Freud*, E. E. Tinterow (Ed.), Charles C. Thomas, Springfield, Illinois, 1970. *Neurypnology*, originally published in London, 1843, was reprinted by Arno Press, New York, 1976.

Edmonston summarizes the work and techniques of Braid, pp. 96-98, and of Lafontaine, pp. 82-86. Lafontaine's two-volume *Mémoires d'un Magnétiseur*, Paris 1886 (an enlargement and revision of the first edition of 1847) is a fascinating personal account of the transition phase from animal magnetism to the beginnings of modern hypnotism. Extracts can be found in Tinterow, op. cit. Durand de Gros' 1860 *Course in Braidism* can be found, abridged, in Tinterow, pp. 390-401.

Laurence & Perry sum up Braid in a single page, 168.

Chapter 14
James Esdaile Introduces Hypnotic Anesthesia

Edmonston, pp. 93-96, summarizes Esdaile's life and Colonel Bagnold's observations on mesmeric practices in Africa and India. Bramwell, op. cit., 1903, gives a more thorough account of Esdaile on pp. 14-21. Bagnold's original reports appeared in the *Zoist*, vol. 6, no. 23 (1848), pp. 250-254, with a commentary by Elliotson on pp. 254-263; and in vol. 7, no. 28 (1850), pp. 443-445.

Esdaile's own account of his mesmeric achievements, *Mesmerism In India*, London, 1846, was reprinted by Arno Press, New York 1976; also in vol. 10 of *Significant Contributions*, by D. N. Robertson, 1977, op. cit.

Chapter 15
Mesmerism's Late Arrival in America

See Edmonston, pp. 59-61 for Elisha Perkins' "tractors"; p. 105 for Charles Caldwell; pp. 106-108 for Charles Poyen in America; p. 109 for Charles Durant; pp. 115-117 for J. Standley Grimes and the electro-biologists; pp. 100-103 for George Sandby and William Scoresby. For a more extended account of Poyen, see E. T. Carlson, "Charles Poyen Brings Mesmerism to America," in the *Journal of the History of Medicine and Allied Science*, 1960, vol. 5, pp. 1211-1232. Carlson with M. M. Sampson has a useful explication of "Perkinism vs. Mesmerism" in the *Journal of History of the Behavioral Sciences*, 1970, vol. 6, no. 1, pp. 16-24.

Caldwell's *Facts in Mesmerism*, Louisville, Kentucky, 1842, has been reprinted by Da Capo Press, New York, 1982. Da Capo has also reprinted (1982) Charles Durant's *Exposition, or a New Theory of Animal Magnetism*, New York, 1837.

Robert C. Fuller, in his *Mesmerism and the American Cure of Souls*, University of Pennsylvania Press, Philadelphia, 1982, provides an excellent overview of the personalities of American Mesmerists in the 1835-1855 period, and their influence and effect on American thought and culture. Fuller carries this overview on into the post-Civil War "New Thought Era," which is more adequately treated in Gail Thain Parker, *Mind Cure in New England*, University Press of New England, 1973. The book is more comprehensive than its title would indicate.

The two-volume compilation of lectures and papers on Mesmerism and its further electro-biological development in America and Britain, by John B. Dods, Joseph Haddock and others, published as *The Library of Mesmerism and Psychology* by Fowlers & Wells, New York, 1854, will repay a search for it by those seriously interested in the subject.

Chapter 16
Liébeault and Bernheim Found the Nancy School

Ellenberger, pp. 86-89, summarizes the careers of Liébeault and Bernheim, and gives a brief account of van Renterghem and Otto Wetterstrand. For more details see Edmonston, pp. 121-123 for Liébeault, pp. 124-127 for Bernheim, pp. 134-136 for Auguste Forel, pp. 137-138 for Wetterstrand, and pp. 139-147 for van Renterghem, van Eeden, Bramwell, and several others who were influenced by or followed the practices of the Nancy School. For its involvement in legal forensics, see Laurence & Perry, pp. 202-206 and 228-231. The French Algerian love-triangle murder, with its involvement of hypnotism, is related on pp. 245-248.

Bernheim's own classic work, *Hypnosis and Suggestion in Psychotherapy*, was first published in French in 1884, with an English translation in 1886, and re-issued in English by Jason Aronson Inc., Northvale, New Jersey, in 1973 and 1993. Much of the book is devoted to Bernheim's techniques and to case histories of his results; however, in chapter 7, pp. 105-124 in the 1993 edition, there is an excellent summary of the development of hypnotism from the time of Mesmer to the 1880s.

Chapter 17
Charcot and the Salpêtrière School

No fully adequate biography of Charcot has yet appeared in any language. The best general account, including the case of Blanche Wittmann, is in Ellenberger, pp. 89-101. Edmonston, pp. 127-128, is concerned principally with Charcot's trance induction techniques. Laurence & Perry, pp. 195-202, describe Charcot's concept of the hysterogenic zones and the ovarian belt; and how he and his assistants staged his lectures and demonstrations of hypnosis-induced hysteria.

There have been numerous editions of Axel Munthe's *The Story of San Michele,* which has remained continuously in print since its publication in 1929 by E. P. Dutton & Co., New York. Munthe's experiences with Charcot at the Salpêtrière are narrated in his Chapter 17.

Chapter 18
Pierre Janet: A Bridge Between Two Centuries

Janet is still without an adequate biography in any language. The closest approach to one is the lengthy chapter, pp. 331-417, that Ellenberger devotes to him. (Janet's encounters with Freud at the 1913 and 1914 medical and psychotherapeutic gatherings are discussed separately on pp. 817-821.)

Some autobiographical material can be found in Janet's two-volume work, *Psychological Healing,* cited in our text (English translation published by Macmillan, New York, 1925); and in the introduction he wrote for Carl Murchison's *A History of Psychology in Autobiography,* Clark University Press, Worcester, Massachusetts, 1930. See also Rev. Walter M. Horton's article, "The Origin and Psychological Function of Religion According to Pierre Janet," in the *American Journal of Psychology,* vol. XXXV, 1924, pp. 16-52. Horton gives a vivid description of the spontaneity and fascination of Janet's lectures, some of which he attended. For the Le Havre tests on Léonie, as interpreted by another participant, see Julian Ochorowicz, *Mental Suggestion,* New York, 1891. For a more critical view of Janet, see *A Treatise on Parapsychology*, by Rene Sudros, London, 1960. Sudros depicts Janet as too restricted and timid in his use of hypnotism.

Chapter 19
Freud's Abandonment of Hypnotism

There are any number of biographies and appraisals of Freud; but an adequate overview of his life and career with analysis of his brief involvement in hypnotism, including the Anna O affair, can be found in the first section (pp. 418-487) of Ellenberger's long chapter on him. The best full-length biography is Ernest Jones' *The Life and Work of Sigmund Freud*, Basic Books, New York, 1953. Its account of Anna O is however seriously incorrect, as Ellenberger makes clear.

Chapter 20
British Hypnotism's Rocky Road

The Myers and Gurney episodes are amply narrated and documented in Trevor M. Hall, *The Strange Case of Edmund Gurney*, Duckworth & Company, London, 1964 and 1980. Although the subject is objectively treated, Hall's personal bias against hypnotism is obvious.

For the British hypnotherapists of the turn-of-the-century period, see Edmonston, pp. 148-152, 161 (Kerr's anti-hypnotism campaign), 170-173; and also the works of those practitioners cited in our text. These books have not been reprinted but some are still generally obtainable through inter-library loan.

George DuMaurier's novels *Peter Ibbetson* (1892) and *Trilby* (1894) have continued to be published in numerous editions. His experience with Felix Mocheles' hypnotizing is described in Leonee Ormond's *George DuMaurier*, University of Pittsburgh Press, Pittsburgh, Pennsylvania, 1960, pp. 74-75.

Chapter 21
"Every Day in Every Way" Charms
the Roaring Twenties

See Edmonston, pp. 173-179 for Sidis, Gerrish, Quackenbos and the Flints; and pp. 180-185 for Emile Coué and Charles Baudouin. Coué's and Baudouin's books cited in our text are still obtainable from some libraries. A new edition of *Self-Mastery Through Auto-Suggestion* by Coué was published in London in 1959.

Muensterberg's disastrous influence on hypnotherapy practice in America is cited in Gay W. Allen, *William James*, London, 1967, pp. 352, 367, and 471. (James called Muensterberg's article in the January 1910 Metropolitan Magazine "sheer buffoonery.") William McDougall's *Outline of Abnormal Psychology*, London, 1926, is more autobiographical than its title would suggest.

The Sally Beauchamp split-personality case is narrated by Morton Prince in his *The Dissociation of a Personality*, New York, 1906. For "Patience Worth," see Walter F. Prince, *The Case of Patience Worth*, Boston, 1927. For "asthenia," see A. J. Cronin, *Adventures in Two Worlds*, London, 1952. John B. Watson's *Behaviorism*, New York, 1928, is partly autobiographical. Georg Groddeck's concept of immune system breakdown was more fully formulated in his *The Book of the Id*, London, 1923, reprinted in 1950.

Chapter 22
The Arrival of Milton H. Erickson

The extant literature on Erickson, including his own numerous writings, is enormous in its sheer bulk. However, almost all of it consists of descriptions and critiques of his methods, techniques and concepts, and case histories of his patients. There is no standard biography and only a small amount of biographical matter in the books treating of him. Edmonston has one page on Erickson's life, followed by 19 pages of his techniques and results, pp. 218-237. Jay Haley in his selections from Erickson's papers, published under the title *Advanced Techniques of Hypnosis and Therapy* (New York 1967), provides some material on Erickson's life and career. Additional biographical data can be found in Haley's 1973 work, *Uncommon Therapy*, W. W. Norton, New York.

The best summations are Jeffrey K. Zeig's in his *Experiencing Erickson*, pp. 7-29, Brunner/Mazel, New York, 1985; and that of Rossi, Ryan and Sharp, pp. 1-61 in *Healing in Hypnosis*, Irvington Publishers, New York, 1983 based on Milton H. Erickson's seminars, workshops and lectures.

Also helpful are Zeig's *A Teaching Seminar With Milton H. Erickson*, Brunner/Mazel, New York, 1980; and S. Rosen, *My Voice Will Go With You*. All of these cited books provide further extensive references on Erickson's philosophy and work.

Chapter 23
Erickson the Master Wounded Healer

Ericksonian Approaches to Hypnosis and Psychotherapy, edited by J. K. Zeig, Brunner/Mazel 1982, has an excellent summation by Jay Haley on Erickson's contribution to therapy, pp. 5-25. See also, in the same volume, S. Rosen on Erickson's values and philosophy, pp. 462-476; I. Secter on Erickson's earlier seminars, pp. 447-454; and C. A. Dammann on Erickson's family therapy, pp. 193-200.

Two collaborative works by Erickson and Rossi, *Hypnotherapy: An Exploratory Casebook*, Irvington, New York, 1979, and *Experiencing Hypnosis: Therapeutic Approaches to Altered States*, Irvington 1981, provide insights into Erickson's concepts and his applications of them.

A wide range of views on Erickson's enduring significance and importance can be found in the July 1988 (vol. XXXVI, no. 3) International Journal of Clinical and Experimental Hypnosis. The entire issue is devoted to transcripts of addresses by prominent speakers in the hypnotherapeutic field, at the 10th Congress of the International Society of Hypnotists, held in Toronto in August 1985. Erickson's eclecticism and avoidance of dogmatic therapies are stressed in the address "Will the Real Milton Erickson Please Stand Up?" by D. Corydon Hammond of the University of Utah School of Medicine, pp. 473-484.

Chapter 24
Future Trends: Hypnotism Comes of Age

The progress of clinical hypnotism in America over the course of the present century is described at length in Ernest R. Hilgard's magisterial work, *Psychology in America: A Historical Survey*, HarcourtBrace Collins Publishers, New York and San Francisco, 1987; it is indispensable for any serious student of the field, and its thorough indexing makes the contents of its over 1000 pages readily accessible to the general reader as well. Also a helpful guide to modern clinical hypnosis is Hilgard's earlier book, *The Experience of Hypnosis*, Harcourt Brace/Harvest Books, New York, 1968. With his wife, Josephine R. Hilgard, Ernest R. Hilgard has written a survey of the latest advances in hypnotherapy for pain, *Hypnosis in the Relief of Pain*, Brunner/Mazel, New York, 1979. A related work is *Hypnotherapy of Pain in Children With Cancer*, by Josephine R. Hilgard and Samuel LeBaron, Brunner/Mazel, 1991. Josephine Hilgard's study of *Personality and Hypnosis: A Study of Imaginative Involvement*, University of Chicago Press, Chicago, 1970 (an expanded second edition was published in 1979) remains a standard work in the field.

Although directed at health professionals wishing to know more about the proper uses of hypnosis, *Hypnosis: Questions & Answers*, edited by B. Zilbergeld, M. G. Edelstien, and D. L. Araoz, W. W. Norton, New York, 1985, will be revelatory for lay readers as well.

Epilogue
What Might Have Been

Coleridge's interest in animal magnetism and his theory of the single and double touch are described in John Beer's essay on *Coleridge's Later Imagination*, pp. 227-233, in the collection of bicentenary studies on Coleridge, titled *Coleridge's Variety*, edited by Beer, University of Pittsburgh Press, Pittsburgh, Pennsylvania, 1973. See also pp. 71-86 in Beer's later work, *Coleridge's Poetic Intelligence*; and the chapter "The Power of the Eye in Coleridge," in Lane Cooper's *Late Harvest*, Cornell University Press, Ithaca, New York, 1952.

Prior to his disappointing visit to Germany, 1798-1800, Coleridge was a close acquaintance of Humphry Davy and keenly interested in the latter's pioneering researches in chemistry, electricity and magnetism. After Coleridge's return, this relationship and interest gradually lapsed. Had Coleridge come back with a confirmed and heightened acceptance of animal magnetism, he might have brought Davy into the same belief, with vast consequences for the reception of hypnotherapy by the British medical and scientific establishment, among whom Davy's stature and credibility had a high rating. See Kathleen Coburn on *Coleridge: A Bridge Between Science and Poetry*, in *Coleridge's Variety*, op. cit.

Dr. Rexford L. North

L ittle did I realize when I set out one cold night in the winter of 1951 to attend a lecture in Boston that I was doing something which would change the whole course of my life. I still remember with vivid pleasure how I felt when I walked through the doors of the Hypnotism Center for the first time. I remember my first impression of Dr. Rexford L. North. He was the very image of a hypnotist—the figure who stepped upon the platform had a dignified professional bearing, long black hair, tiny piercing eyes behind glasses, and a trim Vandyke beard. Dr. North was stone deaf and the inflection of his voice had an eerie quality about it; he nevertheless managed to modulate his voice well enough so it did not clash with the rest of the image he projected.

Charismatic is the impression he made, and we listened spellbound while he enlightened us about ". . . that strange, mysterious power which charms and fascinates men and women, influences their thoughts, controls their desires, and has the power to make you the supreme master of every situation." At the conclusion of his fascinating lecture and demonstration we knew that life was full of alluring possibilities if we signed up for his course in "genuine hypnotism" and mastered the secrets of hypnotic influence. It is no wonder that he was idolized by the students who came to his Hypnotism Center. Those of us who are still alive and active in hypnosis today remember Dr. North with keen affection.

Rexford L. North was by all odds the premiere hypnotist of the late 1940s and early 1950s, as a teacher and a therapist. He was foremost in getting dental hypnosis accepted by the medical and dental authorities of the Boston area, through a series of practical demonstrations of its effectiveness in 1949-50.

Many students of the Hypnotism Center have gone on to careers in the profession. I would like to tell you about one of North's students, who would become an important figure in the field of hypnotism. Martin T. Orne established an influential research center—the Studies in Hypnosis Project at the Massachusetts Mental Health Center under the auspices of Harvard University. The research center was later transferred to the University of Pennsylvania under the name of the Unit for Experimental Psychiatry. Orne was then a professor of psychiatry and in full charge of the program, along with his wife, Emily, who had been associated with the laboratory from the beginning. In 1962, Orne took over as editor of the *International Society for Clinical and Experimental Hypnosis Journal.* The most outstanding among Orne's many contributions to the theory and practice of hypnotherapy has been the clear distinction he drew between the essence of hypnotism—that is, the phenomenon of suggestibility by itself—and the artifacts, or the physical effects produced by hypnosis. Even among the most careful investigators of hypnotic phenomena there had always been some uncertainty about the relationship between the act of suggestion and its results. After Orne, there could no longer be any such intermingling of cause and effect, and this resulted in greater clarity in the definition and application of hypnosis.

In 1951 Dr. North founded the National Guild of Hypnotists. Dwight Damon and I were privileged to see the Guild grow from a small group of enthusiastic hypnotists, most of whom were former students of the Hypnotism Center, to its present status as the world's largest hypnosis organization. Indeed the name National Guild of Hypnotists is now a misnomer, as the Guild has members from all over the world and is truly an international organization.

A cloud of mystery hangs over the fate of Rexford L. North. He disappeared, under still unexplained circumstances, in 1956. Whatever may have been the cause of his vanishing, it cannot detract from what he accomplished in getting hypnosis and its practical applications to the attention of the general public and of the medical profession.

One generation plants the trees; another sits in their shade. Here's to you, Rexford, for planting those trees.

A Word about the Resources of
The National Guild of Hypnotists

The author of this book urges hypnotists to join the world's premier hypnosis organization, the National Guild of Hypnotists, which provides its members with the finest resources in the field of hypnotism. The Guild is a not-for-profit, educational corporation in the State of New Hampshire. Founded in Boston, Massachusetts in 1951, it is a professional organization comprised of more than 10,000 dedicated hypnotists (from 40 countries) committed to advancing the field of hypnotism. The Guild is a resource for members and a vehicle for legal and legislative action.

Dr. Rexford L. North, Director of the Hypnotism Center of Boston, founded the Guild in 1951. Within a short time, local chapters were formed and operating in many major cities throughout the US and Canada. Important resources through the years have been two publications devoted exclusively to the field of hypnotism: *The Journal of Hypnotism* and *The HypnoGram.*

This unique organization encourages an eclectic exchange of ideas, fellowship, mutual trust and cooperation among members – while promoting and protecting the science, art, and philosophy of hypnotism. Dr. Dwight F. Damon, the President of the National Guild of Hypnotists, has made a personal commitment to have hypnotherapy recognized as a separate and distinct profession. The National Guild of Hypnotists is fair-minded and has always assisted wherever needed, helping other groups and individuals regardless of their affiliations.

Each year in August the National Guild of Hypnotists holds the world's largest annual hypnosis educational conference and convention. Hypnotists from all over the world attend this event.

For more information contact:

The National Guild of Hypnotists

P.O. Box 308
Merrimack, NH 03054-0308
(603) 429-9438 (FAX) 424-8066
NGH e-mail address: ngh@ngh.net
NGH Web Page: http://www.ngh.net

INDEX

CPSIA information can be obtained
at www.ICGtesting.com
Printed in the USA
BVHW081229080223
658130BV00005B/26